Restructuring in the New EU Member States

Social Dialogue, Firms Relocation and Social Treatment of Restructuring

P.I.E. Peter Lang

Bruxelles · Bern · Berlin · Frankfurt am Main · New York · Oxford · Wien

Marie-Ange Moreau
& María Esther Blas López (eds.)

Restructuring in the New EU Member States

Social Dialogue, Firms Relocation and Social Treatment of Restructuring

"Work & Society"
No. 63

This book has been published with the support of the European Social Fund (Article 6) in the framework of the research project AGIRE (Anticipating for an Innovative Management of Restructuring in Europe). www.fse-agire.com.

Éditions scientifiques internationales
Brussels, 2008
1 avenue Maurice, 1050 Brussels, Belgium
info@peterlang.com; www.peterlang.com

ISSN 1376-0955
ISBN 978-90-5201-456-2
D/2008/5678/66

Library of Congress Cataloging-in-Publication Data
Restructuring in the new EU member states : social dialogue, firms relocation, and social treatment of restructuring /
Marie-Ange Moreau & María Esther Blas-López (eds.).
p. cm. — (Work & society, ISSN 1376-0955 ; no. 63)
Includes bibliographical references. ISBN 978-90-5201-456-2
1. Corporate reorganizations—European Union countries.
2. Consolidation and merger of corporations—European Union countries.
3. Corporate reorganizations—Europe, Eastern.
4. Consolidation and merger of corporations—Europe, Eastern.
I. Moreau, Marie-Ange. II. Blas-López, María Esther.
HD2746.55.E86R47 2008 338.6094—dc22 2008045149

Bibliographic information published by "Die Deutsche Bibliothek"
"Die Deutsche Bibliothek" lists this publication in the "Deutsche Nationalbibliografie"; detailed bibliographic data is available on the Internet at <http://dnb.ddb.de>.
CIP also available from the British Library, GB

Contents

Part II. Firms Relocation and Social Treatment of Restructuring in the EU New Member States

List of abbreviations

ALMP	Active Labour Market Policies
AMC	Agricultural Marketing Centre
CEE	Central and Eastern Europe
CEEC	Central and Eastern European Countries
CEFTA	Central European Free Trade Agreement
CRCs	Co-operative Research Centres
CSF	Community Support Framework
ECE	East-Central Europe
ECJ	European Court of Justice
EFTA	European Free Trade Association
EMCC	European Monitoring Centre on Change
ESF	European Social Fund
ESRC	Economic and Social Research Council
ETUI	European Trade Union Institute
EU	European Union
EWCs	European Works Councils
FDI	Foreign Direct Investments
GDP	Gross Domestic Product
GDR	German Democratic Republic
GERD	Gross Expenditure on Research and Development
HRM	Human Resource Management
IB	International Business
ILO	International Labour Organization
ISTP	Integrator Supplier Target Programme
ITDH	Investment and Trade Development Agency
MNCs	Multinational Corporations
MNEs	Multinational Enterprises
NMS	New Member States
NORT	National Office of Research and Technology
ODS	Občanská demokratická strana (Civic Democratic Party)

OECD	Organisation for Economic Co-operation and Development
OéT	Országos Érdekegyezteto Tanács (National Interest Reconciliation Council)
OPZZ	Ogólnopolskie Porozumienie Związków Zawodowych (All-Poland Alliance of Trade Unions)
PAYG	Pay-as-you-go
RTD	Research and Technology and Development
SI	Systems of Innovation
SLD	Sojusz Lewicy Demokratycznej (Democratic Left Alliance)
SMEs	Small and Medium-sized Enterprises
UNDP	United Nations Development Programme

Preface

Because of their considerable impact on economies and societies, industrial restructurings give rise to an increasing number of debates and analysis from experts, politicians and social actors. Their aim is to measure the scope of the phenomenon as well as its diversity, to analyse its various components (acquisitions, mergers, externalisations, privatisations, outsourcing, new technologies, production reorganisation, economic layoffs), to document the evolving strategies of companies, in particular transnational corporations. The analysis also relates to legislation (national and EU), international norms (such as those of the ILO) and the public mechanisms aimed at managing this phenomena, minimise its cost on employment, working and life conditions of the workers and populations directly affected.

The book coordinated by Marie-Ange Moreau and María Esther Blas López fits perfectly within these debates by proposing a series of particularly stimulating analysis of restructurings and their management in the new members states of the EU. The first notable point of interest of this book is to have focused on the Central and Eastern European Countries (CEECs) that have joined the EU since 2004, which had not been prominent in the research produced in Western Europe in the past twenty years. In the same way as Asian countries, they were mostly perceived as a threat for activities and employment in Western Europe because of the outsourcing they were the beneficiaries of. By moving east, the book allows for a different perspective on restructurings, by contextualisation both within Europe and the numerous changes which affect these countries.

Considered for a long time as proof of the failure of certain production models affecting certain traditional sectors (steel industry, metallurgy or shipbuilding industry) and associated with site closings and massive layoffs, restructurings now appear to many as diffuse, permanent and complex reorganisation processes of firms, linked to a search for flexibility and competitive advantages.[1]

In the context of this system, what is striking and different with the CEECs is the scope and speed of restructurings since the fall of communism in 1989. As highlighted in this book, the changes caused by

1 See the special edition of *Revue de l'IRES*, "Restructuration, nouveaux enjeux", Vol. 2005/1, No.47, Institut de recherches économiques et sociales, Paris.

privatisations and the adoption of a market economy, combined with the transition towards democracy, are so radical that it would be more suited to speak of the restructuring of whole economies. The speed of change can most notably be perceived in the measuring of growth, employment, unemployment and productivity which have gone through considerable variations in less than fifteen years.

The second contribution of this book is to enlighten us on the restructuring processes by favouring and articulating three dimensions: public policies in employment but also innovation, professional relations and social dialogue in these countries, the impact of EU legislation on work relations. Combined with a specific analysis of transnational strategies in several branches (metallurgy, food industry), this approach appears, in our opinion, to be particularly original and fruitful in order to better identify restructurings, the context in which they take place and that they influence, their social and territorial impact. Indeed, research on restructurings rarely adopts such a point of view, in which societal analysis case studies are so strongly linked. This adds to the value of the book.

Public Policies in Question

Public policies adopted in the 1990s aim to achieve several goals: integrate MNCs to the local economy through tax rebates, innovation programmes and partnerships; combat the increasing unemployment due, first of all, to the privatisation of companies and the reorganisation of their activities, and second of all, to the outsourcing decisions of MNCs.

On the first aspect, the Hungarian situation is particularly telling of the difficulties to integrate MNCs in local political and innovation strategies. Having established tight relations with local actors and suppliers or been integrated to the local territorial, social and economic environment, is of little weight in the outsourcing decisions taken at a higher level. This situation is partly explained by the weakness in the cooperation, on the one hand, between professional organisations and MNCs, and on the other hand, between sectorial policies, governmental policies and local policies. Moreover, from a regulatory policy perspective, it also highlights the importance of this form of cooperation between actors and institutions and the need to rely on intermediary institutions.

Alternating between passive policies (unemployment benefits) and active ones (measures to favour employment), the management of employment in the CEECs does not differ, in its content, from what is done in other European countries affected by unemployment. However, the situations are here once more distinguishable from the western-European countries having well established decentralised institutions playing a role on the job market. In fact, the problem may be less to be found in the actual content of public policies, and more in the lack of sufficient expertise and material resources to implement them.

Social Dialogue and Professional Relations at the Heart of the Changes

The end of the communist regimes in which the State was all powerful paradoxically created a demand for more State intervention in order to put in place economic reforms and minimise their social cost. It also begged the question of the place and role of social partners as well as of the systems of professional relations in the new regimes. The analysis presented highlight the difficulty in reforming the systems of professional relations which, contrary to most Western European countries are not based on sectorial collective negotiations but on the one hand, at the centralised level in tripartite committees, and on the other hand, in companies, at least the largest of those, where unions exist. The obstacles to the implementation of substantial reforms are not astonishing: as has been shown, for example by Colin Crouch,[2] systems of professional relations are deeply implanted in national traditions, which explains the continued existence of their main institutional characteristics and the persistence of a great diversity between countries despite the internationalisation of the economy and globalisation.

The general finding for the CEECs is one of weakness of employee representation (although this varies from country to country, depending on the branches and past compromises), as much in relation to the State which they hardly influence in the definition of labour policies, as in companies where they have a limited influence faced with the increasingly unilateral mode of regulation of employers. Restructurings put considerable pressure on employees and their representatives. Threats (of relocation and lay-offs) condition as much the conduct of the stakeholders as the decisions themselves. Western European companies that move to the CEECs only rarely bring the social dialogue they usually practice in their country of origin, and, in general, they do not mind its absence. However, one can observe changes meant to promote the development of social dialogue and the increase of the autonomous negotiation capacity of stakeholders, as in Hungary. The accession of the CEECs in the EU should accelerate this trend, given the obligation for the states to implement community legislation at the national level.

---

2 Crouch, C. (1993), *Industrial Relations and European State Traditions*, Clarendon Press, Oxford.

The Impact of Community Law on Work Relations

As has been shown, among others, by Marie-Ange Moreau,[3] community legislation that imposed itself through a set of compulsory rules (directives and regulations) in such areas as labour and employment constitutes a foundational base of rights which constitute the European social model. From the middle of the 1970s, community legislation on restructurings focused on the right of concerned employees to be informed and consulted, a trend confirmed by the 1989 Community charter of basic social rights which reaffirms the importance of the rights of "information, consultation and participation of workers".[4] On this point, the added value of the present book is equally important. The analysis shows the ambivalent role played by Community law. On the one hand it encourages the introduction of new forms of employee representation within companies (elected works councils) that are the beneficiaries of the rights of information and consultation, it stabilises tripartite committees, and more generally, promotes and legitimises social dialogue and the role of social partners in the economy by considering them as a major component of the European social model. On the other hand, this legislation can be used in order to reform national labour codes in the direction of an increased liberalisation of its content, and therefore, of a weakening of workers' rights and protections. In doing so, it might reinforce the tendency of certain companies in some countries to disregard existing labour rules.

Do European Works Councils offer new possibilities for action to employee representatives in the CEECs? Here too, the answer is ambivalent. It all depends on the representatives' capacity to get their voice heard in meetings, to mobilise employees, to collaborate with delegates from other European subsidiaries. From defiance between delegates to active collaboration, the analysis reveals a great diversity in practices, but it seems that progressively, cooperation is getting the upper hand. The learning processes that are taking place within these new institutions play an important role in these evolutions. Knowledge challenges are equally present. The institutional framework, laid down by the 1994 directive, among others, does not impose itself automatically. Not only is it interpreted, but there is considerable debate on its content and future. The knowledge aspect cannot be separated from collective action. The implementation of EU legislation in the CEECs confirms

---

3 Moreau, M.-A. (2006), *Normes sociales, droit du travail et mondialisation. Confrontations et mutations*, Dalloz, Paris.

4 See Béthoux, E. (2007), "Restructurations et dialogue social en Europe: état des lieux et perspectives", *Document de travail*, Europe et Société, Paris.

that rules are a source for action and that it is important to analyse on a case by case basis to what extent stakeholders refer to it.

The benefit of this book finally lies in the comparative approach adopted by the authors. It rests on a presentation of the main tendencies in restructurings in Europe and on an attempt to define "the welfare state regimes" of the CEECs, in reference to the classic typology adopted by Esping Andersen.[5] The institutional characteristics and performances of these countries are conducive to considering them as mixed regimes combining certain aspects of the "bismarckian" regimes inherited from their socialist past and, a market-favourable ideology. The comparisons made between the various eastern and central European countries focused on public policies, social dialogue or the impact of EU legislation, bringing to light considerable differences, consequences of varying economic situations, History, compromises reached between the state and the social and economic actors, the choices made by public authorities. Even when the analysis focuses on one country, there are frequent references to neighbouring states, the average situation in Europe or other western States. Comparisons bring to the fore the specificity of each trajectory and dynamics, as well as the common tendencies which are the result, among other things, of the strategies followed by MNCs and the pressure of the internationalisation of economies.

The density of this book, the wealth of its substantial teachings, the use of a comparative and pluridisciplinary approaches that links law, political science, sociology and economy, make it an essential read for those wishing to understand restructurings in the European space and more generally European construction and the European social model.

Annette JOBERT
Sociologist, Research Director at the CNRS,
Institutions et dynamiques historiques de l'Économie (IDHE),
Université Paris X Nanterre

[5] Esping-Andersen, G. (1999), *Les trois mondes de l'État providence, essai sur le capitalisme moderne*, Presses universitaires de France, Paris.

INTRODUCTION

Lights and Shadows of Restructurings in New Member States

Marie-Ange MOREAU and María Esther BLAS LÓPEZ

Professor at the European University Institute in Florence, Labour Law Chair and Senior Lecturer, Doctor in European and Constitutional Law at the University of Saragossa

Restructurings as a consequence of the deindustrialisation process affecting employment are a well-known phenomenon in Western Europe. Beyond this phenomenon and since the 1970s, restructurings in Western Europe have taken on a different aspect due to the transformations in the organisation of companies. They can happen outside the relation to time and space in a process of sophistication of their economic strategies. The opening of markets at a world level as well as the use of technologies in a context of increased financialisation of economic activities allow companies to organise their activities on a global scale, within the framework of processes which are increasingly accelerating (Moreau, 2006 and 2007).

Restructuring processes have multiplied, have become recurring or even permanent: in the "old" Member States, it is common for successive restructurings to take place in important companies because of sectorial economic changes and competition strategies developed on the European market. Until the beginning of the new century, the focus was on mergers and acquisitions (Sachs-Durand, 2004), then on outsourcing of activities and these broad externalisation movements mobilised social actors. Restructurings became increasingly important on the political agenda in countries such as France. Figures show however that Great-Britain and Germany were the most concerned by restructurings within the EU-15 countries.

Restructurings are the consequence of strategic choices made by companies on the European market. Between the access to new markets and the search for better cost management, companies have come up with new ways to distribute their activity, new ways to organise and new standards of management in order to respond to the pressure of international competition.

New Member States have benefited from these new strategies. Outsourcing, direct investments, creation of subsidiaries and joint-ventures, sub-contracting are but only some illustrations of the mobility allowed on the European market, made easier first by the cooperation agreement, and then by the successive enlargements of the Union.

The word "restructuring" has therefore taken on a specific meaning in the 15-member EU, synonymous of job losses or even outsourcing, which is not necessarily shared in the new Member States. It is therefore useful to elaborate a Union-wide definition which would allow the rethinking of European policies from the same analytical starting point, faced with a phenomenon affecting the internal market and European citizens at different levels.[1]

One can therefore analyse restructurings as Petrovski and Gazier (2006)[2] do, as "a complex and multifaceted discrete process of business reorganisation, driven by intentional managerial decisions, whose main objectives is to reinforce or re-establish the global competitive position of the company and whose effects on the workforce and the local economies can be quantitative and qualitative".

One can also adopt the following definition:

> restructurings are today complex, protean and multidimensional processes, including modifications to the organisation, the type, the perimeter and the activities of a company, following multiple economic reasons and objectives chosen by the management and linked to the changes due to the globalisation of the economy, resulting in suspensions of activity, flexibility, reorganisation of the activity, externalisation, both national and international, but also functional and structural expansions and diversifications having major consequences on the structure and quality of employment (Moreau, 2007).

---

1 On the difficulty to reflects on concepts with the same signification see Urban (2007).

2 One can refer to the definition chosen by M. Raveyre for the IRES seminar, dir. Fayolle (2005): "[…] restructurings affecting the entirety of changes of activity and assets of companies, they can manifest themselves as much in the end of activities as in creations, sales, acquisitions or mergers, as well as in outsourcing and externalisation. They are identified by changes in the perimeter and the localisation of activities, in the organisational transformations and in the changes in the legal status of the companies. In this sense, they do not necessarily entail a decrease in employment and activity, but internal and external structural modifications of the company" (Raveyre, 2005: 10).

It remains that restructuring processes are relatively new for the central and eastern European countries (CEEC) since 2004.[3] Restructurings that took place are linked to the economic transition imposed by the market economy and the integration of these countries in the European internal market.

Indeed, from the beginning of the transition, massive restructurings affected industry. Restructurings continued all through the transition with drastic effects on the economy and employment (Kirov, 2004). This transition which took place in the first half of the 1990s had as a consequence a decrease in the growth and employment levels more particularly due to the chocks to offer as well as demand provoked by the loss of traditional markets, the serious disturbance of the chains of offer and the decision-making structures, the liberalisation of commerce and the restrictive macroeconomic policies applied (Havlik, 2006).

The analysis of restructurings at the European level has therefore been able to integrated multiple aspects: on the one hand, restructurings as they are analysed in the old Member States, as strategies aimed at the search for productivity on the European market, on the other hand, restructurings as means of transition in the new Member States (Farell *et al.*, 2007). However, a more thorough analysis is necessary: the EU must take into account what has be called "winning countries" and "losing countries" in the framework of its economic and social cohesion policy.

But the Union must also manage the economic and social consequences of restructurings in the framework of the competition that exists between countries inside and outside the EU. These last few years, mobility outside the EU has added itself to the mobility inside the EU (towards new Member States). And the direct competition of China or India is clear, for example, in Slovenia, Romania or Bulgaria. Companies which had decided to implant production activities in the new Member States have decided to transfer them to China and India. Even if the movement is not clearly identifiable, it shows that the analysis of restructurings in Europe must be set in the context of the global strategies of MNCs.

---

3 According to the Communication from the Commission to the Council and the European Parliament – Enlargement, two years after (EC, 2006: 3-4): "The fifth enlargement of the EU on 1 May 2004 has been the most ambitious in the history of the European Union: the largest ever in terms of number of countries and population acceding to the EU; the most complex, as it brought in the EU ten countries which had experienced very diverse economic, social and political developments", and "Overall, the fifth enlargement, by leading to a larger, more integrated internal market, has created the conditions for the whole European economy to become stronger and more dynamic, hence to be better equipped to face increased global competition".

It is possible to posit as an hypothesis that the EU must therefore take into account two aspects when elaborating for the future its policies regarding restructurings. First of all, it must understand the scope of mobility that exist on the internal market and its economic and social consequences in the old Member States and in the new ones to construct relevant transitions linked to adaptation to change. Second of all, it must undertake an analysis of restructurings in the context of the interaction of competition existing outside the EU, on the level of economic as well as financial activity: nobody could indeed have imagined five years back that major European companies would be controlled by Indian, Chinese or Korean investors.

It is therefore indispensable to identify what restructurings are in the new Member States.

This book aims at contributing to the debate by proposing pluridisciplinary analysis that brings to light legal, but also institutional and sociological aspects. It allows an evaluation of the specific difficulties linked to the adaptation to change that exist in the new Member States and an appreciation of the differences in the phrasing of the debate that exist between the 15-member EU and the new Member States.

In this economic context linked to transitions and successive enlargements, the contributions proposed offer an analysis of restructurings and their management in the new Member States of the EU in the framework of professional relations and social dialogue in those countries. The impact of community legislation on work relations is obviously at the heart of these evolutions and allows for an evaluation of the importance of the *acquis communautaire* (Part 1). The second part of the book is dedicated to the strategies of MNCs in several branches, such as the food industry and metallurgy. It highlights the way its social consequences are dealt with (Part 2).

Part I: Professional Relations, Social Dialogue and Impact of Community Law

It appeared as necessary to start with an analysis of the more important tendencies of work and employment within the enlarged EU, as well as an identification of the more vulnerable workers. Restructurings of entire branches of the economy as well as the expansion of activities linked to the mobility of companies towards new Member States have triggered deep transformations in working conditions. It is demonstrated that the labour market in the recently enlarged EU is not only more and more complex, but also rapidly changing. The difficulty lies in distinguishing long term from short term tendencies, as well as between tendencies due to a progressive evolution, for example in the organisation of labour, and tendencies that are the result of rapid changes in the socio-economic context, under pressure from globalisation and the increase in mobility. Therefore, restructurings not only can be a major determinant of the tendencies of the European labour market, but can certainly also influence other identified determinants (Essay 1).

Given the rapid change in the economic and social context, academics and unionists point a finger at the "excessive" flexibility of working conditions as well as at the development of a unilateral power for the employer in the working relations system in the CEECs. Others identify an "insufficient" flexibility and an excessive role for state protections. The debate on the place of labour norms in the context of world competition therefore takes place in the same way in other EU countries, but in significantly different national institutional contexts.

Secondly, beyond the political reasoning, this book analyses this contradictory diagnosis by reconstructing the influence of three different concepts: 1) the process of economic liberalism, 2) the government-control approach to work relations, 3) the idea of social partnership in Western Europe. Insisting on Poland and the Czech Republic, the author shows how the influence of the diversity of these three notions has contributed to quite permissive work relations that clearly differ from Anglo-Saxon voluntarism: permissiveness does not come from the formal rules, but from their bypassing. During the 1990s, the weakness of actors to regulate and establish a powerful interaction of sanctions creates a dilemma for liberalisation. Moreover, strict state regulation offers little negotiation incentive to employers. A new diminution in this regulation increases the unilateral decision-making on the part of the management, maintaining the collective negotiation of stakeholders at a weak level. As for the impact of the harmonisation of community legislation, it is ambiguous. While it has established new norms and minimal standards in new areas, it also gave stakeholders an opportunity to push the dilemma of liberalisation to its extreme, by not creating the institutions allowing employees to compensate through a power of negotiation, the negative effects of liberalisation (Essay 2).

The place of the welfare state in the new Member States therefore had to be made clearer because of its impact on the process of economic restructuring. Its role is indeed central to identifying social costs, social transfers, social dialogue and social conflicts.

After a brief overview of the evolution of the welfare state in the CEECs, compared to the old Member States, the third chapter analyses the institutional dimension on the historical level and then the achievements of welfare states in the CEECs.

In light of the historical and institutional evolution, welfare states in the CEECs were essentially of a bismarckian character before WWII. It transformed into a universal system under state socialism thanks to full employment. After 1989, several reforms still had a bismarckian character. However, the CEECs' welfare states are a blend linked to an market-oriented market, the choice of universality, as well as combining bismarckian aspects and recent socialist legacies in a very dogmatic way. Therefore, the CEECs have "a minima" welfare states: in comparison to most EU-15 states, social expenditure is low. They are not however a unique and homogenous group because they show important internal differences.

In terms of achievements and challenges, the CEECs laud welfare for all but are in fact relatively poor, because of a low level of income per head (compared to the UE-15). They are also at a fairly low employment level compared to the UE-15, even if it is rising progressively. The CEECs also have a low life expectancy. The situation is different where the inequality of income is concerned: certain CEECs are indeed some of the lowest in Europe, with high levels of social protection due to the redistribution of income and social transfers. Others are within the highest ranking. The situation is the same for the poverty-risk measurements, which vary considerably from one country to the other (Essay 3). As a consequence, the author observes that the differences existing in most new members and the EU-15 countries in terms of social protection and professional relations are constant, considerable and could be durable in the future. Which has a direct incidence in the complex debate where the improvement and the regulation during restructurings are concerned.

The implementation of EU directives on restructurings is indeed insufficient in the CEECs. This aspect is analysed at the end of the first part (Essay 4). The author considers that these directives do not correctly reflect the political, economic and legal situations in the new Member States. Therefore, an effective application requires an improvement in industrial relations, particularly at the branch level. Bipartite dialogue at the national and branch level is relatively new and little developed which explains that collective negotiations take place mostly at the level of the company. The existing case-law on the transfer of companies and massive lay-offs in Hungary illustrates this general tendency in the new Member States. The rights included in these directives mainly aim to protect the interests of workers during the privatisations of companies. However, the respect of the right to information and consultation had serious flaws. However, the cases of Hungary and Poland show that regulation efforts have been made by national government to strengthen the structures of their social dialogue in order to reach the industrial relations levels in Western Europe.

Part II: The Strategies of Multinational Corporations in Certain Branches and Dealing with their Social Consequences

In its second part, the book looks at the role played by Foreign Direct Investments (FDI) in the development of economic activities within the new Member States. The central question is that of the economic and social positive impact at the local level. This depends on the absorption capacities of the host country allowing national stakeholders to integrate the input and know-how of MNCs. Direct foreign investment and local institutions constitute a "system". The effectiveness of this system depends on the extent of the interaction between stakeholders. By referring to the notion of "system" used by R. Narula that explains the links between local societies, MNCs, public institutions and universities as one system, this first contribution of the second part of the book assesses the level of integration of MNCs with reference to the food sector in Hungary. Therefore, despite the efforts undertaken by the government to get MNCs to participate in the local innovation system, it seems that only protectionist measures were successful in preventing the departure of multinational food companies. The reason for this conclusion is that when Hungary joined the EU in 2004, all the protectionist measures were removed. MNCs suddenly engaged in an intense restructuring and shutdown of factories process. There was no longer any obstacle to their global strategies of search for production effectiveness, growth and maximisation of profit. From there, they felt free to relocate somewhere else. Therefore, it is a major challenge to be effective and at the same time responsible at the local level (Essay 5).

The enlargement of the EU in 2004 – through the remodelling of the EU as a job market and a product of the market – weakened the social regulation of the EU and of the national level. More particularly, the way the representatives of the employees, including European Works Councils and Unions, deal with outsourcing and threats of restructurings is difficult to foresee, despite the very strong discourse on "social dumping" and "relocations", which are ill-defined concepts. In this Chapter 6, the author attempt to define the real context of transfer of activities in the new Member States, before considering the way in which the implantation of new activities in these states can influence the German model industrial relations and raw the outline of new industrial relations in the CEECs and of the role of the European Works Council.

This chapter, based on case studies, shows that the impact in terms of broadening of industrial relations is superior to the simple impact on labour, and that it varies depending on the country, the branch of activity and the specificities of the companies (Essay 6).

In a final Chapter, the book analyses the institutional and political foundations of the adaptation of the labour market in the context of the socioeconomic transformation in Central and Eastern Europe. It appraises public policies faced with rising unemployment resulting from industrial restructurings and economic transformations. In Poland, maybe more so than elsewhere because of it economic structure and heavy industry, the branch reorientation of the economy and the restructuring of companies formerly owned by the state into viable private entities, provoked large-scale layoffs which were not entirely compensated by job-creation in the private sector. This analysis of the restructuring framework in Poland shows that the debate on restructurings remains highly conditioned by the nature of the ongoing transitions and the specific institutional context in the new Member States, even if the specific questions linked to the social consequences of restructurings seem similar to those existing in the EU-15 countries. Between 1989 and 2004, the unemployment rate went from nearly zero to a spike of 20%, which becomes a striking social problem during the end of the communist era. Democratic governments faced with this situation have been put under pressure to minimise the effects of unemployment and fight against its spreading. Labour market policies have been implemented to support persons affected by the layoffs and, in certain cases, mass redundancy schemes were put in place. These measures can be categorised following two aspects: the breadth of the protection and the importance of substitution income and measures to promote a return to employment. Thus, in the first years, a certain number of schemes were set up through the universal compensation fund to compensate redundant workers, with provision for specific advantages in certain branches. However, since the end of the 1990s, the labour market has taken the path towards policies promoting return to employment and activation measures, but with a limited impact. In conclusion, the author insists on the existence of two distinct aspects with make it difficult to construct transitions or adaptations to change (Essay 7).

The aim of this book is to identify analytical lines of thought which need to be present when considering the question of restructurings in the EU.[4] It clearly demonstrates that where restructurings are concerned, the

4 These points are here underlined because the book is the result of a seminar organised in the framework of research sponsored by the ESF (article 6), AGIRE. Due to the budgetary restrictions of article 6, the AGIRE research project was not able to establish partners in the new Member States. It therefore was indispensable to in-

terms of the debate are different depending on the countries that are undergo the relocation of activities and those that for the time being are their beneficiaries. It would however be a mistake to consider that the differences are only due to the movement of companies and direct investments towards the new Member States. Indeed, first of all, new Member States are not the sole beneficiaries of direct investment in Europe. Second of all, the international strategies of companies also lead to relocation of activities from the new members states to even more attractive countries, either within the EU (for example Slovenia and Romania), or more often outside the EU.

However there are three important points to be made:

1. It is clear that the debate on restructurings has up to now been linked to economic transitions and not to the strategies of MNCs. There is a causal difference, but on the long run, no differences in nature in restructuring processes.

   It however remains that there are two aspects to the debate within the new Member States: the "old" one, linked to historical transitions, and the "new" one linked to the strategies of companies within and outside the Union.

2. It appears that professional and social relations remain case-specific, because of, in addition to the historical context, the difficult assimilation of the *acquis communautaire*, of its ambiguous character, of the weakness of the stakeholders, and finally, of the differences in the policies adopted by multinational corporations when locating their activity in the new Member States.

   It is not clear that the MNCs also transpose their industrial relations, even when they come from countries with strong social traditions, such as Germany, nor that the European Works Council can play a meaningful role on the general level.

   It also appears that the structures of the social dialogue are weak and therefore cannot be considered as a useful means of elaborating new strategies during restructurings.

3. Finally, the national institutional context seems somewhat limited in circumscribing the negative effects of restructurings, even if there are important differences from one new Member State to another. The professional transition mechanisms must necessarily

clude an analysis on the debate specific to the new Member States in order to avoid misrepresentations due to an approach exclusively based on case studies stemming from France, Germany, Italy, Belgium, the Netherlands and Spain. The different stages and results of the AGIRE project can be found on its website (www.fse-agire.com).

take this aspect into account if they are to be elaborate in Europe in the future (Gazier, 2005).

References

EC (2006), Communication from the Commission to the Council and the European Parliament "Enlargement, Two Years After – An Economic Success", COM (2006) 200 final of 3 May 2006.

FAYOLLE, J. (2005), "Restructurations d'hier et d'aujourd'hui: les apports d'un séminaire", *Revue de l'IRES*, Numéro spécial "Restructuration, nouveaux enjeux", Vol. 2005/1, No.47, pp. 337-359.

FARELL, G., SPERBER, S. *et al.* (eds.) (2007), "Reconciling Labour Flexibility with Social Cohesion. The Experiences and Specificities of Central and Eastern Europe", *Trends in Social Cohesion*, No.17, Council of Europe, Strasbourg.

HAVLIK, P. (2006), "Economic Restructuring in the New EU Member States and Selected Newly Independent States: Effects on Growth, Employment and Productivity", *INDEUNIS Papers*, February 2006, pp. 1-32.

GAZIER, B. (2005), *Vers un nouveau modèle social?*, Flammarion, Paris.

KIROV, V. (2004), "Restructurations industrielles et le jeu des acteurs", *Chronique internationale de l'IRES*, No.90, September 2004, pp. 39-47.

MOREAU, M.-A. (2006), *Normes sociales, droit du travail et mondialisation. Confrontations et mutations*, Dalloz, Paris.

MOREAU, M.-A. (2007), "Restructuring in the European Union: Recent Developments (2005-2006)", in DEGRYSE, C. and POCHET, P. (eds.), *Social Developments in the European Union 2006*, ETUI-REHS, Observatoire social européen and Saltsa, Brussels, pp. 49-67.

PETROVSKI, M. and GAZIER, B. (2006), "Dealing with Restructuring and Change on Sub-national, National and Supra-national Levels, A Review of Recent Litterature", *Cabinet Bernard Brunhes*, January 2006.

RAVEYRE, M. (2005), "Introduction", *Revue de l'IRES*, Numéro spécial "Restructuration, nouveaux enjeux", Vol. 2005/1, No.47, pp. 7-17.

SACHS-DURAND, C. (dir.) (2004), *La place des salariés dans les restructurations en Europe communautaire, Contexte économique, droit européen et comparé*, Presses universitaires de Strasbourg, Strasbourg.

URBAN, S. (2007), "Introduction", in FARELL, G., SPERBER, S. *et al.* (eds.), "Reconciling Labour Flexibility with Social Cohesion. The Experiences and Specificities of Central and Eastern Europe", *Trends in Social Cohesion*, No.17, Council of Europe, Strasbourg.

PART I

INDUSTRIAL RELATIONS AND RECONSTRUCTION OF SOCIAL DIALOGUE STRUCTURES IN THE NEW EU MEMBER STATES

Restructuring in the Enlarged EU

What Effects on the Evolving World of Work?[1]

Daniel VAUGHAN-WHITEHEAD

Senior adviser in charge of wages and other working conditions, International Labour Organization (Geneva)

Introduction

In 2006-2007 a research was carried out by the ILO on 28 countries (current EU-27 and Croatia) with the aim of capturing most important trends in working and employment conditions in the enlarged EU as well as better identifying what are the workers most at risk with regard these new trends. We provide below a summary of the findings of this comparative study, especially with regard the specific role of restructuring.

First, this study concludes that the world of work in the recently enlarged EU is not only increasingly complex, but that it is also changing very rapidly. The whole difficulty consists in distinguishing between those trends that have a long term nature and those which have a rather temporary character; and also between those that are due to a normal and progressive evolution, for instance in work organisation, and those that are due to rapid changes in the general economic and social context, under the pressure for instance of globalisation or EU enlargement. It is in such global changing working conditions that we shall address here the restructuring process.

We shall see below that restructuring is not only representing one major determinant of the trends in the European world of work but that it also may influence many of the other identified determinants.

---

[1] A first draft of this chapter was presented at the workshop "Restructuring in the new EU Member States", organised at the European University Institute in Florence, on 1-2 December 2006.

I. The Major Determinants of the Evolving World of Work

The study has clearly identified six major factors that are explaining most changes in the world of work.

A. The Impact of Governmental Employment Policy: Greater than Expected

The first is the impact of governmental policies. In this regard the general fight against unemployment has clearly led the governments to take action, under the form of regulations or deregulations of the labour market especially to facilitate entry and exit conditions. It is in this context that we can explain the rapid development of more atypical forms of contracts, like fix-term, part-time, through interim agency, self-employment. According to the European Commission (EC, 2006a), 40% of the workers would already be under a non-standard contract. Although permanent contracts remain the majority of contracts in most EU countries, it is also significant that such atypical forms of contracts are not only increasing but are clearly dominating among the new contracts that are signed between employers and individual workers.

First, the rise of *fixed-term contracts* affects the majority of countries. As a percentage of total employment, fixed-term employment increased from 12.1% in 1998 to 14.2% in 2005 in the EU-25, becoming even more widespread in the ten new Member States, with a percentage of 15.6 compared to 14.0% in the EU-15. The most noticeable increases occurred in Poland (from 11.9% of total employees to 25.5%), Portugal (from 17.2% to 19.5%), Sweden (from 12.9% to 16.2%) and the Netherlands (from 11.1% to 14.8%). Conversely, some countries displayed decreases, in particular Ireland (from 8.8% to 2.5%) and the UK (from 7.0% to 5.5%). A few countries presented a percentage of fixed-term contracts well above the average in 2005 (EU-25: 14.2%): the Netherlands (14.8%), Sweden (16.2%), Slovenia (16.8%), Finland (18.1%), Portugal (19.5%), Poland (an exception with Slovenia among the eastern members with 25.5%) and the well-known case of Spain, with 33.3%. In 2005, 54.6% of Spanish employees under 30 were on fixed-terms contracts. Clearly, young workers in the EU-25 are most affected by fixed-term contracts: in 2005, 30.7% of employees under 30 were on fixed-term contracts as against 9.1% for employees over 30.

Figure 1: Employees on Fixed-term Contracts in Member States (1998 and 2005)

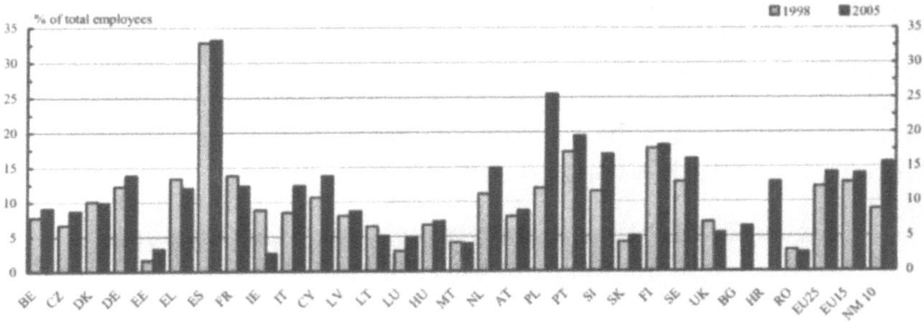

CY, MT, PL: 1998 data are for 2000; LU: 2005 data are for 2004

Source: Eurostat, EU Labour Force Survey.

Another form of temporary work particularly worth taking into consideration is *agency work*. Agency work is most prevalent in the UK, then in Luxembourg, the Netherlands and France, followed by Belgium, Denmark and Finland. Indeed, there appears to be some asymmetry between resort to this type of job and fixed-term contracts: the UK has a high level of agency work but a relatively low rate of fixed-term contracts. Similarly, the decrease in agency work in the Netherlands could be related to the increase in the use of fixed-term contracts. In the same vein, agency work is not important in Spain but it has the highest rate of fixed-term employees. However, many other factors should be taken into consideration to explain these differences, one of them being the flexibility of the Labour Code regarding termination of employment.

As for fixed-term contracts, agency work could be a port of entry to the labour market with a view to a more permanent contract. In Sweden, for instance, some government surveys indicate that around 60% of those hired through an interim agency end up getting employment at the interim agency's customer company. The rate is below 50% in the UK and estimated at 30% in France. It is also true that being a "regular" agency work employee could be a choice: this is estimated to affect 20-25% of employees in France. However, in most cases temporary agency contracts are concentrated on unattractive, low skilled jobs.

Temporary agency work is still a new form of employment in most eastern European Member States. It is often considered that this is due to the use of other forms of irregular contract and particularly "self-employment" (employment on the basis of civil contracts rather than employment contracts). However, agency work is on the rise and this explains government regulation of the matter (see later in this sub-section).

Part-time contracts could also be considered as a form of precarious contract. It is true that part-time work is in many instances a rational choice made to maximise the well being of the household. As such, this form of contract cannot be considered as precarious. However, it could negatively affect workers when it goes together with discriminatory practices – for instance, as regards social protection – in comparison with full-time workers. It also makes a worker's situation more unstable when part-time work is imposed on him.

Figure 2: Part-time Employment in the Total Economy in Member States (1998 and 2005)

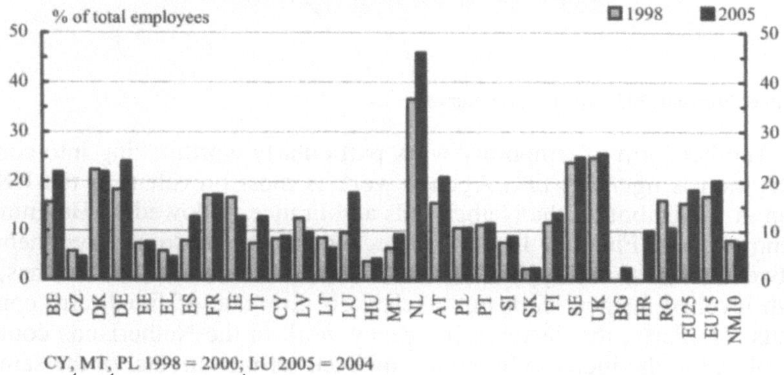

Source: Eurostat, EU Labour Force Survey.

Part-time work has increased in most EU countries, rising from 15.8% of total employment in 1998 (EU-25 average) to 18.4% in 2005 in the EU-25. However, differences remain high among countries. Part-time work remains poorly developed in all the twelve new EU Member States. The main reason is still the low level of wages: workers are keen to work as many hours as possible to improve their income and living standards.[2] On the employers' side, this type of flexibility is not yet integrated in work organisation. Only a slight increase can be noted over the period in these countries.

Undoubtedly, the Netherlands is by far the biggest user of part-time work, accounting for 46.0% of employment in 2005. Furthermore, the percentage has increased drastically, from 36.6% in 1998. Most Northern Europe countries exhibit a high percentage (above 20%): the UK, Sweden, Germany, Austria, Denmark and Belgium. Apart from the Netherlands, the biggest increases have been in Luxembourg (+8.2),

[2] Thus confirming the peculiar nature of part-time work in these countries, already identified in EC Industrial Relations Report 2004 (EC, 2004).

Belgium (+6.2), Germany (+5.8) and Austria (+5.2). It is interesting to note the exception of Ireland, which registered a significant decrease in part-time work (from 16.7 to 12.8).

Although the proportion of men working part-time has increased, particularly in the service sector, women constitute the majority of part-time workers and their share is increasing. We should also note that the percentage of young workers is also rising (18.4% of employees aged 15-29 were on part-time contracts in 2005 as against 16.3% in 2000) maintaining, though to a lesser extent, the gender pattern. In the service sector of the EU-15 in 2005, males aged 15-29 represented 19.3% (10.2% of all males) and their female colleagues 33.2% (38.1% of females as a whole).

These increases have accompanied the growth of the service sector, and particularly activities such as hotels and restaurants, personal services, and so on, which are well suited to the segmentation of working time. In fact the growth of new types of jobs in services also does represent an important explanatory factor behind certain trends in working practices. For instance, in Sweden a new type of arrangement has emerged where employees are put on "stand by" and only work when there is a need for extra work: the number of such part-time arrangements grew from 40,000 in 1990 to almost 145,000 in 2005.

Within the *Hartz* reforms, new legislation in Germany has also encouraged the recourse to a particular type of very short-term, part-time, one-off jobs – so-called mini-jobs paid 400 euros a month – that met an impressive growth with 6.7 million of mini-jobbers being registered in June 2005.

Finally, *self-employment* is a very heterogeneous category. The self-employed can be employers (self-employed with employees) or individual workers under a self-employment contract (self-employed without employees). Partly the latter category has become a flexible form of employment to which enterprises are increasingly having recourse, but which can be quite precarious. Globally, it has increased slightly but steadily over the last decade, representing 10.3% of total employment in 2005 in the EU-25. However, quite large variations could be observed among countries which are not mainly due to variations in agriculture, that generally represents the major part of the self-employed without employees. The growth of self-employment has often been encouraged by incentives provided by the employment national policies.

Figure 3: Self-employed without Employees in Member States (1998 and 2005)

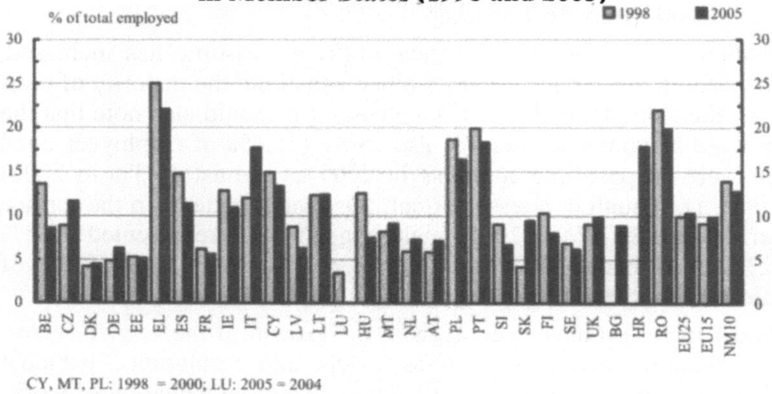

Source: Eurostat, EU Labour Force Survey.

The pace, focus and depth of reforms aimed at introducing more flexibility have been quite disparate among countries. Spain achieved flexibilisation of the labour market early in the 1990s. Germany has also promoted it through financial and tax incentives but also through labour market deregulation, and recourse to new employment forms. In France, the intervention of the government seems to have led not to one major form of labour contract but to an addition of different measures one on the top of the other, something that we could qualify a sort of "patch-work" (Mehaut, 2007). More recently, France decided to abandon its protective armoury of labour legislation in order to facilitate entry and exit from the labour market. A new law has been passed to encourage a new type of two-year contract (the so-called "*contrat nouvelle embauche*") for enterprises with less than twenty employees. A similar contract for young people (*contrat premier emploi*) has also been introduced, which has provoked fierce opposition and had to be withdrawn. The government as an employer has also played a direct role in the development of these types of contract by offering many temporary employment contracts through its public work schemes for young unskilled workers and long-term unemployed. It should be recalled that in many countries, the public sector is a major user of fixed-term contracts. All these measures are aimed at enhancing job creation and reducing unemployment. Action in other areas has also taken place with the same purpose. This was the case in France with the new legislation on the reduction of weekly working time to 35 hours – implemented to boost "employment-sharing" – which, despite a number of drawbacks.

To be emphasised however that the new legislation in the most recent period in EU countries has not only aimed at introducing flexibility but also in some cases at limiting its abuses: it is significant that in the UK for instance a new legislation has been adopted to limit the excesses of the so-called "gang master" phenomenon, that is the exploitation by interim agencies of migrants workers coming from Central and Eastern Europe.[3]

Similarly, the transposition of EC laws had an impact in the new EU Member States, as witnessed by the adoption of the EU working time directive which has led to a rapidly decrease in the working week – as in Poland but also Czech republic and Slovakia – by a few hours.

New legislation – as in Bulgaria – has also contributed to limit the employers' extensive recourse to self-employment – that had become a regular way to replace regular working contracts, and to have employees covered not by the labour code but by the less constraining civil code. Similar legislation is also programmed in other new EU Member States to limit for instance the abuses with regard fix-term contracts, as in the Czech Republic and Poland.

From the public authorities' side we should also remind the importance of health and safety regulations, with definite progress among new Member States that are progressively harmonizing their legislation to EU regulations in this field. However what is also noticed in this field is a gap between such official transposition of the EU acquis and its implementation, something that highlights another key policy tool that is clearly not sufficiently developed yet among the new EU Member States, which is labour inspection. In Poland for instance the institutional weaknesses in this regard explain for a great part the massive recourse to unofficial activities and abuses in terms of working conditions. We should however also point to the need of better labour inspection in older Member States as well, especially with regard subcontracting and associated working conditions.

B. Labour and Capital Mobility: Influential in Both Host and Home Countries

This leads to a second important determinant of working conditions, which is precisely about the impact of labour and capital mobility on working conditions. We observe in particular a general trend toward outsourcing that is influencing working conditions in both the country of origin and the host country.

---

3 At the same time however we have seen the opposition of the UK to the proposed directive on working conditions of interim workers as well as to the removal of its opt-out in the revision of the working time directive.

In Romania for instance most companies in the textile sector are already acting as subcontractors for major EU companies. More than 90% of Romania's production in clothing results from sub-contracting for both large multinational groups and small foreign enterprises. A similar process is also observed in Bulgaria, not only in textiles but also in wood processing industries, and especially for women in certain towns on the border with Turkey and Greece working for generally foreign-owned companies. This massive process of subcontracting in certain host countries has immediate effects on working conditions: Romanian subcontractors for instance are characterised by longer working hours, intensity at work, relatively low wages.

At the same time such outsourcing process is making downward pressure on wages and other labour standards in the home countries, since the threat of relocation may help to water down trade unions' claims. The risk of industrial relocation is particularly putting workers under pressure to engage in greater work intensity and harder working conditions, while also facing significant employment insecurity. This risk is present in all EU Member States as well as future Member States. Significant relocation further east is already affecting the automobile and electronics industries in Hungary. Similarly, a few foreign-owned textile companies have already moved out of Romania further east, for instance to Ukraine.

This trend is not only observed in the private sector but also in the – so far relatively protected – public sector which has started to outsource some of its activities, thus also putting public employees under increased pressure.

Of course there are certain activities that cannot be relocated at all, such as services in hospitals, education, and home services. It is interesting to observe however that it is often in these activities that we assist instead to inward labour migration, precisely to help employers to responding to competitive and labour costs pressures particularly acute in certain occupations as nurses, but also doctors. Certain sectors have also more recourse to migrant workers, such as construction, most of it in the informal sector. This has led many interim agencies to specialise in the delivery of migrant workers in certain sectors, as shown by the gang masters' phenomenon in the UK but also increasing work of migrants through interim agencies in Scandinavian countries.

In this context, the minimum wage appears to be one of the most important income policy tools (Eyraud and Saget, 2005). A few important facts must be underlined on the minimum wage.

First, the proportion of countries with a statutory minimum wage has increased with the arrival of the twelve new EU Member States (among which only Cyprus has no statutory minimum wage but rather a minimum wage determined by sector).

Second the minimum wage has come back quite strongly in policy debates notably in Germany but also at EU level (see the debate on the possibility of having an EU minimum wage).

Third, minimum wages have increased in most countries over the period although in a distinct way. Progression has been particularly high in new EU Member States and candidate countries, with the exception of Poland in the more recent period. This sharp increase follows the very restricted early years of transition during which it was used as a tool to keep all social expenditure under control, and during which the minimum wage remained at a very low proportion of the average wage (Standing and Vaughan-Whitehead, 1995).

Fourth, the percentage of workers covered by the minimum wage shows that its role in protecting low paid workers is quite variable among countries. Only in France, Latvia and Romania is a significant proportion of workers directly affected by minimum wages. In the other countries its impact on low wages seems more limited.

However, and this will be our fifth remark, the minimum wage does protect very low wages, as shown by the British case where a national minimum wage was introduced in 1999. The share of employees on very low pay fell from 12.0% to 9.6% between 1998 and 2004.

C. Restructuring: Direct and Indirect Effects

Beyond mobility, restructuring is a major process in itself that influences working and employment conditions. First, this does clearly affect those workers who are laid off, as shown by the impressive social consequences in Central and Eastern European countries (CEEC). Second, as we shall see in section II, this is also making pressure on remaining workers to accept longer hours, lower wages, and greater flexibility in general in the conditions of work. It is impressive to see for instance how much unemployment in Poland is influencing almost all working conditions. Moreover we observe that the downsizing process carried out by many companies is generally not accompanied by a consequent reduction in the volume of production thus involving a greater burden on remaining employees. This is translated into an increased intensity at work and a greater number of working hours.

The evolution of restructuring is explaining the confirmation of traditional groups at risk as well as the appearance of new categories at risk.

First of all *traditional categories* considered as most vulnerable remain under continuous exposure to the consequences of restructuring.

Clearly, *women* are often the first ones to be the victims of restructuring. This has been clear for instance in Central and Eastern Europe where women have been the first ones to be laid off, a process that has contributed to significantly reduce women's employment rate more than for men in the course of the transition. Women are also more affected by the low-wages phenomenon mentioned above (in the EU-25, 33.8% of women are low-paid as against 17.4% of men), as are young workers (in the EU-25, 40.4% of workers under 30 are low paid, as against 19.3% of workers above 30). They are also often overrepresented among atypical forms of employment that are the first to suffer from the restructuring process. In Denmark, for instance, women with lower-level education are among those most reliant on interim work agencies that are also associated with lower pay and poorer access to training and collective agreements.

Young people remain a category at risk. They are particularly exposed to precarious labour contracts and low wages. Measures taken to secure employment may further harm their working conditions. As an example, the Volkswagen agreement of November 2004 – agreed under pressure to reduce labour costs in the face of international competition – proposed among other things provisions on wage reductions for the newly hired. While the aim of this process was obviously not to affect the current workers of the enterprise it clearly weakened an already fragile category which is most affected by future recruitment, namely young workers.

The temporary work contracts also mainly affect young employees under 30: 52.5% of them are under such contracts in Spain, 44.1% in Poland and 43.7% in Slovenia. The percentage of younger workers with this status has doubled since 1998 in these countries. It is also to be noted that young women seem to be more affected than young men by this form of employment contract, especially in Slovenia, where 51% of women under 30 are affected compared to 38% of their male colleagues of the same age, but also in Finland (48% for women and 32% for men), Sweden (45% versus 33%), and even Cyprus (22% against 14%). The opposite seems to be true for Lithuania (13% for men compared to 5% for women) but also Latvia and Estonia. This may be because of the more permanent nature of employment contracts in the public sector where there is a higher proportion of women than men.

Older people are also more at risk. First, they continue to face discrimination in recruitment because they are considered to be more expensive in terms of labour costs.[4] They also often have more problems

---

[4] See the results of the 57th Eurobarometer survey of fifteen European Union countries in Marsh and Sahin-Dikmen (2003).

in coping with changes in organisation, labour markets and conditions of work. Increased requests for lengthened working time, more unsocial hours or greater mobility may affect their work and productivity. They may be placed in particular forms of atypical employment contracts, as in Germany where the government introduced a new form of contract for those above 50 years of age. Physical conditions at work also impact directly on their employment, and often on their decision to retire, as shown in the UK and Sweden (Humphrey *et al.*, 2003).

The age group most at risk, however, can change according to specific country conditions. For instance, in Hungary – as in Romania – the category most threatened by lay-offs remains workers in their 40s, since the employment of young workers continues to be subsidised and older workers are protected.

In some countries barriers to entry onto the labour market as well as more rapid exit are particularly strong for *minority groups*. In Hungary, Slovakia and many other new and future EU Member States the Roma are primarily affected. In Croatia, the risks are more acute for Serbs – who have no access to state or regional administration – Roma, but also war veterans and disabled people. In Bulgaria *ethnic minorities* such as Roma and ethnic Turks have a much lower level of employment security and problems in terms of health and safety protection.

Immigrants also appear to be discriminated against in the world of work. In Sweden, for instance, there is a strikingly high percentage of working poor among the self-employed, who are dominated by immigrants who have great difficulties finding a place in the regular Swedish labour market. Many immigrant workers do not have a choice other than to adopt self-employed status, unless they manage to enter the Swedish labour market through interim agency work.

Lower educated workers are also more at risk. This is the case, for instance, with regard to interim agency work: while a "freelancer" – for instance, an IT consultant or even a nurse whose qualifications are in demand – can navigate with ease in a job market that offers a diversity of opportunities (although also bringing stress and burnout risks) the low-skilled temporary worker is often compelled to accept less favourable conditions and is thus more vulnerable.

At the same time, we also can identify *new types of vulnerable workers*.

A major new risk in some new market economies in Central and Eastern Europe is related to *restructuring and privatisation* that have led in some cases to massive lay-offs and thus increased both insecurity of employment and the unemployment risk. Some studies identify the positive effects of restructuring on economic growth for instance in

Poland, the Czech Republic and Hungary (Hoshi *et al.*, 2007). At the same time some studies have concluded that privatisation did not always enhance restructuring, especially in CIS transition economies (Djankov and Murrell, 2002) but also in Central and Eastern Europe (Vaughan-Whitehead, 2003).

This process in some cases has also hit *new categories of employees*, especially in sectors most affected by the opening of their country to international markets. Consider the example of the high-level scientists working for the Croatian pharmaceutical company Pliva who were the first victims of the change in strategy decided by the company in order to survive new international competition, to focus more towards generics than fundamental research into new molecules.

No doubt, increased competition within the EU-27 and more generally globalisation have affected new categories of employees, too. We could also mention the white-collar employees of Hewlett-Packard France who in 2005 were most affected by the restructuring and lay-off programme. More generally, we can observe increasing stress on managers and white-collar workers in the EU-25 that may become a determinant risk if it starts to affect their mental and physical health.

Conditions of work and forms of employment have also deteriorated in some countries for *teachers and employees in the health sector* – many of them in the public sector – who are victims of increased stress at work and where there is not always appropriate funding for improving working conditions. This process is particularly acute in the new and future EU Member States, such as Hungary, Estonia, Latvia, Lithuania, but also Bulgaria and Romania. It has brought about a high emigration potential among health employees. Conditions of work for this category of worker – for instance, hospital attendants – have also deteriorated in older EU Member States as the UK or France. More generally, employees in services – as we saw in previous sections – seem to be increasingly confronted by different types of risk. In France, as elsewhere, night work (cleaning teams, and so on) and unsocial hours over the weekend (in supermarkets and other shops) are the most frequent. Moreover, it is often in services that there is the highest proportion of working poor (cleaning or other services to households or elderly and disabled people, and so on). Although these jobs cannot be relocated they are becoming more and more precarious.

New regions may also be at risk. This is typically the case for Eastern Germany (the former GDR) where employees not only suffer from lower wages and working conditions – these differences being clearly observed in the differential contents of their respective collective agreements and with quality of life being directly affected – but also have to face significant restructuring, including industrial relocations (sometimes a few kilometres across the border in one of the new EU Member States) and thus greater unemployment and social exclusion risks. Increased regional differentials in the new and future new Member States, despite their sustained economic growth, is also worrying, as if dual economic development was taking place. In Poland, for instance, the areas most affected by both unemployment and low living standards are the same – the west and north of the country – as those affected in the early transition, that is, 15 years ago, indicating a durable phenomenon of regional fragmentation. Unemployment, for instance, is 40% in the commune of Lobeski (*Zachodniopomorske*) compared to 6.3% in Warsaw.

D. The Rapid Changes in Work Organisation

Another key factor in explaining the changes in working conditions are rooted in the changes in the organisation of work, themselves influenced by the increased competitive context. Technological developments and the forces of globalisation seem to be transforming demands on workers, such as new forms of organisation that require a higher degree of flexibility, lean production, just-in-time, client-oriented activity, job rotation, and quality control. New productive forms of organisation such as Human Resource Management (HRM), but also a new type of trading relationship between subcontractors and main entrepreneur tend to be replacing the traditional employer-employee relationship.

One of the most peculiar processes is the recourse to *shift work* that has been expanding not only in manufacturing but also in services and agriculture. One employee in five in 2004 reported being usually involved in shift work in the EU-25, a global average that hides important differences by country but also by sector of activity – although less by gender. We may observe, first, greater recourse to shift work in the new EU Member States (nearly double that in the EU-15, at between 33 and 19%), which may be explained by the dominance of multinational companies in both industry and services in these emerging market economies (more than 50% of their manufacturing production and 70% of exports) to feed the enlarged EU market. The countries with the highest levels of shift work (in both industry and services) are Poland, Croatia, Slovenia, Slovakia and the Czech Republic.

Shift work is also booming in Portugal (it doubled in industry and services both for males and females), but also in Greece and Austria. It slightly increased in the UK, Denmark and Belgium, whilst it decreased in France and Sweden. In the countries where the phenomenon had not yet developed extensively before 2000 it has since increased significantly, as in Austria and Greece. In the countries where the process had already reached high levels in industry in 2000 as in France, it has slightly decreased since then but has tended to expand in the service sector.

In the new EU Member States the most striking increase in shift work is in industry. This is also a direct consequence of production and sales in the manufacturing sector that require just-in-time production and large-scale operations with 24-hour working and immediate adaptation of the production process to demand.

It is obvious that this expansion of shift work practices is influencing working conditions such as working rhythms – often more intense in companies that have implemented shift work – and working hours, that may be fewer because shared among different shifts.

The increased recourse to shift work has also often led to a parallel development of *unsocial hours*: the countries with a greater number of unsocial hours are often those with more recourse to shift work.

Week-end work in particular has attracted the attention of policy makers and led to sometimes lively debates in society as in Croatia and Slovenia – which organised a referendum on the issue. Week-end work is clearly the most developed in agriculture, followed by services and industry. In 2005 they were the most developed in Slovakia, Malta, Estonia, but also in Austria, Denmark, and France. Since 2000 they have increased the most in Slovakia, Austria, the Czech Republic, France and Italy. They have also slightly increased in Slovenia, Croatia, Spain, Belgium and Portugal. The issue – and in particular working on Sunday – has recently been placed at the core of the public debate in Croatia and Slovenia, in which not only political but also religious representatives have been directly involved.

Figure 4: Proportion of Employees Working Both Saturday and Sunday (2005)

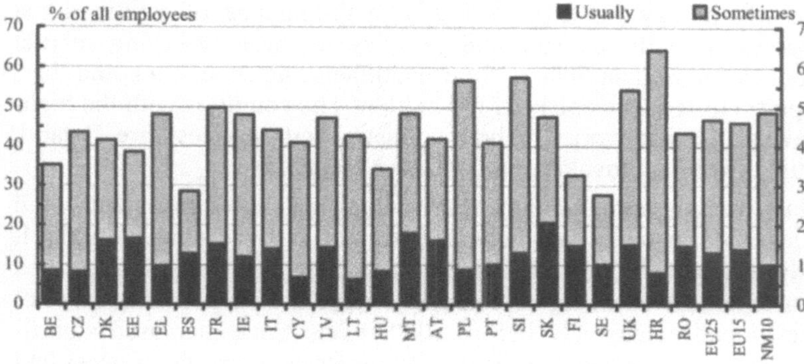

Source: Eurostat, EU Labour Force Survey.

Night work is often developed alongside shift work, which generally involves night-shifts. Night work is well developed in both industry and services in the Slovak Republic and in the UK, though with country specificities. Night work clearly affects more men in the UK – and France – while women in industry are also affected in Slovakia, Malta, Finland and Estonia. There thus seems to be a significant variety in terms of trends between the 25 EU countries which goes well beyond the differences expected between new and older EU members.

Figure 5: Proportion of Employees Usually Working at Night (2005)

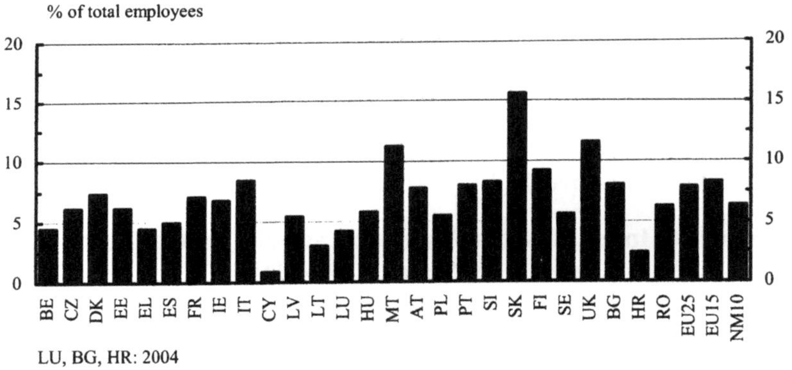

Source: Eurostat, EU Labour Force Survey.

Finally, *stand-by work* has also been developing, a form of working which gives employees no control whatsoever, not only over their working schedule but also their employment schedule since both are decided by the company. Although it affects a small minority of workers on average (less than 2-3%) it has been increasing in some countries, in particular the Netherlands where it affects 2.5% of men and 6% of women and in Sweden (2.5 and 4.5%). Similarly, in Austria today it affects 5% of all employees, and is much more frequent in sectors such as hotels and restaurants and community, social and personal services, where it reaches almost 10%.

Everywhere atypical working hours are increasing, something that has also direct effects on work-family balance.

E. Social Dialogue (or its Absence) Can Make a Difference

Fifth factor, social dialogue is playing a major role in shaping new employment and working conditions. Employers' systematic search for greater flexibility to respond to competitive pressures, the falling trade union membership, the reduced scope of collective bargaining and collective agreement is often explaining the outcome in the respective world of work in individual countries, individual sectors, and individual enterprises. We assist for instance to the increased use of extension clauses at local level, that allow the employer to divert from the higher level collective agreement and which generally results in wage concessions, as witnessed by recent developments in Germany and elsewhere.

Declining trade union density and the scope of social dialogue explain for a great part the current process of wage moderation and concessionary bargaining, whether at the central level as in Ireland or in the process of the decentralisation of collective bargaining. Even in Denmark, where concessionary bargaining is limited, there are examples of major wage concessions at SAS Ground Service in February 2005 or in the Tulip Slaughter Houses in Ringster in December 2004, where 300 workers had to accept wages 15% below the industry level to keep their jobs. Figure 6 confirms that wage rises have been quite moderate in EU-15, particularly in Germany, whereas wage rises in the UK and Finland have been above the EU-15 average.

Figure 6: Index of Gross Wages and Salaries in Real Term in Member States (2000-2004)

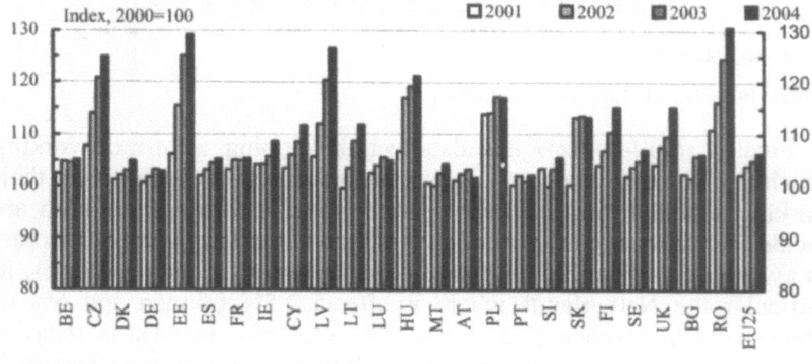

It appears that the highest increases are found in the new EU Member States where wages were the lowest. However, having the highest wage increases does not necessarily mean that the country concerned is a high-wage economy. The majority of low-wage economies (above 30% of employees paid a wage under 60% of the average wage) are in the new Member States, with the exceptions of Portugal and the UK (32.2%), whereas the highest wage economies (under 15%) are from the EU-15: Denmark, Italy, Belgium, Finland and Sweden.

A series of case studies carried out in 2006-2007 have shown concrete cases where the presence of social dialogue may concretely help to improve working and employment conditions (Eyraud and Vaughan-Whitehead, 2007).

While social dialogue can influence working conditions, social dialogue itself is influenced by employment and working conditions. Working under individual contracts or working longer and irregular hours (often at home if self-employed, or at night) clearly diminishes these workers' participation in social dialogue.

The trend is even more striking in new and future EU Member States where low coverage of collective bargaining and low development of social dialogue, at both branch and enterprise level, explain to a large extent the low standard of working conditions and the abuses in the use of atypical work contracts, longer hours, health and safety protection measures, intensity at work. This is the case for self-employment in Poland, often used as a way to shift to civil contracts. Serious drawbacks in the implementation of all EU regulations on health and safety continue to prevail. There is thus a need not only for social dialogue but also for the necessary actors to interact in the new market environment.

At the same time we also see how certain groups of workers are disadvantaged because of their lower access to social dialogue. In Sweden and Denmark collective agreements are not as protective for temporary contract workers – especially those working through interim agencies – which explain the lower wages, longer working time and poorer conditions at work in general. Furthermore, the fact that temporary workers in Germany are covered by collective agreements does not impede adverse conditions for such atypical workers, something that also sheds light on the vulnerability of the trade unions with regard to the interests of such categories of worker.

The trend is even more striking in new and future EU Member States where low coverage of collective bargaining and low development of social dialogue, at both branch and enterprise level, explain to a large extent the low standard of working conditions. In particular, serious drawbacks in the implementation of all EU regulations on health and safety continue to prevail.

F. The Boosting Role of Social Policies: Education, Training, and Social Protection

Finally, there are other conditions and other policies that were found to influence working and employment conditions: these are of course the education policy in a context in which working conditions are found to be the most difficult for unskilled workers. Training is also an essential component since it does represent the major tool eventually at workers' disposal to shift toward better quality and better-paid jobs. According to the findings of our comparative project, training seems to represent the missing link in many of the countries under study.

Other conditions and policies may also release some of the pressures currently on the shoulders of the employees, such as family friendly policies – as increased infrastructure for small children – but also more globally housing and social protection policies.

II. The Transversal Effects of Restructuring

Restructuring is not only one major factor directly influencing working and employment conditions, but it does also influence all the other listed factors.

A. The Threat of Unemployment

By its direct effect on employment and the growth of unemployment, restructuring is putting pressure on the employees to accept any conditions in order to keep their job. This contributes to explain in particular the employees' shift to more atypical forms of contracts as well as more demanding working conditions such as long working hours, stress at work, and sometimes also greater health and safety risks.

Restructuring can lead for instance to "obligatory" *part-time jobs*, especially when the company restructuring decides to reduce its labour costs by shifting part of it full time jobs into part-time jobs. As already mentioned, part-time work may be a positive choice, mainly for the purpose of finding a better balance between work and family. In some cases, however, it is imposed. Figure 3 presents trends in the proportion of part-time workers who would have preferred to work full-time. In both new Member States and EU-15 we can observe an increase in the percentage of "involuntary" part-time workers. It is particularly high though and increasing more sharply in the new EU Member States where the rate of dissatisfaction about part-time is also much higher. We found however also high dissatisfaction among part-timers in countries like Greece, Italy, Spain, France, Finland, Sweden, Denmark and Germany.

Figure 7: Proportion of Employed Working Part-time Because they Could not Find a Full-time Job in Member States (1998 and 2005)

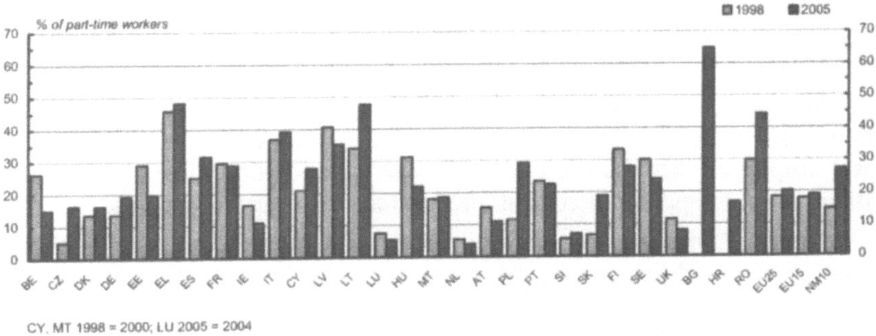

Source: Eurostat, EU Labour Force Survey.

Similarly, *self-employment* is often more a survival strategy than a job seeking strategy. A recent study came to the conclusion that the self-employed in Spain are more at risk of impoverishment (Mercader-Prats, 2005). In Sweden the migrant workers were found to be prevalent among self-employed because they have a problem to find a regular job or are the first ones to be laid-off in case of restructuring.

Certain sectors are particularly concerned by this phenomenon, such as manufacturing and personal services. Manufacturing is the sector in which false self-employment is most likely to be found among the category of self-employed without employees. Although their proportion is not high, we find big increases in the Czech Republic, Estonia, Latvia, Slovakia, but also in Italy, the UK, Austria and Luxembourg. More moderate increases can also be observed in Germany and Ireland. This is not to say that all the increases are due to false self-employment. The specific industrial structures of the countries concerned are also relevant. However, case studies show that this type of self-employed are often regular employees who have been asked by their employer – mainly to avoid social contributions and taxes – to shift from a regular employment contract to a self-employment contract. This is also the case in construction, which in many countries represents the second largest proportion of self-employed without employees after agriculture. Table 1 presents particularly sharp increases in the proportion of self-employed without employees.

Table 1: Self-employed without Employees as % of Total Employed in Construction

	CZ	EE	IT	NL	SK	UK	RO
1998	18.5	5.8	16.4	6.9	9.0	29.5	6.4
2004	31.1	12.8	24.3	11.4	23.9	31.0	13.1

The concerns of the European Commission regarding this problem were expressed in a recent report on free movement of workers across the enlarged EU: "The problem of persons posing falsely as self-employed workers to circumvent the law should be dealt with by Member States" (EC, 2006b: 11).

Alternatively, they may be former employees who were made redundant, as well as unemployed workers who had no choice but to become self-employed. This is typically the case in the restructuring process as it has often happened in central and Eastern European countries.

The phenomenon does also apply to self-employed persons without employees working in the personal services branch. They have increased in number in most countries, with particularly noticeable increases in Italy, Latvia, the Netherlands and Slovakia. The increase is also steady in Germany and the UK. We also find some in the business services sub-sector: the percentage of self-employment without employees rose from 13.3% in 1998 to 15.8% in 2004 in the EU-15, but fell in the eastern EU countries.

Our analysis is confirmed if we look at the self-employed without employees by occupation. We can safely say that the self-employed status of low skilled manual workers is dubious. Interestingly, their share is increasing in most new Member States, and particularly in Latvia (from 6.2% of total self-employment without employees in 1998 to 13.5%), but also in Germany, Spain, the Netherlands, Austria, Finland, Sweden and the UK. This is also true of other occupations such as skilled workers or professionals and technicians.

Although this does not represent a major phenomenon, the trend is steady and defines a population of workers at risk. In some case, the self-employed are quite happy with their status, which gives them more autonomy, but to the detriment of other working conditions, such as irregular income, stress and excessive hours.

Restructuring can also lead to *longer hours and also higher working rhythms* for remaining employees. It is significant to observe than between 2004 and 2005, 10 countries out of the former EU-15 experienced an increase in their weekly working time. At the same time, most new EU Member States are characterised by greater number of working hours. The figures also show a percentage of employees working more than 50 hours a week that is also much higher in the new EU Member States. According to Paoli *et al.* (2002), in 2001, 79% of workers in the twelve new Member States – compared to 48% of workers in the EU-15 – were found to work more than 40 hours a week on average.

The extension of working hours has become a way of coping for both employers and employees. On the employers' side it is a way of responding to peak periods of activity with the same manpower: in this way they limit the payment of social security contributions and avoid costly hiring/firing procedures. From the employees' side accumulating the number of hours during the week has become the main way of increasing low basic wages and of obtaining the supplementary means necessary for family survival. It is mainly low wages that impel workers to accumulate extra working hours. However, longer working hours are often due not to the employees' wishes but to the employers' requirements. As an example, 30% of extra working time is involuntary in Poland and thus does not correspond to a free choice on the employees' side.

Figure 8: Average Usual Hours Worked by Full-time Employees (2000 and 2005)

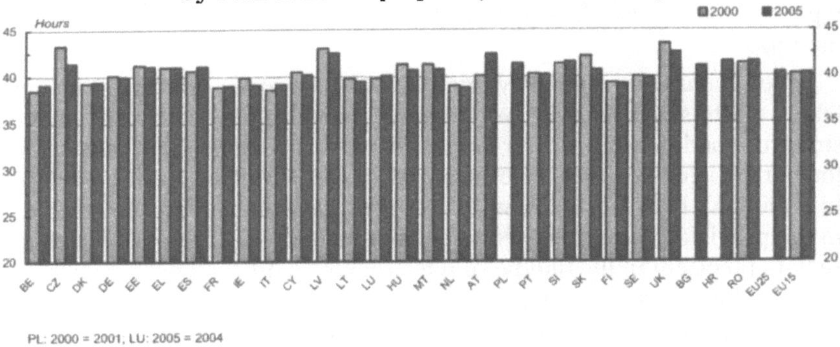

Source: Eurostat, EU Labour Force Survey.

It is also significant to observe that the longest number of hours in transition countries of Central and Eastern Europe has been recorded in the early transition when restructuring was particularly widespread in all sectors of the economy. The number of working hours then started to decline in the late 1990s and early 2000s first because restructuring started to slow down, and then because of changes in national labour laws mainly to fall into line with the EU working time directive along EU membership – for example, a reduction in the maximum weekly working time in Poland from 42 to 40 hours between 2001 and 2003, with similar decreases in the Czech Republic and Slovakia.

Between 2004 and 2005, and in contrast with former EU-15, only two out of the ten new EU Member States have experienced a – very moderate – increase in working hours, Lithuania and Slovakia. As a result, a sort of convergence seems to be operating, with the average for the new Member States (41.9) being now comparable to that in the EU-15 (41.8). This is partly due to a slight increase in working hours in the

EU-15 (from 41.7 in 2000 to 41.8 in 2005) – notably through the greater use of overtime – but also a rapid catching-up process in the new EU Member States.

If we look at the figures on working time of those only working full-time, Greece remains in first place, but with Austria (44.3 hours a week) not far behind, followed by Poland (43.3), the UK (43.2), the Czech Republic and Slovenia (42.9), Latvia (42.8), Cyprus and Spain (42.4).

B. Outsourcing or Recourse to Migration to Reduce Labour Costs

At the same time, companies which have to carry out restructuring are in the process of searching any possible solution to reduce labour costs, and consequently often have recourse to outsourcing, thus reducing even further the already poor prospects of local employees to keep their job.

The recourse to migrant workers is also a way to attempt reducing labour costs since migrant workers are generally ready to work under stressful conditions for lower wages. It is not by chance that most new temporary agencies that have emerged in the recent years in countries like the UK, but also Sweden or Denmark have specialised themselves in the provision of migrant workers from the new EU Member States to sectors precisely in the middle of a restructuring process, as in construction, textile, and automobile.

This may have direct on working and employment conditions. In the UK while the extensive migration from new EU Member States especially Poland was found to have positive economic effects on growth and employment, it also led to some adjustments on the labour market. It did contribute to the general process of wage moderation and also led in many cases to some lengthening of working hours or intensification of working rhythms.

It is interesting to note in that respect that the minimum wage has been revisited in some countries as an anti-dumping tool. This is the case in Germany where the statutory minimum wage fixed for specific branches are specifically based on regulations introduced to implement the EU Directive on the posting of workers in the framework of the provision of services. More recently, a debate to extend it to all sectors notably through the introduction of a statutory national minimum wage has taken place following the arrival of migrant workers and the differences observed in terms of wage standards between the western and eastern länders. Similarly in the UK the adjustment of the national minimum wage has been influenced by increased inward migration and the activities of the labour providers also often known as "gang masters" (Low Pay Commission, 2006). Conversely the minimum wage has been presented in Latvia, Poland and Romania as a possible tool for stopping the emigration of workers, a debate that is also currently going on in other new EU countries. As an example, healthcare workers' representatives in Poland have called for the introduction of minimum pay rates in the sector to prevent the exodus of doctors and nurses seeking higher wages elsewhere in the EU.[5]

C. The Organisation al Impact on Remaining Employees

Restructuring is also influencing the organisation of work since the companies that have laid-off people generally have to change work organisation in order to continue their production with a reduced labour force, something that is possible only through extending the number of working hours especially unsocial hours over the week-ends. Similarly many companies under restructuring prefer to have recourse to temporary agencies in order to have access to a cheap labour force without any constraining conditions in terms of the length of their working contracts.

D. Placing Employers in a Dominating Bargaining Position

Finally restructuring is influencing social dialogue since it clearly places the employer in a dominating negotiation position, with workers' representatives generally having to accept painful tradeoffs at local level in order to limit layoffs, such as wage concessions, or extensive working hours.

From this point of view, certain trends in social dialogue may contribute to modify the overall context of work organisation. This could be the case with the development of more decentralised agreements on flexibility, which could become more constraining for workers. Take, for example, the new two-year collective agreement reached in the construction sector in Sweden on 9 November 2005, in exchange for a pay increase. It introduces more work flexibility by introducing the possibility for employers to agree schedules of work directly with individual workers or teams. However, the union refuses to go further in terms of individualising working relations (particularly regarding wage negotiations), which would indeed impose high pressure and stress on workers. Similarly in the Netherlands, draft legislation approved in late 2005 proposes to grant more responsibility for working conditions and the achievement of health and safety goals on the shop floor to employers and employees. The trade unions oppose this because they fear such

---

5 See "Health Care Workers Demand Sectoral Minimum Wage", *European Industrial Relations Review*, November 2006.

new regulations will progressively replace existing – more central and protective – regulations governing working conditions. A similar risk exists when companies subcontract risky tasks to small subcontracting firms, where social dialogue does not exist and working conditions are much more permissive.

At the same time wage competition due to low cost labour arriving from some eastern European EU countries, however limited,[6] does also have a negative impact on vulnerable categories of the labour force. Apart from affecting in the first instance immigrants themselves, a vulnerable category, it most affects the priority at-risk sectors identified above: hotels and restaurants, construction, and so on. In Sweden, the forestry sector is also affected. In the same country, one of the most publicised examples is the case of the Latvian construction firm which had not signed up to the collective agreement for the Swedish construction industry. The firm was therefore legally able to fix lower labour standards for its employees, including lower wages. The same has happened in countries not applying statutory minimum wages like Denmark and Germany.

The Swedish example shows that the traditional labour protection system does not always meet new challenges. In particular, the absence of a national system of minimum wages allows enterprises to "legally" introduce lower standards for workers coming from the eastern part of the European Union. Indeed, other types of protection exist. In Sweden, the Latvian case cited above has, for example, pushed the white-collar union of salaried, technical and clerical workers and the engineering industry employers' federation to negotiate an agreement at the branch level which, among other things, requires that "the union be informed of the employment conditions offered to new immigrants at the point when work permits are sought from the immigration authorities".[7] The German answer has been based on the EU Directive on posting workers, introducing statutory minimum wages in certain sectors, in particular construction. In this country, the Posted Workers Act has been extended to address the problem of wage dumping. The recent ferries dispute in Ireland is also illustrative of the trend: the company wanted to replace 543 seafarers with cheaper labour from eastern EU countries. Finally, an agreement was signing imposing the payment of at least the Irish minimum wage.[8]

---

6 The European Commission Report on the Functioning of the Transitional Arrangements (EC, 2006b) shows that the risks of massive migration flows have clearly been overestimated, together with their effects on local labour markets.

7 *European Industrial Relations Review*, July 2005, page 16.

8 *European Industrial Relations Review*, January 2006, page 9.

E. Many Trapped into Low Pay-low Quality Jobs

The basic reasoning behind the flexibilisation of labour contracts is that by making hiring and firing easier, it helps the employees victims of restructuring and unemployed in general (and particularly the medium/long-term unemployed, young people and ageing workers) to find a job more easily. Even short-term experience acquired through a series of precarious jobs may facilitate access to more secure jobs. This policy may be effective and it could be a stepping-stone for more regular employment. However, it could also be a dead end. The main risk with temporary contracts is that they may constitute a trap that undermines the long-term employability of these categories of worker.

In most countries, temporary jobs, whatever the type of contract, are low-skilled jobs. In Hungary, the majority of fixed-term jobs are semi-skilled or unskilled and the proportion is rising: 69.7% of fixed-term jobs were unskilled in 2001, 81.1% in 2003. Similarly, in the Czech Republic temporary work is concentrated among the lowest skilled tasks and attracts less qualified workers, of whom 20% are in the age group 20-24 and 25% above 55. In addition, while traditionally restricted to a few sectors, like retail or agriculture, it is now tending to spread to all economic activities. In Germany, the rise of temporary work has mainly occurred in the low qualified segment of the labour force (Jahn and Rudolph, 2002a and 2002b). In addition, fixed-term contracts have been used for the temporary replacement of workers – and this affects also the public sector. In Denmark, many temporary jobs are the result of the leave-of-absence schemes facilitated by the government, which benefit permanent workers.

The same is true of temporary agency work. In France, such work is highly concentrated on low-skilled blue-collar and young workers, and while fixed-term contracts can be used as a screening device for hiring, they also more often end in unemployment. With such low skilled jobs it is difficult for these categories of workers to acquire enough qualifying experience to find better jobs. The difficulty is made worst by the fact that the length of fixed-term contracts is generally very short. In 2005 in the EU-25, 42.4% of fixed-term contracts were for less than six months and the percentage is even increasing (from 35.2% in 1998 to 43.7% in 2005 in the EU-15).

Such a pattern may become a structural dimension of the labour market as enterprises may institutionalise the use of fixed-term contracts in their work organisation (or re-organisation) structure. Studies in the UK suggest that during the late 1990s employers reduced the scope of their internal labour market (characterised by relatively secure and well paid jobs) and shifted many jobs to the secondary labour market, entailing in many instances the contracting of temporary workers from employment agencies (Grimshaw and Carroll, 2006). In other words, by allocating the lowest skilled tasks to temporary workers, they have denied them the opportunity of increasing their skills by on-the-job training and have trapped them in a low-skilled-jobs cycle. This is also true of formal training. In most EU countries temporary workers have much less access to training. A recent study has shown that in the EU-15, enterprises invest less in training for temporary workers (Nienhüser and Matiaske, 2006).

Governments have generally accompanied flexibility of the kind that leads to more employment rotation with significant training programmes, although in recent years the relevance of current training practices and arrangements has been put into question. Even in Denmark, where the upgrading of the labour force is identified as a central precondition for maintaining the Danish welfare system, training within companies has diminished in recent years and has neglected less skilled workers. In that country, however, unemployed people have relatively good access to national training facilities. Spain is among the lowest investors in training programmes – only 25% of employees receive training – and it does not seem to have played a central role in government employment policy. Germany's renowned vocational training system is also under threat. In 2005 the number of vocational training seekers increased by 0.6%, whereas the number of training positions offered within the vocational training system decreased by 9.3%. The situation of vocational training is even more worrying in the former GDR. In 2004 every fifth job seeker in the former West Germany and every second job seeker in the former GDR was without any vocational training. This situation obviously does not help them to increase their chances on the labour market, while also impeding future efforts to find a higher quality job. Unpredictable economic fluctuations, together with the cost of training, explain the reluctance of enterprises to offer training positions.

It is still the case that those who suffer the most from insufficient training are the categories of worker who need it the most: the low educated, women, immigrants and temporary workers (OECD, 2003).

Conclusion

This article identifies the main factors that may explain most recent trends in the world of work in the enlarged EU.[9] It shows that a number

[9] Many were confirmed by the recent (2005) European Working Conditions Survey (Parent-Thirion *et al.*, 2007).

of factors explain the current evolution of working and employment conditions. Government policies are playing a major role. The intensification of the flows of labour, capital and trade of goods and services brought up by the EU enlargement and globalisation is also leading to a progressive transformation in the organisation of work and working and employment conditions. Restructuring is influenced itself by such internal and external pressures. It does also contribute to accelerate the changes in the world of work. Restructuring is first influencing working conditions directly, as shown by its direct implications on those groups – such as women, unskilled, younger and older workers, migrants – that remain traditionally most vulnerable to the firing process or to the casualisation of working contracts, imposed part-time or self-employment that may follow the restructuring.

At the same time restructuring is also influencing working conditions indirectly – through its influence on all other identified major determinants of the world of work. Restructuring is notably making pressure on remaining workers to accept longer hours, lower wages, and greater flexibility in general in the conditions of work. Through all these effects restructuring may also contribute to generate a vicious circle of low pay-low quality jobs for a certain number of workers. This calls for a new approach to restructuring, based on anticipation of changes and the quality of work, and that would pay more attention to the trends here-identified, and especially to the vulnerability "traps", and to the conditions that may constitute possible entry to such longer-term vulnerability.

References

DJANKOV, S. and MURRELL P. (2002), "Enterprise Restructuring in Transition: A Quantitative Survey", *Journal of Economic Literature*, Vol. XL, September 2002, pp. 739-792.

EC (2004), *Industrial Relations in Europe 2004*, Office for Official Publications of the European Communities, Luxembourg.

EC (2006a), Green Paper "Modernising Labour Law to Meet the Challenges of the 21st Century", COM (2006) 708 final of 22 November 2006.

EC (2006), *Industrial Relations in Europe 2006*, Office for Official Publications of the European Communities, Luxembourg.

EC (2006b), Communication from the Commission to the Council, the European Parliament, the European Economic and Social Committee and the Committee of the Regions "Report on the Functioning of the Transitional Arrangements Set Out in the 2003 Accession Treaty", COM (2006), Brussels.

EYRAUD, F. and SAGET, C. (2005), *The Fundamentals of Minimum Wage Fixing*, International Labour Organization, Geneva.

EYRAUD, F. and VAUGHAN-WHITEHEAD, D. (eds.) (2007), *The Evolving World of Work in the Enlarged EU – Progress and Vulnerability*, EC-ILO, International Labour Organization, Geneva.

GRIMSHAW, D. and CARROLL, M. (2006), "Adjusting to the National Minimum Wage: Constraints and Incentives to Change in Six Low Paying Sectors", *Industrial Relations Journal*, Vol. 37, No.1, pp. 22-47.

HOSHI, I., WELFENS, P. and WZIATEK-KUBIAK, A. (eds.) (2007), *Industrial Competitiveness and Restructuring in Enlarged Europe*, Palgrave MacMillan.

HUMPHREY, A., COSTIGAN, P., PICKERING, K., STRATFORD, N. and BARNES, M. (2003), *Factors Affecting the Labour Market Participation of Older Workers*, Report, No.200, UK Department for Work and Pensions Research.

JAHN, E. and RUDOLPH, H. (2002a), "Zeitarbeit — Teil I: Auch für Arbeitslose ein Weg mit Perspektive", *IAB Kurzbericht*, No.20, Institut für Arbeitsmarkt- und Berufsforschung, Nürnberg, 28 August 2002.

JAHN, E. and RUDOLPH, H. (2002b), "Zeitarbeit — Teil II: Völlig frei bis streng geregelt: Variantenvielfalt in Europa", *IAB Kurzbericht*, No.21, Institut für Arbeitsmarkt- und Berufsforschung, Nürnberg, 29 August 2002.

LOW PAY COMMISSION (2006), "National Minimum Wage – Low Pay Commission Report 2006" (www.lowpay.gov.uk), London.

MARSH, A. and SAHIN-DIKMEN, M. (2003), "Discrimination in Europe", Report for the European Commission, DG for Economic and Social Affairs.

MEHAUT, P. (2007), "France: Patchwork – Tensions between Old and New Patterns", in EYRAUD, F. and VAUGHAN-WHITEHEAD, D. (eds.) (2007), *The Evolving World of Work in the Enlarged EU – Progress and Vulnerability*, EC-ILO, International Labour Organization, Geneva.

MERCADER-PRATS, M. (2005), "La pauvreté menace les jeunes espagnols au moment où ils s'émancipent", *Économie et Statistique*, No.383-384-385, Institut National de la Statistique et des Études Économiques, December 2005, pp. 384-385, pp. 75-89.

NELANDER, S. and GODING, I (2005), "Anställningsformer och arbetstider 2005", *Ett faktamaterial om välfärdsutvecklingen*, No.64, LO, Stockholm.

NIENHÜSER, W. and MATIASKE, W. (2006), "Effects of the 'Principle of Non-discrimination' on Temporary Agency Work: Compensation and Working Conditions of Temporary Agency Workers in 15 European Countries", *Industrial Relations Journal*, Vol. 37, No.1, January 2006, pp. 64-77.

OECD (2003), *Employment Outlook*, Organisation for Economic Co-operation and Development, Paris.

PAOLI, P., PARENT-THIRION, A. and PERSSON, O. (2002), *Working Conditions in Candidate Countries and the European Union*, European Foundation for the Improvement of Working and Living Conditions, Dublin.

PARENT-THIRION, A., FERNÁNDEZ MACÍAS, E.; HURLEY, J. and VERMEYLEN, G. (2007), Fourth European Working Conditions Survey, European Foundation for the Improvement of Working and Living Conditions, Dublin (http://www.eurofound.europa.eu/pubdocs/2006/98/en/2/ef0698en.pdf).

STANDING, G. and VAUGHAN-WHITEHEAD, D. (eds.) (1995), *Minimum Wages in Central and Eastern Europe: From Protection to Destitution*, Central European University Press, Budapest.

VAUGHAN-WHITEHEAD, D. (2003), *EU Enlargement versus Social Policy? The Uncertain Future of the European Social Model*, Edward Elgar Publishing, Cheltenham.

VAUGHAN-WHITEHEAD, D. (ed.) (2005), *Working and Employment Conditions in New Member States – Convergence or Diversity?*, ILO/EC, International Labour Organization, Geneva.

Resolving Liberalisation Dilemma

Labour Relations in East-Central Europe and the Impact of European Union

Katharina BLUHM

Assistant Professor of Sociology at the Friedrich Schiller-University in Jena

Introduction

The expansion of the European Union is seen by many – according to the perspective of the observers – as a worrying or hopeful intensification of the institutional regime competition. Among the subsystems often analysed in this way are the labour relations in East-Central Europe. Their characterisations, however, have been interestingly divergent. On the one hand, descriptions like "an entrepreneur's paradise" (Tenbrock, 2004), "laboratory for labour-relations" or "freedom-loving East-European system" (Fickinger, 2004) fill Western newspapers. Scholars often characterise the relations as being of "maximal" or "excessive" flexibility that gives management a unilateral decision-making power in setting working conditions (Ladó and Vaughan-Whitehead, 2003; Meardi, 2002). Even the metaphor of the "Trojan horse of Americanisation" is employed to describe the worries expressed among Western European unionists (Meardi, 2002).

Heribert Kohl and Hans-Wolfgang Platzer (2004), on the other hand, stress the etatism of these labour relations, due to the decisive role of the state and the substantial weakness of the independent collective bargaining actors. While evoking similarities to France in this respect, Kohl and Platzer see more reasons to refer to East-Central Europe as a separate model of labour relations. Conservative politicians, domestic and foreign employers and industry representatives in the countries themselves complain about "too little" flexibility for their part. German investors also contribute to this debate, criticising the "meticulous interventions of the state" and demanding more flexible working conditions.

In this chapter I will show that the conflicting perspectives of the almost "excessive" and "too little" flexibility, between etatism and management unilateralism do fit together, as each of them filters out other contradictory aspects. I argue for the theoretical differentiation between the concept of flexibility and what I call permissive institutional regulation. The "excessive flexibility" has not been caused by a lack of regulation but rather by a remarkable gap between the formal rules and actual practice in East-Central Europe during the 1990s. This gap created a labour relations system that was permissive by deviation.

A further retreat of the state from regulation, however, had to face a *liberalisation dilemma*, as the collective bargaining partners are either not willing or too weak to step in. Thus, the state risks only strengthening managerial unilateralism. In this situation, the impact of the EU-accession has been quite ambivalent. Pushing for social dialogue on the one hand, the harmonisation with the *acquis communautaire*, the EU common law, also provided the opportunity for national players to press for a resolution of the liberalisation dilemma in spite of the weaknesses of the collective bargaining system.

In the first part of my chapter, I will clarify why it is useful to differentiate between flexible adjustment and permissive regulation. I will then outline the conflicting influences on the institutionalisation of labour relations in Poland and the Czech Republic, which must be taken into account in order to understand the recent structure. Finally, I shall trace the intended and unintended effects of the *acquis communautaire.*

I. Conceptual Clarification: Flexible Adjustment and Permissive Arrangements

The term flexibility refers to actual adjustment of the work supply to the demand, which can have numerous meanings attached to it: It can refer to an *external numerical flexibility*, e.g. the ease of hiring and firing, or to the *nominal or real wage-flexibility*. Flexibility can appear as the flexible application of a time-budget, in which, instead of personnel, the work-time is extended or reduced. Finally, another form is *functional flexibility*, in which the no-longer-needed labour is applied to new tasks through additional job training and internal labour markets. The various forms of flexibility can, to a limited extent, substitute each other, which also contributes to the multi-dimensionality of the flexibility concept. Different institutional settings support different ways of flexible adjustment (*cf. e.g.* Sengenberger, 1987; Streeck, 1991; Walwei, 1996; Hall and Soskice, 2001).

In order to distinguish the difference between the institutional setting and actual adjustment to the market within this setting, I call less regulated systems *permissive.* Permissive institutional systems are those with low levels of standardisation and regulation that bind plant-level actors in one way or another. Regulation and standardisation can take the form of state-imposed norms or collective agreements. No institutional system supports all four ways of adjustment equally. Highly regulated labour relations can, therefore, not be automatically equated with inflexibility; just as little, as weakly regulated labour relations allow flexible adjustment without any restrictions.

II. Competing Influences on Labour Relations in Poland and the Czech Republic

For the institutionalisation of labour relations in East-Central Europe (ECE),[1] three concepts were influential in the 1990s: a) the concept of the *intervening and regulating state* which, inherited from the state socialist past, is still present today – despite the liberal rhetoric of new elites; b) the *Continental-European model of "social partnership";* and c) *the Anglo-Saxon liberal-market model, which* parts of the new political and economic elites ideologically prefer, while distancing themselves from the European social-partnership model.

The significance of each conceptualisation varies from country to country and in the longitudinal view. Among the ECE-countries Estonia as the most liberalised country and Slovania with a developed corporatist system build the extremes (Buchen, 2007). In both countries, different elite groups shared a similar view on the labour relations system. This has not been the case in the former *Visegrád* states. The institutionalisation of labour relations remained a battle field among different groups during the 1990s and EU accession process. Weighing the influence of the three concepts in Poland and the Czech Republic, much speaks in favour of seeing the Czech Republic more strongly under the influence of the social-partnership model, while in Poland, through the close relationship of labour unions and political parties – the heritage of the Solidarność movement – there is a tendency to solve labour-policy problems with the help of state intervention. That is, institutionalisation in Poland alternates more markedly between economic liberalism and etatism.

1 The term East-Central Europe stresses the narrow perspective on countries in the first and second wave of EU accession.

Figure 1: Conflicting Concepts for Institution Building

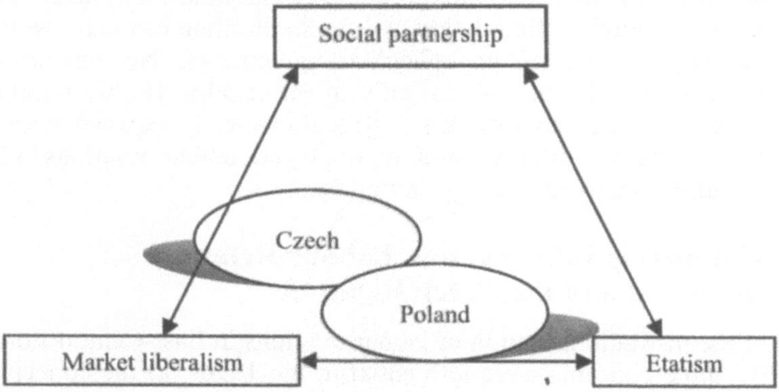

A. The Concept of Social Partnership

Few ECE-countries have, in their reform of labour relations, taken a specific European nation as their model. The German "dual" system – consisting of union representatives and works councils – was widely discussed in the early period. Despite promotion by German unions and investors, the dual system was neither adopted by Poland nor by the Czech Republic, nor, with a few exceptions, in other transition countries.[2] Among the declared opponents of the dual system were the unions, who only saw it as a fundamental threat to their own existence (*cf. e.g.* Federowicz and Levitas, 1995; Pumberger, 1998; Vickerstaff and Thirkell, 2000; Kohl and Platzer, 2004).

However, the idea of a "return to Europe" did include the concept of an idealised model for Western European capitalism. Sarah A. Vickerstaff and John E.M. Thirkell define this as a model linking "hard budget constraints" of the market economy with strong collective actors and negotiations *at all levels* (1997: 19f).

The *legal equipment* of the Polish and Czech *union organisations* is therefore presentable in a European comparison, in regards to the protection of plant union committees against dismissal, as well as rights to information and consultation; although their co-determination rights have not reached the German level. Founding plant-level union organisations is, formally, easy. In the Czech Republic three members are sufficient to establish a union organisation in a workplace (ten in Poland); a company is then obligated by law to make collective agree-

2 The exceptions were Hungary and Slovenia, who oriented themselves to the German or Austrian system, and in the case of Slovenia, even quite extensively.

ments with the unions for *all the employees* – in Germany this only a *de facto* practise not a legal rule.

That the orientation towards the social-partnership model in the formation of labour relations has been more pronounced in Czech than in Poland, can be demonstrated by the corporate governance system, all-binding coverage clauses, and tripartism.

The Czech corporate governance system foresees an employee representation on the supervisory board of stock companies, an idea incompatible with a liberal, Anglo-Saxon conception of corporate governance, but which is widespread in Continental Europe (Schulten and Zagelmeyer, 1998). The regulations chosen in the Czech Republic are very close to the Austrian ones in this respect. Also, in Poland there are employee representatives on the supervisory boards. However, this applies only to former state companies under the 1996 Law on Commercialisation and Privatisation. The participation of employees or other stakeholders was granted only as a transitional solution. Among the post-socialist reformers it was hardly disputed that the absence of a self-interested private owner was one – if not *the* cause – of the failure of the socialist state's reforms in the 1980s. Employees therefore were only to have a role in the corporate governance system, if they themselves had shareholder rights. In this way the shareholder concept, in contrast to the stakeholder approach, came to be the preferred ideology (Weinstein, 2000).

The Czech legislation sponsored by the socialist-liberal coalition of 1991, furthermore, originated with the premise that the decisive negotiation level should be above the company level; only wages higher than those agreed on in collective bargaining should be negotiated at the workplace (Cornejowá and Fassmann, 2003: 10). To support the development of an above-company bargaining level, the Collective Bargaining Act of 1991 contained – as in a number of other continental European countries – clauses on the all-binding nature of collective agreements (Traxler and Behrens, 2002; OECD, 2004). The Czech state had the right to declare agreements reached with several employers also as binding for other employers, who were not participants in the negotiations and not a member of the employers association involved.

In Poland, state support for the above-company level is limited to firms in the state sector. Besides, all-binding coverage clauses are only prescribed for exceptional cases (Polish Labour Code, Art. 241[18]). From the beginning the Solidarność preferred "company-close" bargaining above all. Therefore, they rather eased plant-level collective arrangements.[3]

It was the Continental European social partnership that served as the direct model in the creation of the Czech *tripartite councils*, which were already created in the early 1990s by the social-liberal coalition in Prague (Horalek and Formanova, 2002). In these national- and regional-level councils, representatives of government, industry branches and unions meet to discuss wage and employment polices. Helmuth Wiesenthal has accurately characterised the Eastern tripartism as "pre-emptive corporatism" (1995). The state involved potential veto players, even though the unions and employers' associations did not have the organisational strength to claim such a position.

That the Continental European social partnership was the model, underscored Milan Stich, a leading Czech union official and politician, in an interview: "We saw that the social partnership, as a model for the representation of interests, functions in other European countries, and understood its creation as a part of our fitting in with these countries" (cit. after Wielgohs, 2001: 127).

In Poland, tripartism has not been the first choice of the new elites. The first Solidarność-era governments tried to impose their austerity policy through an indirect wage-tax (*popiwek*). Only when this approach failed in 1993, was a tripartite commission created. From the point of view of Solidarność, "pre-emptive corporatism" meant "dealing in" none other than their competitor organisation – the All-Poland Alliance of Unions (OPZZ) – which, under the martial law of the 1980s, had been set up by the Polish state as the organisation opposing the then-forbidden Solidarność (Wielgohs, 2001: 141). Solidarność, therefore, preferred to take direct political influence, at least as long as its coalition with other parties held the government. This became trend-setting for the OPZZ. In general, the move of high-rank leaders from collective associations towards politics is quite common for the Polish political landscape.

---

3 Until the labour-law reform of 2002, it was relatively easy for unions to win recognition as representative collective actor. Up to 2002 union committees could be founded even directly prior to negotiations without risking exclusion. Contracts lasted until a new one was concluded, and the number of committee members was not exactly determined legally. This led to the curiosity that union activists did use the body as a safe haven against redundancy by expanding the number of committee members extraordinarily.

B. *Predominant Market Liberalism Among the New Political Elites in the 1990s*

Despite its stronger orientation towards social partnership, the plant level has established itself as the decisive collective-agreement level in the Czech Republic as in Poland (*cf.* Carley, 2002; Ladó, 2002; Kohl and Platzer, 2004). In broad parts of the private economy no collective agreements at all are concluded. The coverage rate of collective agreements – as in Anglo-Saxon countries – correlates largely with the actual organisational strength of the unions.

In the Czech Republic the union organisation rate is, at 30%, similar to that of Germany; however, the coverage rate, e.g. the portion of all employees under collective agreement, is only 35%, while for all of Germany this figure is placed at c. 75%. In Poland the decline of the unions – having split into three federations – is dramatic. Here, the degree of organisation, at 18% (or even lower), is similar to Spain's. The formal coverage rate for collective agreements, however, lies at only c. 30%, which is blamed on state concerns and the public sector, where in the 1990s only sector agreements were allowed. In Spain formal coverage is 80% because of all-binding clauses.

The low rate of coverage in Poland and the Czech Republic not only indicates the lack of interest of employer and industry federations in collective bargaining, but also a lack of *state support* at the time of institutionalising the collective agreement level; this was equally true of Poland and the Czech Republic, despite their different initial situations.

The practical application of the existing all-binding coverage clause in the Czech Republic is symptomatic for East-Central Europe.[4] The liberal-conservative government under Vaclav Klaus, in office in 1992-1997, categorically refused to extend multi-employer agreements to other companies, using the justification that this would be impermissible support of cartel formation and acting against the free play of market forces.

Only with the Social Democrats' accession to power in 1998, was this instrument again utilised, however, not without being juridically contested and hindered by government officials and conservative politicians as "intervening in the freedom of private enterprises", so that even in following years only few collective agreements at the above-company level could be extended to other enterprises (Cornejová and Fassmann, 2003: 10; Uhlír *et al.*, 2003). Eventually, the clause had to be abolished, as the constitutional court decided that an extension of collective agreements to employers not being member of the negotiating association

4 Exceptions had been Slovenia and to some extent Slovakia.

contradicts the constitutional rights. Thus the new Labour Code, which is in force since January 2007, only binds the members and those employers who left the employers' association while the higher-level collective agreement was in effect. In addition to this, trade unions also conclude contracts on behalf of non union members (Czech Labour Code 2006, Part II., Ch.V, Sec 24 and 25[2a]). Both regulations are quite similar to the German law and represent weak forms of coverage clause.

In the *tripartite councils* not much initiative was taken towards strengthening the autonomous sectoral collective agreements in the course of the 1990s. The commitment of the governments to the tripartite councils revealed itself to be unsteady. Moreover, they were used mainly an instrument for legitimating state wage *controls* in the beginning. That was supposed, according to the theory of shock therapy, to prevent rapid wage growth in the wake of price liberalisation and make the region an attractive investment site for foreign capital. Critics rightly point out that this "illusionary corporatism" has only little to do with the West-European post-war class-compromise, which, as is known, was meant to *couple* wages to increases in productivity (Ost, 2000: 504).

One of its consequences is that the state left the *institutionalisation* of the collective bargaining system to the unions alone. These, however, were – because of problems of privatisation and de-industrialisation, as well as their own legitimation, professionalisation and structural problems – too weak to impose a system of wide coverage in the face of marginally interested employers. Therefore East-Central Europe also differs from the "romance" labour-relation system of France or Spain, where the state instead of the weak collective actors, at least to date, actively supports the generalisation of collective standards.

C. The Etatist Heritage

The *etatist tradition* of former planned-economy systems, with its heritage of detailed *regulation by labour law*, is in a relation of tension with market-liberal rhetoric and the social-partnership orientation. Before the transformation of 1989, autonomous collective bargaining on the *sectoral* or *regional* levels was either not legal or practically non-existent, and instead, labour law set down not just general minimum standards and regulations, but regulated labour conditions in detail. In contrast to the legal principle of civil-rights, socialist law followed the rule: "Whatever is not explicitly permitted is forbidden".

After 1989, new laws were introduced in the transformation countries on freedom of association, collective agreements and the right to strike. Beyond that, guarantees for job security were liberalised. Yet, a complete reform of labour laws was not a priority task, so that the basic formal principle, wholly or in part, remained. To that extent it is impossible to speak of *"permissive" regulation of working conditions*.

One of its consequences is that many issues concerning *working conditions* in collective agreements are identical to the same points in the existing labour codes. Above all, regulation of *work-time* and *overtime*, including overtime bonuses, remained strongly state regulated in the labour codes of Poland and the Czech Republic up to the harmonisation with the *acquis communautaire*. Exceptions were officially possible, but mostly only through *special regulations*. Even if the unions were supposed to agree to them, the exceptions did not become a regular object of *collective agreements*.

In light of the weakness of the collective bargaining level, a *dilemma* is nevertheless hindering a further *retreat by the state* from regulation and standardisation of working conditions: Detailed state rules and standards offer employers little incentives to engage themselves in collective bargaining. To make independent collective bargaining more attractive, the state must retreat from detailed norms. Here, conversely, the chances are greater of only increasing the unilateral decision-making power of management – and, in effect, not strengthening the autonomous bargaining power of weak employee representations.

From their position of weakness, the unions – but also some of the political elites – tend to rely on etatist regulation and look to state intervention for solutions to socio-economic problems (Voß, 2003; Kohl and Platzer, 2004). This is particularly true for Poland, where the privileged access of the unions to the political arena was exploited in the 1990s to make *even more stringent* state norms and surveillance. Thus in the reform of the Labour Code in 1996, the state labour inspectorate's power to oversee the maintenance of collective agreements and labour norms was extended, whereby, for example, *in all enterprises* labour inspectors had to be elected.

III. Permissive Labour Relations Through Deviation

Detailed regulations accompanied by weak monitoring and sanction mechanisms, invite "informal" deviation from the prescribed norms and thereby widen the legal grey area. This is especially true in a region where in the past "bending the rules" was often quite functional or even a civil virtue. One indicator of the gaps between regulation, monitoring and sanctions are the state labour-inspectorate's frequent denouncements of law-breaking by firms (Janicki, 2001). Even labour-law jurisdiction does not seem to be able to sufficiently narrow these gaps.

To put it tersely: During the 1990s, labour relations in East-Central Europe had not been permissive at the normative level, which was still predetermined by the state in many respects. But they had been permissive out of the weakness of actors and institutions in actually holding companies to the letter of the law, in monitoring them and, if necessary, applying effective sanctions. In other words, the institutional system of labour relations was permissive through deviation. And this had consequences. It created *zones of uncertainty* for managers, as they could not be sure *how* the environment is going to react to informal infractions, or freer interpretations of regulations.

Above all, the risk grows when management takes decisions deviating not only from official norms but also from usual practices and containing the potential for conflict with employees. This risk can vary from constellation to constellation and is thus *situational*. The *type of company* is significant here. Generally, local small and middle-size companies have the greatest room for free action because union representations are almost totally absent at that level; such firms more easily avoid the attention of state authorities and local unions. This proves to be also generally true for middle-size operations of foreign investors.

Large multinationals, on the other hand, are sensitive to image problems and therefore subject to greater attention on the part of the state and media than domestic firms. They must be highly aware of the possibility of media-effective scandals arising through their actions. Among large firms, the former state enterprises make up the bulk of the decisive support for unions and the collective-agreement system in East-Central Europe, as the pre-1989 workplace-level union representations still largely exist. There, generous interpretations of labour laws are possible only together with, and not against, the unions. Green-field sites can, on the other hand, more easily avoid employee-organizing attempts of unions, whereby again multinationals with an Anglo-Saxon background have it easier than large German firms, whose works councils at home monitor production shifts abroad (Bluhm, 2007).

A. Institutionally Supported Flexibility

What kind of flexibility, in the adjustment of labour supply and demand, is encouraged by the above-sketched state of labour-relations institutionalisation in East-Central Europe? Besides the relatively great *freedom of decision of management in wage setting*, caused by the weakly developed collective agreement level, the ECE labour relations of the 1990s tend to support an *external, e.g. numerical flexibility*. Protection against redundancy clearly appears to be more liberal than in the Continental countries with a strong etatist tradition (France, S. Europe), or in those with well established collective-agreement norms (Germany). At the same time, however, it is stricter than in Anglo-Saxon countries (*cf.* OECD, 2004 and 2006; World Bank Group, 2006).

The formal redundancy procedure in the Czech Republic is assessed by the OEDC, in a comparison of countries (2004: 71f; 2006: 18), as even one of the most rigid (after Portugal), and therefore its further liberalisation is given high priority.[5] Already in the 1990s, Polish unions have achieved a limitation of two years on fixed-term contracts. They also exert influence on the *selection* of employees to be given notice in mass redundancies. Termination in cases of legitimate absence, e.g. sickness, is not possible in either country. The liberalisation of guarantees against redundancy is therefore also in Poland and the Czech Republic a main topic in the political discussion.

With regard to *flexible work-time arrangements*, the labour laws have revealed themselves particularly rigid, since they remained oriented to a standardised, extensive shift-scheme that was convenient for the needs of state-socialist economies of shortage, stated briefly, up to the reforms surrounding EU accession. The *extensive work-time regime* allowed long regular work-weeks of 40-43 hours in a round-the-clock shift system, at least on weekdays. Also, overtimes on short notice, often at month's end – the busy period in planned economies – fit well into this work-time regime. But it did, for example, *not permit* the collection of overtime hours throughout the year and their compensation through time-off. In other words: the extensive work-time regime fit well into the producer markets of planned economies, where vulnerability to disturbances resulted, above all, from unpredictable material supply and delivery. It is much less suitable to volatile post-fordist buyer markets. If one omits traditional seasonal work, for the entire 1990s work-time flexibility remained limited in transformation countries, because unequal distribution of work-time over the year was formally restricted.

Flexible work-time regimes are an important topic, particularly for German investors. Transferring the concept of "work-time accounts" with year-end equalisation – which reflects a compromise between work-time cuts and flexibility concluded by the IG Metall and the employers' association in the 1980s in Germany and since then enjoys wide acceptance – to East-Central Europe was often not possible. German expatriates attempting to establish working-time accounts in Polish or Czech subsidiaries usually failed in the attempt to transfer the model (Bluhm, 2001 and 2007). Here, the uncertainty zones come into play. The difficulties of implementing working-time accounts cannot only be ascribed to restrictive legal standards but also to customs and interests of the actors involved. Neither unions nor the employees could

5 Otherwise fixed-term contracts had been possible without limitation. This was changed after EU accession.

be convinced to abandon the usual practice of overtime as a "second pay-envelope." Because of their low wages, the offer of overtime compensation in the form of time off from work was totally unattractive, while for the unions, contrary to their German counterparts, the accounts were little more than a new Western management technique. Thus, neither the Polish nor the Czech institutional system could support flexible work-time regimes. The situation changed only slowly, with the EU accession.

IV. Intended and Unintended Effects of the *Acquis Communautaire*

In the early years after the transformation, the European Union followed a *demand-oriented* policy, which is, reacting primarily to requests of national ministries in the region (Wade, 2001: 178). For the phase of institution-building in labour relations in East-Central Europe, the EU was only one external actor among others. With the beginning of direct accession talks and the harmonisation of national laws with community law from 1997 onwards, the EU began actively and systematically to intervene in the institutional system and observe the progress of reforms.

The transposition of EU law to the accession countries is sometimes called pure "window dressing", because such an institution transfer, facing the enormous gap between "law in the books and law in action", has no effective influence on practice (Weiss, 2004: 24). This assessment, however, fails to recognise the internal political instrumentalisation of the EU accession and the EU rules that affect the dilemma of liberalisation, wherein the weight of competing concepts – market-liberal, social partnership and etatist – is subject to change. Three important areas of active influence of the EU in the accession environment can be observed: the tripartite councils, securing information and consultation rights of employees, and the further liberalisation of labour law.

A. Tripartite Councils

A central demand of the EU in the area of labour relations was improvement in the "social dialogue" – *below* the national level – between the collective representatives of the employers and employees. As the "social dialogue", first set down in the agreements of 1986, is meanwhile anchored in various EU directives and became an immediate component of community law (Art. 138 and 139; Vaughan-Whitehead, 2000; Weiss, 2004).

Most of the accession countries have met this demand by *legalizing the status* of the tripartite councils and extending them to the *regional* level, where they were not yet existing (Voß, 2003). In this way, the "pre-emptive" or "illusionary corporatism" has taken on a new function: it becomes a regional instrument in the European multi-level political system, through which the countries seek to improve their chances for European structural funding. Further, as the EU demanded social dialogue in the transformation of the *aquis* into national law, the tripartite councils became a platform for the struggles surrounding the labour reform. In sum: the EU contributed significantly to the institutionalisation of ECE tripartism (Vickerstaff and Thirkell, 2000).

B. Implementation of a Dual System

With the EU directive on securing information and consultation rights of employees (approved in 2002 by the European Parliament as Art. 27 of community law), political pressure grew in accession countries to consider once more a non-union interest-representation body in workplaces, that is, a dual system, since the unions less and less could fulfil the function foreseen by this new law.

Here the Czech solution also paved the way for other countries (Kohl and Platzer, 2004). In the "Czech model", an employee council must be set up in sites with more than 50 employees, if no workplace union organisation is present; it has fewer consultation rights[6] and no voting or collective-agreement functions. Theoretically, the council must dissolve itself immediately if a union organisation is formed and no other arrangements are met, even if union organisers can gather no majority of employees behind it.

In Poland, the struggle surrounding a solution continued up to 2006. In 2005 two alternative propositions were handed to the lower house of Parliament (*Sejm*). While the government had foreseen a more extensive law, the competing proposition of the Polish unions follows the "Czech model". Two years after accession, the Polish parliament agreed to a "Polish model" that establishes employee councils also in sites where unions exist, but gives them a strong foothold in the new councils, which are furnished with basic information and consultation rights only.[7] In sum, unions in both countries did not grasp the chance to

6 Most of all, trade unions only have consultation rights with regard to remuneration and appraisal of employees, employee training and vocational training (education) (Czech Labour Code 2006, Part XII).

7 In workplaces where unions exist they received the right to vote for, and determine, the candidates. Only if there is no union at the site do the employees elect their council directly. As in the Czech case the employer must have a staff of more than

promote a council system as strongly as possible, but opted rather to keep the competitors weak.

C. New Labour Codes

The need for labour law reform mandated by the *acquis* offered the opportunity and legitimisation for those actors an important step in further liberalisation. This was not necessarily an intention of the harmonisation with community law, which was actually only meant to secure certain minimum standards in order to hinder exploitative labour practices (Weiss, 2004: 11). A consequence of the transposition is, nevertheless, that internal pressure for liberalisation *in* the accession countries, as well as the institutional competition *between* the accession-countries, increased. This holds especially true for the ECE-countries where the concept of labour relations has been contested during the 1990s.

A Polish industrial federation, for example, demanded that labour laws in Poland should contain *only minimal standards* that in no case go "beyond EU norms" because of the developmental lag of the Polish economy (PKPP, 2001: 2). Even if such demands were not realised, European integration, the adjustment to European standards and the intensification of competition on the internal European market came to express the struggle surrounding the liberalisation of labour law. Meanwhile, shrinking the state's regulation by widening the range of independent bargaining objectives means, above all, widening management's room for action and reducing the uncertainties of its labour-policy decisions.

In Poland, under the coalition led by the Social Democrats (SLD), 2001-2005, the assumption of the *acquis* into national law was associated with a partial *lowering* of the existing (formal) standards and a stricter *regulation* of the existing generous representational rights of the unions, in which a three-year "opt-out clause" for companies in economic crisis is included. This allows them a justified exclusion from the part of the labour law that regulates the rules and obligations of an employment relation (including collective agreements). Beyond that, the very high (but often not paid) overtime bonuses were reduced, though they are still higher percentage-wise than those in the Czech Republic. Companies with fewer than 100 employees were again freed from the obligation of electing work-inspectors and employees' rights to days off (to seek new work) after giving their own notice of termination was abolished. Besides this, legislators set out the restriction on fixed-term

---

50 people. State enterprises with the traditional Polish labour council, which is still in place for this sector, are excluded from the new law.

contracts until EU accession. Polish employers did *not* prevail over the disputed reduction in paid sick-leave days which, after union protests, was reversed by an amendment in 2003, nor did they succeed in the introduction of more flexible working-time schemes at the first glance. The number of overtime hours may not exceed 150 hours per year and individual; the period for which the overtime work can be calculated remains four month at maximum. However, collective agreements, *as well as* workplace regulation and even individual contracts of employment, may set up other arrangements by which individual overtime work may peak to more than 400 hours per calendar year (Polish Labour Code 2005, Sec. VI, Ch. V, Art. 151 §4).

With the new regulation, the battle surrounding the liberalisation of labour law was in no way over. One of the employers' federations, "PKPP Lewiatan" (existing since 1999), has declared the liberalisation of the Labour Code to be one of its central tasks. For them, more labour flexibility is still a major issue[8], while the nationalist party "Law and Justice" (PiS) won the election of 2005 with the slogan "solidary Poland contra liberal Poland".[9]

The Czech Republic, with an amendment to the labour laws in 2000, began a comprehensive discussion of the reform of the Labour Code in the completely new edition, in which in 2006 the old *formal basic principle* was definitively replaced with a new *liberal* basic principle: Instead of "Anything not permitted is forbidden", now valid is only "Permitted is anything not forbidden".

The government lead by the Social Democrats (1998-2006) thereby attempted to make collective bargaining attractive for employers by increasing freedom from state regulation dependent on the existence of collective agreements. This principle was employed in the flexibilisation of working time. As in Slovakia and Hungary, also the new Czech Code extended the upper limit for overtime work, as well as the equalisation period to twelve months. Although the Labour Code does keep the limit of 150 hours of overtime work within one calendar year, it excludes overtime work for which the employees were granted time off, implying that overtime work can be accumulated up to 416 hours per individual and year (Czech Labour Code 2006, Part III, Ch. IV, Sec. 93).

However, the Social Democrats did tie the full usage of the new flexible time regime to the existence of collective bargaining with unions. After a hot debate about the access of non-unionised enterprises

---

8 See the shortage list published by the association (PKPP, 2006).

9 *Ibid.*

to the new time regulation, the Code determined that *only* relevant collective agreements may permit unevenly scheduled working hours over the whole period of 52 consecutive weeks (twelve months), otherwise equalisation must be done during 26 consecutive weeks. This compromise is identical with the German regulation. At the same time, the Social-Democratic-led government coalition was attempting to extend the idea of incentive setting for collective agreements to other areas of regulation.

The way of resolving the dilemma of liberalisation, however, met with massive rejection on the part of employer federations and the liberal-conservative Civil Party (ODS). These actors justify their opposition with the imposed limitations on flexibility. According to the ODS parliamentarian Vlastimil Thlusty: "This aim of the Czech government goes completely against the tendency not only in Europe but all over the world. So, I think it is necessary to go in the opposite direction, which means to improve the flexibility of the Czech market" (Asiedu, 2005).

Thus, the counter-proposal introduced to parliament by the opposition-conservatives foresees another resolution to the liberalisation dilemma: It simplifies the redundancy procedures by freeing the employer from the obligation of a written termination justification, allowing termination in the case of longer illness, extending the free-month trial period to twelve months, and giving the unions the right to represent only their members (not all employees).

This counter-proposal of the liberal-conservative Civil Party at the end of November 2005 provoked the greatest demonstration in Prague since the "Velvet Revolution" of 1989, for which unions throughout the country mobilised their members in support of the government's proposal. Thus, the failure of the opposition proposal due to the legislature's majority situation in early 2006 represents only a pause before a further fighting round in the resolution of the liberalisation dilemma. The balance of market-liberal, social-partnership and etatist concepts in labour relations is still more fluid than steady. Yet in contrast to the Polish regulation, the new Czech Labour Code succeeded in combining liberalisation with providing stronger incentives for collective bargaining so far.

Conclusion

Because of the specific mixture of social partnership, market liberalism and etatism, it is justified to think of labour relations in East-Central Europe of the 1990s as a distinct type (Kohl and Platzer 2004). Its etatist legal tradition and institutionalised tripartism, make it different from Anglo-Saxon voluntarism, but also – because of the weaker states – it is different from the "romance" etatist model. In comparison to corporatist systems, the collective bargaining between the wage parties above single enterprises is widely absent. Whether, and in how far this type of labour-relations represents a stable configuration must be cautiously considered in light of the already present "inner differentiation" and deserves an extensive examination that, however, was not the aim of the present essay.

The assumption of a relationship of tension between the concepts of social partnership, market liberalism and etatism offers a heuristic means of analysing the institutionalisation of labour relations and its contradictions and, thereby, highlights the differences between the ECE countries, which would become even broader if we include further countries in the picture. Thus, in the Czech Republic, the social-partnership-model orientation – also among elites – plays a much greater role than it does in Poland, where over decades a pendular movement between etatism and market liberalism has taken place.

Common to both constellations are above all, up to the latest Labour Code reforms, permissive arrangements by deviation that are based on a weakness of actors and institutions. Those observers, who assume as a common characteristic of East-Central Europe, a "maximal" or "excessive" flexibility in labour adjustment, see above all the weakness of the collective regulatory level but filter out the effect of the etatist heritage.

The internal political debate in Poland and the Czech Republic about "too little" flexibility in labour relations is troubled by the etatist labour-law tradition. "Flexibilisation" of the labour market becomes a catch word for the resolution of the liberalisation dilemma by ultimately strengthening managerial unilateralism. Yet, it would be wrong to dismiss this critique as pure ideology. The restrictions on work-time flexibility mean in fact an institutional disadvantage in the competition with neighbouring Western countries. And in spite of the successful introduction of new working-time regulations in the Czech case, "constraints" are only changing slowly in this respect, as employers must overcome unions and employee reluctance (*cf.* Cardiff Report, 2005).

If we consider the role of the EU in this situation, we must note ambivalent impacts. On the one hand, the EU has contributed to the stabilisation of tripartism in East-Central Europe, set new standards (above all in the area of anti-discrimination) and extended rights to information and consultation to non-union employee groups. On the other hand, harmonisation became an internal political instrument for carrying further the liberalisation of labour law. Thus, instead of regulation, deregulation is occurring. This unintended effect results from the demand of the accession process that candidates synchronously re-elaborate their labour law. An intensified institutional competition in East-Central

Europe has accompanied pressure on the states to legitimate their regulation. This pressure is based not only on the difference between the minimum standards of community law and the stricter, national regulations; it is also a matter of the ability of locations to compete in the internal European market, and globally. The arguments and positions hardly differ from those debated in Western Europe. In that respect, it is Europe itself that is causing the pressure for convergence – here as well as there.

References

ASIEDU, D. (2005), "New Czech Labour Code Mobilises Trade Unions into Action after Sixteen Year Slumber", Talking Point, available at http://www.radio.cz/en/article/73207, 15 April 2008.

BLUHM, K. (2001), "Exporting or Abandoning the 'German Model'? Labour Policies of German Manufacturing Firms in Central Europe", *European Journal for Industrial Relations*, No.2, pp. 153-173.

BLUHM, K. (2007), *Experimentierfeld Ostmitteleuropa? Deutsche Unternehmen in Polen und der Tschechischen Republik*, VS-Verlag, Wiesbaden.

BUCHEN, C. (2007), "Estonia and Slovenia as Antipodes", in LANE, D. and MYANT, M. (eds.), *Varieties of Capitalism in Post-Communist Countries*, Palgrave, Basingstoke, pp. 65-89.

CARDIFF REPORT (2005), National Reform Programme of the Czech Republic (Lisbon Programme), available at http://www.mfcr.cz/cps/rde/xchg/mfcr/hs.xsl/cardiff_report.html, 22 March 2006.

CARLEY, M. (2002), "Industrial Relations in the EU Member States and Candidate Countries", *European Industrial Relations Observatory on-line*, http://www.eurofound.europa.eu/eiro/2002/12/study/tn0212102s.htm, available at http://www.eurofound.europa.eu/eiro/2002/07/feature/tn0207104f.htm, 18 November 2002.

CORNEJOVÁ, H. and FASSMANN, M. (2003), "The Czech Republic – Legal Framework and Experience 2001-2002 plus forecasts for 2003", available at http://www.etuc.org/ETUI/CBEurope/Creports/2003/RepCzEN.pdf ("downloaded" not available), 9 January 2004.

CZECH LABOUR CODE (2006), No.262/2006 Coll, (English Version), available at http://www.mpsv.cz/files/clanky/3221/labour_code.pdf, 2 May 2007.

FEDEROWICZ, M. and LEVITAS, A. (1995), "Poland: Councils under Communism and Liberalism", in ROGERS, J. and STREECK, W. (eds.), *Works Councils: Consultation, Representation, and Cooperation in Industrial Relations*, University of Chicago Press, Chicago, pp. 283-312.

FICKINGER, N. (2004), "Ein Laboratorium für Arbeitsbeziehungen. Systemwettbewerb zwischen angelsächsischem und europäischem Modell", *Frankfurter Allgemeine Zeitung*, 2 April 2004.

HALL, P. and SOSKICE, D. (2001), "An Introduction to Varieties of Capitalism", in HALL, P. and SOSKICE, D. (eds.), *Varieties of Capitalism. The Institutional*

Foundations of Comparative Advantage, Oxford University Press, Oxford/ New York, pp. 1-70.

HORALEK, M. and FORMANOVA, J. (2002), "Wirtschafts- und Sozialpolitik in der Tschechischen Republik", *Politikinformation Osteuropa*, No.99, Electronic ed., FES Library, Bonn.

JANICKI, M. (2001), "Wolny Najmita", *Polityka*, No.12, http://polityka.onet.pl/162,1024466,1,0,2290-2001-12,artykul.html ("downloaded" not available), 9 January 2004.

KOHL, H. and PLATZER, H.-W. (2004), *Arbeitsbeziehungen in Mittelosteuropa. Transformation und Integration. Die acht neuen EU-Mitgliedsländer im Vergleich*, 2nd ed, Nomos, Baden-Baden.

LADÓ, M. (2002), "Industrial Relations in the Candidate Countries", *European Industrial Relations Observatory on-line*, available at http://www.eurofound.europa.eu/eiro/2002/07/feature/tn0207102f.htm, 15 April 2008.

LADÓ, M. and VAUGHAN-WHITEHEAD, D. (2003), "Social Dialogue in Candidate Countries. What For?", *Transfer*, No.1, pp. 64-87.

MEARDI, G. (2002), "The Trojan Horse for the Americanisation of Europe? Polish Industrial Relations Towards the EU", *European Journal of Industrial Relations*, Vol. 8, No.1, pp. 77-99.

OECD (2004), *Employment Outlook*, Organisation for Economic Co-operation and Development, Paris.

OECD (2006), *Economic Policy Reforms: Going for Growth*, Organisation for Economic Co-operation and Development, Paris.

OST, D. (2000), "Illusory Corporatism in Eastern Europe: Neoliberal Tripartism and Postcommunist Class Identities", *Politics and Society*, No.4, pp. 503-530.

PKPP (2001), "Programme" (accepted at the PKPP General Assembly meeting on 21 February 2001)", Polska Konfederacja Pracodawców Prywatnych Lewiatan, Warsaw (http://domino-www.enternet.com.pl/prywatni.nsf/SubPages) ("downloaded" not available), 25 June 2003.

PKPP (2006), "Czarna Lista Barier", Polska Konfederacja Pracodawców Prywatnych Lewiatan, Warsaw, available at http://www.prywatni.pl/upload/plik/czarna_lista_barier_final_1222_2976709.pdf, 15 March 2006.

POLISH LABOUR CODE (2005), available at www.polishlaw.com.pl, 17 July 2005.

PUMBERGER, K. (1998), "Rohrstock – Kapitalismus oder soziale Partnerschaft? Anmerkungen zu Gewerkschaften, Management, Arbeitgeberverbände und Arbeitsbeziehungen in der Tschechischen Republik", Aktualisierte Version, Friedrich-Ebert-Stiftung, Prag.

SCHULTEN, T. and ZAGELMEYER, S. (1998), "Board-level Employee Representation in Europe", *European Industrial Relations Observatory on-line*, available at http://www.eurofound.europa.eu/eiro/1998/09/study/tn9809201s.htm, 15 April 2008.

SENGENBERGER, W. (1987), *Struktur und Funktionsweise von Arbeitsmärkten. Die Bundesrepublik Deutschland im internationalen Vergleich*, Campus, Frankfurt a.M./New York.

STREECK, W. (1991), "On Institutional Conditions of Diversified Quality Production", in MATZNER, E. and STREECK, W. (eds.), *Beyond Keynesianism. Socio-Economics of Production and Full Employment*, Edward Elgar Publishing, Aldershot, pp. 21-61.

TENBROCK, C. (2004), "Real Existierender Kapitalismus", 9 September 2004, page 26.

TRAXLER, F. and BEHRENS M. (2002), "Collective Bargaining Coverage and Extension Procedures", *European Industrial Relations Observatory on-line*, available at http://www.eurofound.europa.eu/eiro/2002/12/study/tn0212102s.htm, 15 April 2008.

UHLÍR, J. (2003), "Tarifautonomie – auch ein Modell für die Beitrittsländer?" Dokumented Presentation at the Third International Conference of the Otto Brenner Foundation, Berlin, 25 and 26 April 2003.

VAUGHAN-WHITEHEAD, D. (2000), "Social Dialogues in EU Enlargement: Acquis and Responsibilities", *Transfer*, No.3, pp. 387-398.

VICKERSTAFF, S.A. and THIRKELL, J.E.M. (2000), "Instrumental Rationality and European Integration. Transfer or Avoidance of Industrial Relations Institutions in Central and Eastern Europe?", *European Journal of Industrial Relations*, Vol. 6, No.2, pp. 237-251.

VICKERSTAFF, S.A. and THIRKELL, J.E.M. (1997), "Eastern European Labour Relations. Transference, Imitation, Imposition", in BRADY, J. (ed.), *Central and Eastern Europe – Industrial Relations and Market Economy*, Oak Tree Press, Dublin, pp. 15-35.

VOß, E. (2003), "Entwicklung der industriellen Beziehungen und Unternehmenskulturen in Polen. Länderstudie im Rahmen des Projekts. Arbeitsbeziehungen und Unternehmenskulturen" in Polen (http://www.boeckler.de/pdf/mbportal_moe_laenderstudie_polen.pdf).

WALWEI, U. (1996), "Flexibilität und Regulierung des Beschäftigungssystems: Optionen und Effekte", *Mitteilungen aus der Arbeitsmarkt- und Berufsforschung*, No.29, pp. 219-227.

WEINSTEIN, M. (2000), "Solidarity's Abandonment of Worker Councils: Redefining Employee Stakeholder Rights in Post-socialist Poland", *British Journal of Industrial Relations*, No.1, pp. 49-73.

WEISS, M. (2004), "Enlargement and Industrial Relations: Building a New Social Partnership", *International Journal of Comparative Labour Law and Industrial Relations*, No.1, pp. 5-26.

WIELGOHS, J. (2001), "Varianten erfolgreicher Privatisierungspolitik – Die Konditionierung und Steuerung der Unternehmensprivatisierung in Estland, Polen und der Tschechischen Republik", in WIESENTHAL, H. (ed.), *Gelegenheit und Entscheidung. Policies und Politics erfolgreicher Transformationssteuerung*, Westdeutscher Verlag, Wiesbaden, pp. 93-168.

WIESENTHAL, H. (1995), "Pre-emptive Institutionenbildung. Korporative Akteure und institutionelle Innovationen im Transformationsprozeß postsozialistischer Staaten", *Working Paper AG TRAP*, No.95/4, Max-Planck-Gesellschaft, Berlin.

WORLD BANK GROUP (2006), "Doing Business. Benchmarking Business Regulations", available at http://www.doingbusiness.org/ExploreTopics/HiringFiring Workers, 22 March 2006.

Welfare States and Restructuring in Central and Eastern Europe

Maarten KEUNE

Senior Researcher at the European Trade Union Institute (ETUI-REHS)

Introduction

Since 1989, the New Member States (NMS)[1] of Central and Eastern Europe (CEE) have been going through a profound process of restructuring. The systemic dimension of this restructuring process concerned the transformation of state socialism system into capitalism, which can largely be considered as finalised. A second, more macro-level dimension concerns a continuous and ongoing process of reforms resulting from regime competition, e.g. competition between countries for investment. Regime competition amounts often to attempts to offer investors with cheaper and/or more flexible production conditions including low wages, low taxes and contributions or high labour market flexibility. Such competition for capital takes to some extent place at a global scale but is more concrete within the EU, in particular among the new members (see the contributions in Galgóczi *et al.*, 2006; Bohle, 2008). A third and closely related micro dimension is the continuous adaptation of enterprises to global competitive pressures and their search for ever-higher profit margins. This is manifested in a variety of development, including the constant search of capital for more advantageous locations, conditions and ways to organise their organisation and value chains (*ibid.*).

The extent to which restructuring processes are translated into negative social effects like poverty, inequality and unemployment depends to a large degree upon the characteristics of the welfare state. The welfare state can cushion the impact of restructuring by providing individuals or

---

1 The NMS under discussion here are the eight Central and Eastern European countries that entered the European Union in May 2004, e.g. the Czech Republic, Estonia, Hungary, Latvia, Lithuania, Poland, Slovakia and Slovenia.

groups with income guarantees, subsidised employment creation initiatives, assistance in finding new employment and others. As a result, restructuring processes create demands for (increases in) welfare by those affected and their representatives. At the same time, there are pressures for welfare state retrenchment. Sometimes it is argued that the welfare state may affect enterprise competitiveness and the attractiveness of a country for foreign investors in a negative way by the costs it implies trough employer social contributions. Also, some underline the negative effects of "excessive" welfare provision on risk taking and motivation to work. Finally, welfare state expenditure often makes up a sizeable share of government expenditure, but governments are often under pressure to limit such expenditure and balance their budgets, not the least because of the economic criteria set by the EU economic architecture.

Within this context, the present chapter discusses how the welfare states in the NMS have developed. Two main dimension of this development will be reflected upon. Using Esping-Andersen's three worlds of welfare typology (Esping-Andersen, 1990 and 1999), the institutional side of the welfare state will be examined. These three welfare regimes each represent a group of countries which historically have had broadly similar (though certainly not identical) welfare states. The core characteristics of the three welfare regimes can be summarised as follows (Esping-Andersen, 1990; Hemerijck *et al.*, 2006):

- The liberal regime is based on utilitarian market principles and is characterised by targeted, needs-based, means-tested entitlements; low replacement rates; general revenue financing; underdeveloped public social services apart from Beveridgean health and education systems; and poor family services, often market-based and hence not accessible for all.
- The social democratic or Nordic regime is characterised by citizenship-based universal entitlements; generous replacement rates; general revenue financing; a broad supply of social services beyond health and education, and active family policy encouraging gender egalitarianism and women's integration in the labour market (albeit with a noticeable degree of gender segregation).
- The Bismarckian or continental regime is characterised by employment-related social insurance and a contribution-biased revenue dependency; an important role of social partners in managing the welfare state; very unequal levels of generosity in transfer programmes; very modest levels of public social services beyond health and education; and passive family policies premised on the conventional male-breadwinner family.

These welfare regimes will be treated like Weberian ideal types rather than as fully representing empirical cases. Empirical country cases will always include elements of more than one of these regimes and are attributed to one or another of them on the basis of their dominant characteristics rather than because they perfectly fit the type. Indeed, real-life welfare states are all hybrids to some extent. For the NMS it will be established to what extent they contain elements of the three ideal types.

The second dimension of welfare state development that will be discussed is welfare state performance. Here the emphasis will be on what outcomes welfare state development has produced in terms of income, poverty, inequality and employment. Here the NMS welfare states will be compared to each other as well as to the EU-15 countries.

The structure of the chapter is as follows. In section II the historical context of post-1989 welfare state development will be reviewed. Section III analyses the reform of welfare state institutions in post-socialist Central and Eastern Europe, using the three worlds of welfare typology. Section IV considers welfare state performance in the new Member States in terms of income, poverty, equality and employment, and compares this performance with the rest of the EU. Section V presents conclusions.

I. The Welfare State Before 1989

The historical development of the welfare state in the CEE countries differs markedly from that in Western Europe. Whereas in Western Europe welfare state development has been a fairly gradual process characterised by strong elements of continuity and path-dependence, in CEE this has been much less the case. The CEE countries have undergone two fundamental, systemic changes, from capitalism to state-socialism in the 1940s and back to capitalism after 1989, and on both occasions the complete array of social and economic institutions were called into question, resulting in radical institutional change. This does not mean, however, as will be discussed below, that there is no continuity between these different historical periods.

In the late 19th and early 20th century, the welfare state in CEE countries initially emerged – as in the German context – as a response to the "social question": with advancing industrialisation the urban working class grew rapidly and the ruling elites started to increase social rights to improve the situation of industrial workers and prevent them from engaging in political protest (Keune, 2006a). For example, in the Czech lands, the frontrunner where industrialisation was concerned, in the 1880s new labour and social legislation reducing the role of the market was introduced. The roots of the welfare state emerged, with laws to restrict child labour, limits set on working time and the introduction of a system of labour inspection, accident insurance and health insurance. Welfare state development was further speeded up following pressure from the growing labour movement as well as, in certain countries (noticeably Czechoslovakia in the inter-war era), the strengthening in the position of social democratic parties.

The emerging welfare states in the CEE countries largely followed the employment-related insurance-based Bismarckian welfare state model (Keune, 2006b; Potůček, 2004; Cerami, 2005). They established firm distinctions between occupational groups and generally favoured urban industrial workers over agricultural workers. Large welfare disparities could be observed across inter-war CEE, with the highly industrialised Czechoslovakia belonging to the more affluent European countries while Poland or Hungary were far more agricultural and more deeply affected by poverty.

After WWII, with the emergence of state socialism in the CEE countries, dramatic institutional change affecting all areas of society was on the agenda. The welfare state became centrally regulated by the one-party state in a nationalised economy and it also increasingly acquired a universal character. However, this was not so much because welfare entitlements became based on citizenship, as in the Nordic welfare model, but rather because the emergence of full employment, a by-product of rapid industrial growth and a continuous shortage of labour, led to universal coverage of welfare arrangements (Baxandall, 2003; Róna-Tas, 1997).[2] Indeed, the core of the welfare system remained firmly employment-based. This employment-based character was further strengthened by the fact that welfare entitlements were often provided through the state enterprise (Kornai, 1992) and that trade unions were involved in the management and provision of welfare.

Welfare arrangements in state-socialist CEE had an equalising effect in terms of income and social rights. Even so, important differences prevailed between elites and non-elites, between priority sectors and non-priority sectors, and within the enterprise between groups with more and those with less bargaining power. The state-socialist system, characterised by continuous labour shortages, also required women to enter employment and facilitated female employment by providing extended maternity leave and child-raising benefits as well as ample and free childcare facilities. However, little changed in terms of the house-

---

2 Full employment was initially not part of the state socialist discourse. It was only after full employment was achieved as a result of labour shortage that it became part and parcel of the state socialist discourse (Baxandall, 2003).

hold responsibilities of women who bore a double burden, while the division of labour also remained sexist (Deacon, 2000; Fodor, 2005). The shortage of labour, combined with a low retirement age and low pensions additionally led to the widespread practice of the working pensioner.

However, not all welfare entitlements were employment based. For example, the state subsidised food, housing, and transport, and maintained a formally free health system and education system, although some formally free services were not in fact entirely free (tipping of doctors, for example, was standard practice). There were, furthermore, differences in the actual shape this system took in the various countries and over time.

The state-socialist welfare states have been evaluated in a variety of ways, combining normative and efficiency arguments. One of the main ways to characterise the pre-1989 CEE welfare states has been Kornai's "premature welfare state", a welfare state that exceeded the means of the economy and was, moreover, wasteful (Kornai, 1992). Indeed, the inefficient character of CEE welfare states, exemplified by the low quality of many universal and free services, queues, underemployment, limited choices in consumption, and a generally low standard of living, has often been underlined. The pre-1989 CEE welfare states have also been accused of being paternalist and overly interventionist, of excluding choice, and of favouring the elites. At the same time, pre-1989 welfare states have been credited with reducing poverty, increasing equality, universal and free health and education services, and high employment levels.

II. Post-1989 Welfare State Developments

In the years 1989-1991, the state-socialist system was abandoned in favour of democratic capitalism. The first half of the 1990s was characterised by a deep economic crisis across the entire CEE region, the depth of which nonetheless varied substantially. By 1994, all NMS had seen their Gross Domestic Product (GDP) drop, with GDP losses – as compared to the 1989 level – ranging from 8% in Poland to almost 50% in Latvia. Many enterprises collapsed and others downsized or rationalised. Also, inflation had exploded (reaching up to 1000% in the Baltic countries in 1992), full employment had come to an end and unemployment rose rapidly. Women and working pensioners were often the first to be dismissed.

The depth of the crisis of the early 1990s dampened the initial optimistic expectations of a speedy and unproblematic "transition" to capitalism which would rapidly replace and outperform the obsolete state-socialist economy. Job losses reached up to 30% and unemployment skyrocketed. As the new political elites feared that the high social costs of the initial crisis would undermine the support of the population for economic and political reform, radical economic reforms were accompanied by more cautious welfare state reforms. Indeed, in these initial years the welfare state was, to an important extent, used as a buffer with the aim of absorbing the most dramatic social effects of the restructuring of the economy, in particular loss of income through loss of employment.

One important way of absorbing part of the employment and income losses was the widespread use of early retirement provisions and disability pensions for redundant workers (Fultz and Ruck, 2001; Müller, 2002). As a further means of reducing the impact of employment losses, previously largely non-existent unemployment benefit schemes were set up around the region (Nesporova, 1999). In addition, all NMS introduced a minimum wage to put a wage floor in the labour market. Finally, social assistance schemes were introduced to prevent those without others means of existence from falling into poverty.

This endeavour succeeded only partially. By the mid-1990s, the NMS had returned to economic growth and brought inflation under control but inflation had often already depleted the real value of wages and benefits, leading to increasing poverty. Employment rates remained low and unemployment high. In addition, welfare schemes had come under severe financial strain because of the dramatic increase in numbers of benefit recipients, unfavourable demographic developments and falling tax and social contributions (Rhodes and Keune, 2006).

As a result, from the mid-1990s onwards welfare state reform moved to the top of the political agenda, but this time with a view to reducing costs and increasing efficiency, reducing welfare dependency and changing incentive structures and governance systems. Much of the political elites considered that the welfare state had become a problem instead of a facilitator of reform because of it budgetary implications and its presumed negative effects on regime and enterprise competitiveness and on the motivation of the unemployed to seek employment. Yet reform has proved difficult for two reasons. First, economic crisis and growing poverty had led to increasing social needs and demands for welfare. Second, democratisation created institutional opportunities for political parties and trade unions to block extensive retrenchment, preventing government elites from cutting taxes and spending at will (Campbell, 1996). Indeed, welfare state reform has been a hot political issue and has been heavily contested. Even so, profound institutional change has taken place on a number of welfare state dimensions. Let's briefly consider some of its main elements.

Where pensions are concerned, state-socialist pension systems were largely financed on a pay-as-you-go (PAYG) basis through transfers from state firms to the state budget, direct contributions by workers being rare and retirement ages low (Fultz and Ruck, 2001; Guardiancich, 2004). As of 1994, far-reaching reform of pension systems – which accounts for the largest share of social expenditure – was on the agenda. This was as a result of budgetary and demographic pressures, but also of strong advocacy of reform from the World Bank which was pushing for privatisation and individualisation of savings (World Bank, 1994).

Firstly, all NMS introduced adaptations to the traditional pension scheme, maintaining or even strengthening the link to employment. The adaptations included, for example, a raise in the retirement age, a change in benefit formulae, and improved collection of contributions. However, not all countries did this in the same way: Poland and Latvia made pensions more individualised, more dependent on lifetime contributions and life expectancy, more earnings-related and less redistributive (Fultz, 2003); Hungary retained the traditional system but reduced redistribution to low-income workers; the Czech Republic and Slovenia, on the contrary, increased redistribution to the benefit of low-wage workers (Stanovik, 2002; Mácha, 2002).

Hungary, Poland, Latvia, Estonia and Slovakia went a step further and introduced, alongside the public pillar, mandatory, commercially managed, individual savings accounts, thus partially shifting pension risks from society to the individual, strengthening the link to employment and reducing risk pooling and redistribution (Müller, 2002; Fultz, 2003). Finally, all NMS introduced voluntary supplementary pensions. Hence, pension reform in the NMS has combined elements of convergence – a stronger relation of pensions to employment histories, an increasing pension age and the introduction of voluntary schemes – with elements of divergence in the form of mandatory private savings accounts (or not), the importance of the market in pension provision and a greater or lesser degree of redistribution. Hence, a general Bismarckian trend is mixed with some egalitarian and market elements.

Something similar can be observed in health care. Whereas, before WWII, most CEE countries had a Bismarckian system of health insurance, under the state-socialist system free universal health care was provided by the state. After the demise of state socialism, all NMS opted for a Bismarckian-type health insurance system under which the insured, in return for the payment of health insurance contributions, receive health care services (Cerami, 2005). However, this Bismarckian orientation is combined with the strong universal and egalitarian aspirations that were prevalent during the state-socialist period. Today, the state largely continues to guarantee the provision of health services to the non-insured, while it also covers the deficits of the newly established health insurance funds (Cerami, 2005). Most systems also operate on the principle of solidarity whereby the premiums paid by the insured are not risk- but income-proportionate (see, for example, Hungarian Ministry of Health, Social and Family Affairs, 2004). These Bismarckian and universalist dimensions were subsequently further combined with market influence, including market-based services (Cerami, 2005).

Where unemployment benefits are concerned, all NMS set up unemployment benefit systems after 1989 to soften the effect of employment losses and facilitate labour market mobility. Following the Bismackian logic, benefits are financed by contributions (although in some countries complemented by taxes), and eligibility as well as the level and duration of benefits are tightly linked to the individual employment and wage history. The link with previous employment is however weakened by the fact that minima and maxima apply to duration and levels of benefits. Initially, these systems were often relatively generous, offered benefits for long periods of time and with relatively high replacement rates, and provided benefits to most of the unemployed. For example, the proportion of the unemployed receiving benefits in 1991 was 79% in Poland, 77.1% in Hungary and 65% in Czechoslovakia. Over time, however, eligibility criteria have been tightened, and the level and duration of benefits reduced. The proportion of those in receipt of benefit declined dramatically as a result and in 2001 amounted to 20% in Poland, 49.7% in Hungary and 34.9% in the Czech Republic. This rapidly declining coverage, combined with falling levels and duration, means that, whereas at the start of post-socialist transformation relatively generous and almost universalistic unemployment benefit systems prevailed, within the course of some ten years this was transformed into low-coverage and low-benefit systems (Keune, 2006a; Spieser, 2007). At the same time, the decline in expenditure on unemployment benefits was not translated into increased expenditure on active labour market policies, which has remained low. A possible exception on both accounts is Slovenia where, as will be discussed below, social expenditure is substantially above that in the other NMS.

Where family policy and maternity benefits are concerned, an ILO comparative study concludes that, since 1989, the reform of family benefits has been incremental and continuous and has included a tendency towards the de-coupling of family benefits from employment status, the introduction of universal benefits as well as means-tested benefits, and the equalisation of benefits for men and women providing childcare (Fultz and Steinhilber, 2003). At the same time, only limited changes were introduced concerning maternity benefits, which have been retained as a form of employment-related social insurance (*ibid.*).

This overview of a number of components of the welfare state in CEE shows that, to a large extent, their institutional characteristics are Bismarckian, with largely insurance-based benefits as well as fairly strongly employment-related factors defining benefits. However, this does not mean that NMS welfare states are simply on a Bismarckian track, for universalist aspirations from the state-socialist era also play a significant role, while the market is increasingly important as a governance mechanism. Moreover, targeted social benefits aimed at poverty relief have been introduced in some areas, while the provision of unemployment benefits, in spite of the contributory basis and the link to employment histories, has become minimal in most countries. Hence, reforms have not been uni-directionally conceived with reference to a single institutional logic or model, but include elements of various models. Given such institutional terms, welfare states in the NMS do not simply fit one of the traditional welfare-families typology developed for the EU-15. Rather, each NMS welfare state presents its own mix of elements of the four welfare regimes. Institutionally, the inclination towards the Bismarckian system is clearly strongest, but with a significant role also played by market-orientation, targeting and universality. In other words, these countries have combined their Bismarckian and state-socialist heritages with the market ideology projected onto the region in the past fifteen years (see also Cerami, 2005: 143-144).

III. Welfare State Performance

In this section welfare state performance is discussed in terms of a number of indicators referring to income, poverty, inequality and employment, comparing the NMS countries both with one another and with the EU-15. First however a view is needed of the level of welfare expenditure, key to understanding performance. Table 1 provides an overview of the percentage of GDP allocated to social expenditure. It clearly emerges that, in comparison with the EU-15, welfare expenditure in CEE is low. The Baltic States are the lowest spenders in Europe but Slovakia, Hungary, the Czech Republic and Poland are also among the low spenders. Slovenia is the exception with a level of expenditure that outperforms three EU-15 countries.[3] Hence, in terms of social expenditure, the CEE countries belong to the minimal welfare states of the EU, where social transfers are lowest. Their expenditure also re-

[3] The structure of social expenditure in the eight is however very similar to the EU-15 average, with the main portions of expenditure directed towards pensions and health (Keune, 2006b).

mains below that of the "traditional" Bismarckian countries of the EU-15. Hence, whereas, as discussed above, their institutional logic may be, to a large extent, Bismarckian, in terms of expenditure they are at or below the level of the worst performers among the liberal and the Southern European countries so that their welfare states might best be described as minimal Bismarckian. The only apparent exception here is Slovenia which is closer to the traditional Bismarckian countries of the EU-15. In addition, there are no signs of "catching up" in this respect. In the longer term there is no clear pattern in the development of social expenditure in the NMS and in most of them it is quite stable over time. This also means that the economic growth of recent years does not necessarily lead to a higher share of GDP spent on social protection. What is more, between 2003 and 2004 social expenditure declined in all NMS except Estonia.

Table 1: Expenditure on Social Protection (2004 – % GDP)

Sweden	32.9	Slovenia	24.3
France	31.2	Luxembourg	22.6
Denmark	30.7	Hungary	20.7
Germany	29.5	Spain	20.0
Belgium	29.3	Poland	20.0
Austria	29.1	Czech Republic	19.6
The Netherlands	28.5	Slovakia	17.2
EU-25	27.3	Ireland	17.0
United Kingdom	26.3	Estonia	13.4
Italy	26.1	Lithuania	13.3
Greece	26.0	Latvia	12.6
Portugal	24.9		

Source: Eurostat.

Turning to the performance indicators, a first key indicator is the average level of income, expressed by GDP *per capita* corrected for purchasing power (Table 2). Differences among the NMS are large: in 2006, GDP *per capita* in the poorest of the eight, Poland, is only 61.2% of that of the richest, Slovenia. Poland, Latvia and Lithuania make up the poorer group of the NMS, a middle group consisting of Slovakia, Hungary and Estonia, with a richer group constituted by the Czech Republic and Slovenia. Since 2001, however, differences between NMS have diminished as especially the Baltic countries, then the poorest NMS, have been growing faster than the richer NMS. The exception to this trend is Poland, which has seen its relative position worsen recently.

In comparison to the EU-15, GDP *per capita* is far below the average of the EU-15 in all NMS. Only Slovenia and the Czech Republic have a *per capita* GDP above that of the poorest old Member State (Portugal). Clearly, in spite of the differences among tem, the NMS as a group make up the low-income part of the enlarged EU. Hence, there is much less social cohesion in the enlarged EU than was the case before May 2004. Nonetheless, the differences are getting smaller for, whereas in 2001 five of the eight NMS had a GDP *per capita* below 50% of the EU-25 average, in 2006 they all exceed this threshold. Indeed, average yearly GDP growth in the NMS has been much higher in 2001-2006 than in the EU-15 and all NMS have improved compared to the EU-25 average. In other words, there is some convergence in terms of income across the EU-25, even though this process is slow and differences are still large.

Table 2: GDP *per Capita* in Purchasing Power Parities (PPS) (EU-25=100, 2001-2006)

	2001	2006
Poland	46.1	51.3
Latvia	37.1	53.3
Lithuania	40.1	54.8
Slovakia	48.7	60.2
Hungary	56.9	63.4
Estonia	43.7	65.0
Czech Republic	65.8	76.0
Slovenia	73.9	83.6
EU-15	109.5	107.8
EU-15 min-max	73.2-214.6	70.3-257.0

Source: Eurostat.

The situation is very similar where wages and compensation are concerned (Table 3). In Euro terms, total compensation per employee in the NMS stands at around one-third of the EU-25 average (Hungary, Czech Republic) or lower. The positive exception is again Slovenia but even here compensation remains below 60% of the EU-25 average. Clearly, the NMS are the low wage countries of the EU. Again real wages in the NMS have been increasing faster than those in the EU-15 and some conversion can be observed. At the same time, wage growth in most NMS remains behind productivity growth and the wage share in GDP is declining. Indeed, not unlike the situation in the EU-15, there are strong pressures for wage moderation stemming from the demands from enterprises and investors (sometimes reinforced by the threat of relocation), regime competition, budgetary considerations, and the often weak position of organised labour.

Table 3: Yearly Average Compensation per Employee (2006 – Euro)

Latvia	6,294	EU-25	34,480
Lithuania	7,785	Italy	34,480
Slovakia	8,410	Sweden	39,980
Poland	9,377	Austria	41,170
Estonia	10,090	United Kingdom	41,380
Czech Republic	11,900	Germany	41,790
Hungary	12,430	Ireland	42,090
Portugal	18,840	France	42,980
Slovenia	20,090	Denmark	43,730
Spain	28,510	Netherlands	45,870

Source: AMECO.

Given the low levels of average income and wages, the welfare state plays a key role in ameliorating poverty and reducing income disparities. Table 4 provides an overview of the levels of relative poverty in the EU before and after social transfers.[4] Interestingly enough, where poverty after transfers is concerned, in spite of low social expenditure, four of the eight NMS perform better than the EU-25 average of 16% and the Czech Republic and Slovenia, e.g. the richest two NMS, are among the countries with the lowest levels of poverty in the EU. These four NMS have relative poverty levels comparable to the Nordic and Bismarckian countries.

On the other hand, the poorest NMS (Poland) and those with the lowest social expenditure (the Baltic States) perform worse than the EU-25 average, while Poland and Lithuania have the highest poverty level of all. These four have poverty levels characteristic of the liberal and the Southern European countries.

As shown by Table 4, although the level of poverty before social transfers is of importance for the level of poverty after social transfer, these transfers themselves seem to have a decisive impact. On average, social transfers (including pensions) reduce poverty levels from 43% to 16% in the EU, a reduction of 27 percentage points. On average, pensions are responsible for 17 percentage points of this reduction and other social transfers for 10 percentage points. In the countries with poverty levels lower than the EU-25 average, e.g. the Nordic and the Bismarckian countries as well as four of the NMS, the impact of the welfare state is stronger: social transfers reduce poverty by 26-37 percentage points. In the countries with poverty levels above the average,

4 The poverty indicator refers to the share of persons with an equivalised disposable income below 60% of the national median. Hence it is an indicator of income distribution rather than absolute poverty.

e.g. the liberal and Southern European countries and the Baltic States with their low levels of expenditure, the impact of social transfers is much more limited and hovers between 19-24 percentage points. The only exception here is Poland, where the impact of transfers is clearly above the average with 30 percentage points, but where poverty before transfers is also the highest of the EU-25. Hence, the welfare state impact in Poland is comparable to Bismarckian and Nordic countries, whereas the outcome in terms of poverty, because of the high pre-transfer level, rather resembles the liberal and Southern European countries.

Table 4: At-risk-of-poverty Rates After and Before Social Transfers (2005)

	A: Poverty after social transfers*	B: Poverty before social transfers (old age and survivor pensions counted as income before social transfers and not as social transfers)*	C: Poverty before social transfers (pensions included in social transfers)**	C-A
SE	9	29	42	33
SL	10	16	37	27
CZ	10	21	39	29
NL	11	22	37	26
AU	12	24	43	31
FI	12	28	40	28
DK	12	31	39	27
SK	13	22	40	27
DE	13	24	44	31
FR	13	26	45	32
HU	13	29	50	37
BE	15	28	42	27
EU-25	16	26	43	27
EE	18	24	39	21
IT	19	24	43	24
LV	19	26	40	21
UK	19	29	43	24
GR	20	23	39	19
ES	20	24	39	19
PT	20	26	42	22
IE	20	32	40	20
LI	21	26	42	21
PL	21	30	51	30

Note: data refer to the share of persons with an equivalised disposable income below the risk-of-poverty threshold, which is set at 60% of the national median.
* Slovenia is 2003 ** Slovenia and UK are 2003
Source: own elaboration based on Eurostat.

The differences between male and female poverty are fairly small in the NMS, as in the EU-25 in general (Table 5). More important are the levels of child poverty. With the sole exception of Slovenia, child poverty is higher than average poverty, the difference reaching up to 8 percentage points in the Czech Republic and Poland. Hence, families with children are particularly affected by low income, and family benefits do not sufficiently compensate for this.

Table 5: Poverty after Social Transfers, 2003-2004 (%)

	Total	Women	Children
Czech Republic	8	8	15
Slovenia	10	14	9
Hungary	12	11	17
Lithuania	15	15	17
Latvia	16	17	19
Poland	17	14	23
Estonia	18	20	20
Slovakia	21	19	30
EU-25	16	17	20
EU-15 min-max	11-21	10-22	9-23

Source: Eurostat.

Table 6: Inequality of Income Distribution Top/Bottom Income Quintile Share Ratio 2005

Slovenia	3.1	EU-25	4.9
Sweden	3.3	Ireland	5.0
Denmark	3.5	Spain	5.4
Finland	3.6	Italy	5.6
Czech Republic	3.7	UK	5.6
Austria	3.8	Greece	5.8
Slovakia	3.9	Estonia	5.9
France	4.0	Poland	6.6
Hungary	4.0	Latvia	6.7
Netherlands	4.0	Lithuania	6.9
Belgium	4.1	Portugal	8.2
Germany	4.1		

Note: Slovenia is 2003
Source: Eurostat.

The picture that emerges from the poverty data is confirmed by data on the inequality of income distribution comparing the top and bottom quintile (Table 6). Slovenia and the Czech Republic are among the most equal countries in Europe, the former being even more equal than the

Nordic countries – although at a much lower absolute income level. Income distribution in Slovakia and Hungary is also clearly more equal than the EU-25 average and these are placed among the Bismarckian countries. The Baltic States, with their low social expenditure, and Poland belong to the countries with higher levels of inequality, together with the liberal and the South European countries.

Finally, the employment rate is an important indicator for the performance of the welfare state. In 2006, the employment rate in the NMS varied substantially, from 53.9% in Poland to 68.8% in Estonia (Table 7). What is more, all NMS improved their employment rate compared to 2001, but to a highly variable extent. It was close to stagnant in Poland, Hungary and the Czech Republic, while increasing rapidly in the Baltic States. On the one hand, this is a reflection of differences in economic growth. However, in the Baltic States especially, outward migration plays a significant role here also. In Poland, where outward migration is substantial as well, this seems, for the time being, to affect only the unemployment rate.

Table 7: Employment Rate (15-64 years) 2001-2006, Second Quarter (%)

	Total		Males		Females		M-F difference	
	2001	2006	2001	2006	2001	2006	2001	2006
PL	53.7	53.9	59.2	60.2	48.3	47.8	10.9	12.4
HU	56.1	57.3	62.9	63.9	49.6	51.1	13.3	12.8
SK	56.7	59.3	61.8	66.9	51.8	51.6	10.0	15.3
LT	58.1	63.7	59.5	66.4	56.9	61.1	2.6	5.3
CZ	65.0	65.3	73.1	73.6	56.9	56.8	16.2	16.8
LV	58.9	65.5	61.9	68.2	56.1	62.9	5.8	5.3
SI	63.6	67.1	68.5	70.8	58.6	63.3	9.9	7.5
EE	60.8	68.8	65.1	71.3	56.9	66.4	8.2	4.9
EU-15	63.9	65.9	73.0	73.4	54.9	58.5	18.1	14.9
EU-15 min-max	54.5-75.9	58.9-76.9	68.1-82.7	67.0-80.8	40.9-72.6	46.7-73.2	5.0-29.9	3.6-27.1

Source: Eurostat.

In all NMS the male employment rate is higher than the female rate. Differences are, however, much smaller in the Baltic States and in Slovenia – which are in line with the Nordic countries on this indicator – than in Poland, Hungary Slovakia and the Czech Republic, where they resemble the Bismarckian countries of the EU-15 (but remain below the very high level of gender differences observed in the Southern European countries).

Where the wider European context is concerned, in 2006 Slovenia and Estonia had employment rates just above the EU-15 average but still substantially below the best performers; in Latvia, the Czech Republic and Lithuania they were just below the EU-15 average; and in Slovakia, and especially Hungary and Poland, they were quite far below the
EU-15 average (Poland and Hungary being the worst performers of the entire EU-25). Between 2001 and 2006, the employment rate in five NMS increased more rapidly than the 2 percentage points increase for the EU-15: Estonia (8.0 percentage points), Latvia (6.6), Lithuania (5.6), Slovenia (3.5) and Slovakia (2.6). However, in Poland (0.2), the Czech Republic (0.3) and Hungary (1.2), the employment rate is falling further behind the EU-15 average. Indeed, the latter three seem to be suffering from a well-known Continental disease: jobless growth.

Conclusions

This chapter set out to examine the institutional characteristics as well as the performance of the welfare state in the NMS, within the context of a continuously restructuring economy and the demands and counter pressures this restructuring process implies. Post-1989 welfare state developments took place within a historical context which fist of all consists of the initial Bismarckian style welfare state that started to emerge in the late 19th century to address the social question and was further developed in the interwar era. In the pre-war welfare state entitlements were employment-related and insurance-based and favoured some social groups over others, in particular urban industrial workers over agricultural workers. Under the state socialist system welfare entitlements continued to be firmly linked to employment but acquired a universal character because of the emergence of full employment. At the same time a number of truly universal elements with no connection to employment were introduced. The state socialist welfare state managed to reduce poverty and increase equality and employment levels, and to offer universal and free health and education services. This was however achieved at the cost of a low average level of income, the lack of basic freedoms, high underemployment and low levels of efficiency and choice.

After 1989, following the deep economic crisis of first half of the 1990s and the resulting employment and income losses, the demands on the welfare state increased rapidly. Initially, the welfare state was largely used as a buffer to soften the social impact of radical economic change and to address public discontent. A number of new welfare programmes and policies were introduced including a minimum wage, unemployment benefits and social assistance. However, because of falling employment levels and rising numbers of benefit recipients the welfare state came under severe financial strain and from the second half of the 1990s onwards, it moved more to the centre of political conflict. Much of the CEE political elites, often inspired or supported by the international financial institutions and company interests, considered that the welfare state had become a problem instead of a facilitator of reform and sought to implement welfare state reform focused more on cost containment, reduction of welfare dependency and improved governance. But such reforms have not been popular and have spurred opposition as well.

The combination of the institutional heritage of a strongly employment-related welfare state which also included important universal elements and the stronger market orientation of post-1989 reform pressures meant that today the NMS present a mix of the elements of the worlds of welfare. Bismarckian elements clearly dominate but universality, targeting and markets all play significant roles too, although their weight differs among the NMS. At the same time, in terms of social expenditure the NMS are at the bottom of the EU and clearly are minimal welfare states. Hence, the NMS could be termed "minimal Bismarckian" welfare states. The exception to this is Slovenia which also in terms of social expenditure comes closer to the traditional Bismarckian countries of the EU-15.

Noticeable, however, in spite of their broad institutional similarities, the performance of the NMS welfare states is quite divergent. They are all low-income and low wage countries compared to the EU-15 average, even though they have been catching up with this average in recent years. Among the NMS income levels nonetheless differ widely. Where poverty and inequality are concerned, two very divergent groups emerge. The countries where inequality is high are those where welfare expenditure is lowest (the Baltic States) or where welfare problems are highest (Poland). In these countries welfare expenditure is much less successful in reducing pre-transfer inequality than is the case in the other four, much more equal cases.

What can be expected for the future of the welfare state in the NMS? Considering the fact that economic growth has been high in CEE and is likely to continue to be substantial in the coming years, the standard rule of thumb would suggest that the increasing level of economic development will lead to equally increasing wages and social expenditure and therefore to higher levels of welfare. However there are several factors that question such a positive relationship between growth and welfare.

One is simply the observation that the substantial economic growth most NMS have experienced in the past decade has not led to higher social expenditure and has not been matched by similarly high wage growth. Another is that regime competition and the insistence of capital on wage moderation and reduction of taxes and social contributions are unlikely to diminish, resulting in continued pressure on wages and social expenditure as discussed above.

A final factor that has not yet been touched upon is European Monetary Union (EMU). All new EU members are required to enter EMU at some point, even though no specific entry date has been set, and recently Slovenia was the first NMS effectively to join. Preparation for and participation in EMU is a serious challenge for the new members and is having, or is expected to have, a profound impact on their policies, politics and public institutions (Dyson, 2006).[5] Two of these effects are of particular interest for the present discussion.

One is that entry into EMU means that the individual countries lose certain instruments for adjustment to economic imbalances and shocks, in particular the exchange rate and the interest rate. As such, they will have to rely more on other available adjustment mechanisms in case of asymmetric shocks, in particular wage flexibility, labour market mobility and/or fiscal policy (Dyson, 2006: 20). Insofar as this means pressure for greater flexibility in collective bargaining and in the labour market, it poses an obvious challenge to social solidarity (*ibid.*), the likely effect being that the weaker groups on the labour market will see their relative position worsen, with the ensuing risk of increased working poverty and social polarisation.

The other effect is that EMU entry implies strict inflation, public expenditure and public debt criteria. The inflation criterion as such adds to the above-mentioned pressure for wage moderation, which is further increased, where the public sector is concerned, by the deficit and debt criteria. In addition, the EMU criteria put pressure on public expenditure in general and social expenditure in particular (Rhodes and Keune, 2006). Hence, decreasing social expenditure and a subsequent increase in poverty and inequality are among the possible effects of preparation for and entry into EMU. This applies particularly to the new members that suffer from the combination of high social risks with high budget deficits and/or high public debt, e.g. Poland, Slovakia and Hungary (*ibid.*). It comes as no surprise that these countries have recently begun to delay their planned entry into EMU because of opposition from certain sections of the population to the austerity programmes required to meet EMU criteria.

The new members without serious problems in terms of deficits and debt, e.g. the Baltic countries, face less pressure of this kind. However,

---

5 See Keune (2008) for a further discussion of this issue and of the general impact of EU accession on the NMS welfare states.

considering that today their levels of social expenditure are very low and their levels of inequality and poverty are among the worst in Europe, EMU entry may well foreclose the future option of increasing welfare spending and improving these countries' social situation through an expansion of their minimal welfare states.

References

BAXANDALL, P. (2003), "Postcommunist Unemployment Politics: Historical Legacies and the Curious Acceptance of Job Loss", in EKIERT, G. and HANSON, S. (eds.), *Capitalism and Democracy in Central and Eastern Europe: Assessing the Legacy of Communist Rule*, Cambridge University Press, Cambridge, pp. 248-288.

BOHLE, D. (2008), "Race to the Bottom? Transnational Companies and Reinforced Competition in the Enlarged European Union", in VAN APELDOORN, B., DRAHOKOUPIL, J. and HORN, L. (eds.), *Neoliberal European Governance and Beyond – The Contradictions and Limits of a Political Project*, Palgrave/MacMillan, Basingstoke, Hampshire.

CAMPBELL, J. L. (1996), "An Institutional Analysis of Fiscal Reform in Postcommunist Europe", *Theory and Society*, Vol. 25, No.1, pp. 45-84.

CERAMI, A. (2005), "Social Policy in Central and Eastern Europe. The Emergence of a New European Model of Solidarity?", PhD thesis, University of Erfurt, Germany.

DEACON, B. (2000), "Eastern European Welfare States: The Impact of the Politics of Globalization", *Journal of European Social Policy*, Vol. 10, No.2, pp. 146-161.

DYSON, K. (2006), *Enlarging the Euro Area. External Empowerment and Domestic Transformation in East Central Europe*, Oxford University Press, Oxford.

ESPING-ANDERSEN, G. (1990), *Three Worlds of Welfare Capitalism*, Polity Press, Cambridge.

ESPING ANDERSEN, G. (1999), *Social Foundations of Post-industrial Economies*, Oxford University Press, Oxford.

FODOR, É. (2005), "Women at Work. The Status of Women in the Labour Markets of the Czech Republic, Hungary and Poland", *Occasional Paper*, No.3, United Nations Research Institute for Social Development (UNRISD), Geneva.

FULTZ, E. (2003), "Recent Trends in Pension Reform and Implementation in the EU Accession Countries", paper presented at the International Labour Conference, Geneva, 10 June 2003.

FULTZ, E. and RUCK, M. (2001), "Pension Reform in Central and Eastern Europe: Emerging Issues and Patterns", *International Labour Review*, Vol. 140, No.1, pp. 19-43.

FULTZ, E. and STEINHILBER S. (2003), "The Gender Dimensions of Social Security Reform in the Czech Republic, Hungary, and Poland", in FULTZ, E.,

RUCK, M. and STEINHILBER, S. (eds.), *The Gender Dimensions of Social Security Reform in Central and Eastern Europe: Case Studies of the Czech Republic, Hungary and Poland*, International Labour Office, Budapest, pp. 13-41.

GUARDIANCICH, I. (2004), "Welfare State Retrenchment in Central and Eastern Europe: The Case of Pension Reforms in Poland and Slovenia", *Managing Global Transitions*, Vol. 2, No.1, pp. 41-64.

HEMERIJCK, A., KEUNE, M. and RHODES, M. (2006), "European Welfare States: Diversity, Challenges and Reforms, " in HEYWOOD, P., JONES, E., RHODES, M. and SEDELMEIER, U. (eds.), *Developments in European Politics*, Macmillan/Palgrave, Basingstoke, Hampshire, pp. 259-279.

HUNGARIAN MINISTRY OF HEALTH, SOCIAL AND FAMILY AFFAIRS (2004), Health and Social Services in Hungary: 2004 – Year of Changes, Budapest, May 2004 (http://www.eum.hu/download.php?docID=331).

KEUNE, M. (2008), "EU Enlargement and Social Standards: Exporting the European Social Model?" in ORBIE, J. and TORTELL, L. (eds.), *The EU and the Social Dimension of Globalisation*, Routledge, London and New York.

KEUNE, M. (2006a), "Creating Capitalist Labour Markets: A Comparative-Institutionalist Analysis of Labour Market Reform in the Czech Republic and Hungary, 1989-2002", PhD thesis, European University Institute, Florence.

KEUNE, M. (2006b), "The European Social Model and Enlargement", in JEPSEN, M. and SERRANO, A. (eds.), *Unwrapping the European Social Model*, Policy Press, Bristol, pp. 167-188.

KORNAI, J. (1992), *The Socialist System: The Political Economy of Communism*, Oxford University Press, Oxford.

MÁCHA, M. (2002), "The Political Economy of Pension Reform in the Czech Republic", in FULTZ, E. (ed.), *Pension Reform in Central and Eastern Europe*, Vol. 2, *Restructuring of Public Pension Schemes: Case Studies of the Czech Republic and Sloven*ia, International Labour Office, Budapest, pp. 75-112.

MÜLLER, K. (2002), "Pension Reform Paths in Central-Eastern Europe and the Former Soviet Union", *Social Policy and Administration*, Vol. 36, No.2, pp. 725-748.

NESPOROVA, A. (1999), *Employment and Labour Market Policies in Transition Economies*, International Labour Organization, Geneva.

POTŮČEK, M. (2004), "Accession and Social Policy: The Case of the Czech Republic", *Journal of European Social Policy*, Vol. 14, No.3, pp. 253-266.

RHODES, M. and KEUNE M. (2006), "EMU and Welfare State Adjustment in Central and Eastern Europe", in DYSON, K. (ed.), *Enlarging the Euro Area. External Empowerment and Domestic Transformation in East Central Europe*, Oxford University Press, Oxford, pp. 279-300.

RÓNA-TAS, Á. (1997), *The Great Surprise of the Small Transformation. The Demise of Communism and the Rise of the Private Sector in Hungary*, The University of Michigan Press, Ann Arbor.

SPIESER, C. (2007), "Labour Market Policies and Union Politics in Post-Communist Poland: Explaining the Peaceful Institutionalisation of Unemployment", *Politique Européenne*, No.21, pp. 97-132.

STANOVNIK, T. (2002), "The Political Economy of Pension Reform in Slovenia", in FULTZ, E. (ed.), *Pension Reform in Central and Eastern Europe*, Vol. 2, *Restructuring of Public Pension Schemes: Case Studies of the Czech Republic and Slovenia*, International Labour Office, Budapest, pp. 19-73.

WORLD BANK (1994), *Averting the Old Age Crisis*, World Bank, Washington DC.

The Impact of European Law on Regulating the Labour Law Dimension of Corporate Restructurings in Central and Eastern Europe

Nikolett HŐS[1]

Researcher at the European University Institute, Florence

Introduction

Under the free movement provisions of the EC Treaty, labour is viewed as a production factor and it is claimed that its internal mobility will contribute to the efficient allocation of resources in the common European market. In this way also the labour markets of the Member States are getting increasingly involved in the common market and begin to function according to its principles and rules. However, traditionally, labour law and social policy considerations were not considered necessary to achieve the ambitious economic goals of the integration project. In the influential Ohlin Report it was claimed that the benefits of a functioning single market would enable governments to realise the objectives of promoting improved working conditions and an improved standard of living best at national level. Strong social partners, employers' organisations and trade unions were expected to effectively commit national governments to steadily adhering to these common objectives (Ohlin Report, 1956: 112). As result of the post-1945 consensus of the founding Member States of the European Community on full employment and on strengthening the welfare state, this approach was felt to be acceptable in the 1950s (Deakin, 2006: 87). This inceptive consensus was gradually eroded by the further enlargements of the EU (Scharpf, 2002). A few decades later – namely in 2000 – the launch of the Lisbon Strategy indicated that this approach has not fully lived up to the expectations of the founding fathers. While preparing for

[1] I am grateful to Prof. Marie-Ange Moreau and Prof. Radnay József for their comments on an earlier version of this chapter.

the last two enlargements, in which ten Central and Eastern European countries (CEEC) have joined the European Union, the EU set itself a new strategic goal that is to become the most competitive knowledge based economy in the world (European Council, 2000). Growing unemployment was identified as one the most worrying problems of the European economy, therefore the Commission invited the Member States to commit themselves to improve their labour market institutions. In order to regain the conditions of full employment, the Open Method of Coordination was institutionalised which was designed to connect the highly diverse national welfare states to each other (Zeitlin, 2005).

However, changes in the traditional approach were already visible as early as in the 1970s when three Directives were designed to ensure that the interests of the employees will be taken into account when the establishment of the common market and the following restructuring of the national economies will have a negative impact on employment relations (Shanks, 1977). According to *Hepple*, Community labour law came into being in the shape of the Directives on collective redundancies,[2] acquired rights of workers on the transfer of undertakings[3] and insolvency[4] (Hepple, 2005: 202). These Community measures together with the directive on the European Works Councils[5] and most recently the framework directive on information and consultation[6] established rights to information and consultation to the workers and their representatives. In this way European labour law gradually legitimised the role of the social partners in the economic and financial-decision making of the employer on corporate restructurings. On the other hand, the growing areas in national labour law where the impact of European rules play an important role increased also the value of effective enforcement of national labour laws from a European perspective (Bercusson, 2005).

---

2 Council Directive 80/987/EEC of 20 October 1980 on the protection of employees in the event of the insolvency of the employer, OJ L 283 of 28 October 1980, pp. 23-27.

3 Council Directive 77/187/EEC of 14 February 1977 on the approximation of the laws of the Member States relating to the safeguarding of employees' rights in the event of transfer of undertakings, businesses or parts of undertakings or businesses, OJ L 61 of 5 March 1977, pp. 26-28.

4 Council Directive 75/129/EEC of 17 February 1975 on the approximation of the laws of the Member States relating to collective redundancies, OJ L 48 of 22 February 1975, pp. 29-30.

5 Council Directive 94/45/EC of 22 September 1994 on the establishment of a European Works Council or a procedure in Community-scale undertakings for the purposes of informing and consulting employees, OJ L 254 of 30 September 1994, pp. 64-72.

6 Directive 2002/14/EC of the European Parliament and of the Council of 11 March 2002 establishing a general framework for informing and consulting employees in the European Community, OJ L 80 of 23 March 2002, pp. 29-34.

Social dialogue procedures, including the similar information and consultation procedures of the Directives could be viewed also as instruments of effective enforcement of Community labour law at national level.[7] This contributed to a process in which the emerging economic model of the EU has gradually been embedded into a "European Social Model". The latter is built into a constitutional context characterised by the engagement of the workers' and employers' organisations (Bercusson, 2002: 213). Nevertheless, one should be realistic when assessing this evolution, since the EU has still two faces. While it has strong powers to realise its economic objectives, despite the fifty years evolution and development of European employment law the EU has still less powerful means to enforce its social objectives in the Member States.

From the perspective of this evolution several scholars contested the capacity of the industrial relation and collective bargaining system of the Central and Eastern European countries to carry out the tasks attributed to them by the EC Treaty and different labour law directives (Weiss, 2006, Ladó and Vaughan-Whitehead, 2003). How have the Central and Eastern European states coped with the task of implementation, while carrying out reforms in their national labour laws after the collapse of the Communist regime? Especially that the directives did not properly reflect the reality of these countries. The former concept of regulating the labour market in CEE was characterised by central administrative intervention, where the status of the state as an employer ruled out the possibility of conflicting interests between employers and employees. Furthermore, the phenomenon of "path dependency" is used to describe the reality in several CEE countries. Namely, in the new institutional and legal frameworks the old practices still prevail and continue to undermine the effective functioning of the collective bargaining system for instance (Kollonay Lehoczky, 2004).

This chapter intends to point out in general those difficulties which can undermine the effective enforcement and application of the abovementioned European directives in the new Member States.[8] After giving an overview about the role and the importance of social dialogue in the current social governance of the EU the chapter will assess the recent developments on sectoral social dialogue and the implementation of several directives related to business restructurings. The fifth section

---

7 As to the role of information and consultation from the perspective of effective enforcement of European labour law see Malmberg (2003).

8 This chapter was presented at a workshop at the European University Institute in December 2006, therefore the term new Member States refers to those Central and Eastern European countries, which joined in the EU in 2004 (the Czech Republic, Estonia, Latvia, Lithuania, Hungary, Poland, Slovenia and Slovakia).

will review the implementation of the framework directive on information and consultation from the perspective of reforming the industrial relation systems of the Member States. In several cases the chapter concentrates on the developments in Hungary, but on many occasions the experiences of other Central and Eastern European countries will be addressed as well. The last section of the chapter will conclude and it will be argued that despite the rather moderate short term impact of the Directives, in a long-term implementation can contribute to the consolidation of the current system of industrial relation and it might improve also the legality of the labour relations as whole.

I. The Role of Social Dialogue in the Current Social Governance of the EU

Social dialogue is a key feature of the "European Social Model". This means the involvement of European social partners in EC policy-making,[9] active role of the national social partners in the national implementation[10] and as described above in the enforcement of EC labour law. Therefore an ILO report identified, as one of the key challenges for the future in CEE the consolidation of the processes and institutions of social dialogue (Bronstein, 2003). The increasing involvement of the social partners into the social governance of the EU is part of a new concept for integrating national labour laws. This new procedural approach has allowed more space for deliberation and national level discretion which is claimed to facilitate also political agreement over harmonisation in the EU.

With the accession criteria and, more importantly, with the transposition of the *acquis communautaire* this new approach was transferred to the new Member States. One of the so called "Copenhagen Criteria"[11] required the then candidate Central and Eastern European countries to have a *functioning market economy*, as well as the capacity to cope with competitive pressures and market forces within the European Union. The attempts made by the enterprises to adapt to the competitive pressures of such a functioning market economy led to increased practices of diversification and the reorganisation of their framework and processes of production (Bronstein, 2003). The desire to establish the best legislative framework to cope with economic pressures shifted the

---

9 Article 138-139 of the EC Treaty.

10 Article 137 (3) of the EC Treaty.

11 The Copenhagen Criteria were set by the European Council in 1993 and they were reinforced by the European Council in Madrid in 1995. See http://ec.europa.eu/enlargement/enlargement_process/accession_process/criteria/index_en.htm (access date: 13 May 2008).

attention of the subsequent governments to increase the freedom and managerial prerogatives of the enterprises in determining their most effective work organisation. However, it was common ground that without external legal constrains employers and managers tended to ignore the negative social consequences of these decisions. Therefore this increased the value of labour laws and other areas of the legal system which provided for a better articulation of non-market values in competitive market economies.

These changes in the economy were reflected also in the new regulatory concept of EC social and labour law. The changing conditions of internal and international competition require a concept of central intervention which does not attempt to perfect the market, because this would presuppose that the central legislator knows and will know for all possible cases the best solution and the best outcome (Deakin, 2006). As Deakin has put it, the "main issue is not simply whether regulatory intervention can cure particular market failures, but rather how successful the regulatory framework is in creating an environment which is favourable to the emergence of high-trust employment relationships" (Deakin and Reed, 2000: 25). Therefore, a desirable regulatory policy of the central legislator might be one which facilitates the consolidation of those autonomous processes in a legal system where conciliation and negotiation about diverse interests and exchange of best practices of all the stakeholders in the world of work will be possible.[12]

The ILO emphasises also the role of social dialogue within the governance of the workplace and in the field of labour law reforms. If labour law reforms are based on a solid foundation of social dialogue, it is more likely that the final outcome will address the real challenges of the world of work and that it will facilitate effective enforcement. This could be a powerful way to avoid the establishment of "model labour laws" (Bronstein, 2003) and the gap between "the law on the books and law in practice" in Central and Eastern Europe (Weiss, 2006). At the level of the workplace this means involving especially the elected representatives of the employees in the economic and organisational decisions of the employer and limiting their managerial prerogatives, although remaining under an obligation to cooperate. Nevertheless, the obligation to disclose information to workers' representatives is a prerequisite of meaningful social dialogue between the parties. This

12 The regulatory technique which extensively relies on the "autonomous processes of adjustment" in order to steer the market towards common goals and objectives has been called by Simon Deakin and Catherine Barnard as *reflexive harmonisation* (Deakin and Reed, 2000).

explains why the European legislator also focused on strengthening the right to information and consultation in the Member States.

Nevertheless, it has been contested whether the current industrial relations systems in CEE will be capable of supporting the effective enforcement of those European directives which are based on this new regulatory concept. Two of the possible explanations for the alleged shortcomings must be highlighted, namely the phenomenon of "path dependency" or the "repercussion of the past" and the concept of the undertaking.

In Central and Eastern Europe, the transformation from a centrally planned to a market economy required the consent of the social partners and the society in order to the serious economic reforms to be legitimised. Moreover, decentralised autonomous social dialogue was expected also to contribute to the process of replacing the former central administrative regulation of employment laws.[13] It was, however, presumed that local and sectoral level collective agreements would only gradually come to play the key role assigned to them, namely to regulate workplace employment relations. In the meantime, it was revealed that the process of how the current institutional structures of collective bargaining were arrived at, especially the political role of the trade unions in the former Communist regime and their social recognition, was and is so important, even today, that the old practices still prevail and undermine the effective functioning of the new institutions (Kollonay Lehoczky, 2004). That is, it has been shown that both employers and employees can be reluctant set up works councils and trade unions (Vašková *et al.*, 2005, Kollonay Lehoczky, 2004). Employers generally try to avoid the elections of works councils and works councils exist mostly in those undertakings which had established trade unions before the 1990s.

The second problem might be that contemporary labour law in Hungary is still based on the taylor-fordist models of production and work organisation, which have also furthered the spread of so-called atypical employment relationships (Kiss, 2007: 2).[14] This concept of the enterprise generally neglects other levels of economic decision-making within an organisation, which economic can affect the interest of the employees. It can be extremely important in the regulation of collective labour law. If the undertaking is perceived as an organisation with several establishments under the governance of a single management

13 On the contrary, in other European countries – in a broad comparison – the consolidation of trade unions and employers organisations in the second half of the 20th century constrained their involvement in legal and political decision-making.

14 Such as fixed-term and part-time work, temporary agency work, self-employment.

then the industry or sectoral level is likely to be the best level at which to effectively influence the enterprise's main line of business (Morin, 2005). The new Member States have to take into consideration also that the organisation of work has become considerably more complex with the vertical disintegration of the enterprise. Outsourcing, relocation and subcontracting are all examples of challenges both for the legislators and for the functioning of industry level bargaining. The attempt by the legislator to react to the changes in the organisation of the firm can be best observed in the rules on the transfer of undertakings. For instance, in contrast with the European Directive the Hungarian rules on the transfer of undertakings[15] including the rules on information and consultation and the responsibility of the employers for the remunerations of employees, are also applicable to takeovers by the acquisition of share capital.[16] This could be interpreted as an attempt of the legislator to create a legal link between the management and the centre of economic and financial decision-making of the enterprise.

Sectoral level social dialogue can be the best level also for a strategy which intends to influence the negative social consequences of relocations, as a common form of corporate restructurings. Depending on the different sector or industry the intensity of relocations to Central and Eastern Europe is very diverse. Recent research carried out in Hungary has shown that companies relocating to the country follow very different strategies, their motivation and the ultimate realisation of relocations can be also very diverse (Hunya and Sass, 2006).[17]

II. Developments on the Filed of Sectoral Social Dialogue

Social dialogue in most of the new Member States has been characterised by the dominance of the tripartite negotiations at the national level and collective bargaining at the workplace level. In contrast,

15 The Labour Code uses the term "legal succession in the person of the employer".

16 According to the prevailing view in the literature the directive is not applicable to share sales and takeovers by the acquisition of share capital (Barnard, 2006).

17 Hunya and Sass assessing the relocation cases within the period of 2003 and 2005 have identified at least five different strategies for relocations, in Hungary. These involve those companies, which are moving very fast whenever there is as an increase in their production costs. Whereas others are rather reorganising their processes of production and workplaces very often in order to remain competitive on the market. Especially, in the service sector managers favour long-term investments. The authors highlight the importance of the European Restructuring Monitor (EMCC) in providing statistical data on vertically integrated, export-oriented investment developments in Europe. However, they criticise the results of EMCC research because they are not enough accurate. The EMCC has identified only three relocation cases in Hungary, while the authors have found at least fifteen cases.

sectoral level social dialogue and collective bargaining is relatively underdeveloped in most of these countries. In *Hungary*, it was mainly attributable to historical reasons. When the legislator drew up the new Labour Code (Act XXII of 1992, LC) in the early 1990s, it pointed to the importance of collective agreements at the sectoral level as well. However, as mentioned above it was expected that the consolidation of those representative bodies which could realise this objective would take a longer time. Therefore, the legislator considered it important to insert minimum requirements into the Labour Code for the protection of the workers, when these collective agreements were not existent. The rule that the LC only stipulates minimum requirements for the world of work was incorporated into the Act itself and became the most important governing principle of interpretation.[18] This concept of the Labour Code was criticised as being based on the misapplication of the European traditions and undermining the development of collective agreements and their regulatory function. In addition, it contributed to the establishment of a "statically" structured national labour law which is unable to follow changes in the economy and in the labour market (Kiss, 2007: 1-2).

Nevertheless, the new LC also counted on the commitment of the subsequent governments in strengthening the role of autonomous collective bargaining in the regulation of employment relationships. It emphasised that such a system would only work if the law gave legal guaranties for the establishment and gradually involved the social partners in regulating the world of work. However, the developments which followed showed a less straightforward approach. The rules on trade unions have been amended at least twelve times during the past fifteen years in Hungary. A most recent amendment of the LC – coming into effect from 1 April 2007 – subjected the right of the works council on the allocation of welfare resources to the provision of a collective agreement. This overrules a former decision of the Supreme Court (EBH 2004/1148) and with this the legislator eliminated also the only substantial co-determination right of the works council. Since there are no statutory de minimis requirements for the content of collective agreements in the LC it may happen that the works council will not

---

[18] Section 13 (3) stipulates that a collective agreement and an individual contract of employment can only deviate from those rules on employment in the statue which allow derogations and only in those cases if it is in favour of the employee. This must be read in conjunction with s76 (4), that the parties can agree on any question in the contract of employment. But the agreement can not be contrary to a statue or a collective agreement unless it lays down a more favourable protection for the employee. In practice, several collective agreements only implement the rules of the Labour Code without any difference.

have any influence on the decision of the employer (Bankó *et al.*, 2006: 238-241.). This historical evolution reveals that the market economy environment was established without any social and legal environment to encourage the social partners to maintain and continuously operate social dialogue with each other (Czugler, 2004). It is important from the perspectives of sectoral social dialogue, since the new sectoral level institutions will be built into this overall system of collective bargaining.

During the EU accession negotiations, the European Commission criticised Hungary because of its weaknesses in the field of autonomous social dialogue. Therefore in 2001, in the framework of an institutional twinning with Denmark, a PHARE-project was set up to strengthen autonomous social dialogue at the sectoral level. Both the representatives of the government and the social partners seemed to be committed to enhancing the functioning and the organisation of social dialogue in Hungary.[19] In 2004, the government and the social partners signed an agreement about the institutional framework of sectoral social dialogue until such time when the legal rules on autonomous social dialogue are adopted by the Parliament. A decisive impetus towards the adoption of such an act was given by the Hungarian Constitutional Court in 2005, when it concluded although regarding the current system of national level tripartite dialogue, that it lacked democratic legitimacy. The Court ordered the Parliament to adopt the appropriate legal rules until March 2006 in order to clarify the legal status of the national tripartite council (OÉT). The government decided to adopt two statutes with various criteria for the institutional framework of national and sectoral level social dialogue in December 2006.[20]

The preamble of the bill on *bipartite social dialogue* stipulates that the purpose of the act is to lay down the institutional framework for bipartite social dialogue at sectoral level and to promote its evolution. Some authors have pointed to the fact that a clear relationship and coordination between the various levels of collective bargaining is important, because they give a certain amount of stability to industrial relations as a whole (Casale, 2003: 15). Bipartite dialogue between employers' and workers representatives can improve the effectiveness of tripartite negotiations and the representativeness of the social partners (Vaughan-Whitehead, 2003: 243). Both the Hungarian legislator and

[19] In July 2002 the social partners and the representatives of the government concluded an agreement in the national tripartite council about the further development of the industrial social dialogue in Hungary.

[20] The law on sectoral social dialogue was based on the above mentioned agreement between the government and the social partners in 2004.

several scholars expect that the spread of sectoral collective agreements will contribute to the consolidation of the national system of industrial relations as a whole (Prugberger, 1999; Czugler, 2004).

Without any clear and detailed rules on collective bargaining at the sectoral level, the existing sectoral level committees have only carried out deliberation and consultation. Therefore it was an important question how to identify those legal rules and regulatory techniques which would allow and also advance the conclusion of sectoral level collective agreements. For this to be achieved the legislator has to make the employers interested and has to cerate real bargaining positions. *Czugler* argued that it is important to draw on the models and solutions of other EU Member States, but she cautiously warned the public from a direct transposition of one or another model, because the structure of employee involvement is always embedded into the labour market characteristics and traditions of the given country. A direct transposition would thus risk also undermining the existing and organically developed system and functioning of several sectoral and subsectoral organisation s and would also be contrary to the principle of freedom of organisation (Czugler, 2004).

The institutional framework in the proposed act is based on sectoral social dialogue committees at three levels (sectoral, sub-sectoral and sector-specific levels). In these committees the representatives of the employers and employees carry out *autonomous social dialogue* with respect to all relevant questions related to industrial relations and employment. The bill confirms that the task of these committees is to facilitate the balanced development of the given sector by furthering appropriate conditions of employment, preserving peaceful labour relations and improving the legality of the processes of the labour market. In the framework of these committees, the representatives inform each other about the economic and social developments, carry out consultations and publish joint opinions and recommendations. The negotiations in the sectoral committees can lead to the conclusion of collective agreements, which will be applicable to the members of the employers' organisations and their employees. The two sides of the committee can jointly request the extension of the collective agreement to the whole industry.[21] In addition, administrative authorities having competences in the given sector either have to give information or, at the request of the committees, have to enter into consultation about all

21 The national tripartite council and the competent ministers have a right of opinion before the minister takes its decision.

the economic and social issues which concern the interests of the workers.[22]

Although the law stipulates that sectoral dialogue is governed by the mutual agreement of the parties, the draft statute lays down detailed rules on the procedure for establishing a sectoral committee and how an organisation can join a committee. Furthermore, it specifies the criteria for the way in which an organisation can qualify as a sectoral level organisation for interest representation, as well as the criteria for assessing *representativeness*. Meeting these criteria is to be measured by a new institution, the Committee for Confirming Participation,[23] which consists of two delegated members of the government and an additional four members from the social partners. Legal remedy is granted by the labour courts against the decisions of the Committee. The government carries out tripartite consultations with the social partners in the Council of the Social Dialogue Committees.[24]

The bill lays down the criteria which an organisation must meet in order to participate in sectoral level dialogue *in general*. It is important that the association shows a certain degree of stability, since it has to pursue its activity for more than two years. Furthermore, it has to meet the specific quantitative criteria to qualify as an organisation for industry-level interest representation. On the side of the trade unions, these criteria are based on the number at how many employers the trade union has established representatives and how it correlates with the number of employees in the given sector.[25] An employers' organisation qualifies as an institution for industry-level interest representation when its member organisations employ at least 5% of employees in the given sector or when at least 40% of the employers in the relevant sector are members of this organisation or its member organisations. In order not to exclude smaller organisations, the bill stipulates that if the employers' organisation is unable to fulfil the above-mentioned criteria it can still qualify as a sectoral level organisation if it employs at least 80% of

22 Section 4 of the bill.

23 *Részvételt Megállapító Bizottság.*

24 *Ágazati Párbeszéd Bizottságok Tanácsa.*

25 According to section 7 of the bill a trade union qualifies as an institution for interest representation when, a) it has in the given sector at least by ten employers established representation and its members amounts to 1% of the employees in the given sector or, b) it has in the given sector at least by three employers established representation and its members amounts to 10% of employees in the respected sector, or c) at those employers where it has established representation and where the candidates of the trade union received at the works council elections three years before handling in the request to the Committee for Confirming Participation as much of the votes which amount to 5% of the employees in the given sector.

the workforce in the given sector. It furthermore permits the representatives to set up coalitions to fulfil these requirements.

The proposal sets different quantitative requirements for representativeness, which are designed to identify those organisations which have a right to take part in the decision-making of the committees. Representativeness is based on the following criteria: the results of the previous works council election, number of active trade union members, and coverage of collective agreements, involvement in the tripartite negotiations or in international organisations in the given sector. For the employers' organisations, the first two criteria is different namely, the number of workers employed and the net annual income of the represented economic organisations, which must be assessed. However, the law stipulates that the criteria for representativeness for the purposes of negotiations and consultations can also be regulated by the mutual agreement of the parties.

Contrary to the sectoral level social dialogue, all CEE countries created *national tripartite councils* in the early 1990s. In Hungary, the involvement of the social partners into national-level decision making dates back to the late 1980s. This institutional structure for interest representation in economic and social matters was built into the system of political decision-making without any legal rules on its legal status and legitimacy. Apart from a short period between 1998 and 2002, national social dialogue is based on a tripartite agreement and on the mutual recognition of the parties. The Hungarian national tripartite council (National Interest Reconciliation Council – OÉT) consists of nine national employers' organisations and six trade unions as well as government representatives. The Labour Code lays down that the government must carry out conciliation in the OÉT regarding issues on industrial relations and employment relationships which are of national importance. According to a governmental decree, this obligation on conciliation means, in general, a commitment for negotiation with a view to concluding an agreement with the social partners.[26] Despite this declaratory statement, the law does not give any details on the nature and legal status of these agreements. Therefore, in the reality, the agreement reached in the Council is not binding for the government, and the fate of the legislative proposal is subject to the majority decision-making in the Parliament (Kiss, 2005). The Labour Code also stipulates those fields where the proposal or decision of the government is dependent on the consent of the OÉT. These include especially the intro-

26 Governmental decree number 1094/2002 (VI. 8).

duction of new rules on collective redundancies[27] and decisions about the national minimum wage.[28]

The Hungarian Constitutional Court (*Alkotmánybíróság, AB*) decided that the lack of any statutory regulation on the national tripartite council is unconstitutional because, beyond its right to consultation and consent on certain legislative acts the OÉT can exercise functions of executive power as well.[29] The Constitutional Court interpreted Article 4 of the Constitution, which stipulates that unions and other representative bodies shall protect and represent the interests of employees, members of co-operatives and entrepreneurs. As the majority of the judges argued, in a democratic constitutional state based on the rule of law, representation of the diverse interests of the society is of special importance. It contributes to better democratic governance, based on a more comprehensive conciliation of interests. That is, "the effective involvement of the social partners in public decision-making and the legislative process must be considered as giving substantive meaning to the notion of "democratic" in the constitution". Nevertheless, Article 4 of the Hungarian Constitution defines only *in general* the functions of representative bodies for representing the interests of the employees. Therefore, and in pursuance of earlier decisions of the Court, there are no constitutional requirements for the substance or the operation of the tripartite interest-conciliation. According to the Court, only the type of involvement taken on by the representatives is of constitutional significance, in the exercise of pubic power in the field of employment policy. However, as the Court argued, beyond its traditional consultative functions in economic and social matters OÉT carries out managerial and decision-making functions which can be classified as part of the functions of an executive power. Namely the Court addressed the role of OÉT regarding the Governing Body of the Hungarian Labour Market Fund. The latter is a special tripartite forum for interest-conciliation in employment policy. The members of the OÉT have the right to nominate the employers' and employees' representatives of this body. As a result the representativeness of this institution is based on the OÉT and in this way it derives its legitimacy from an institution whose democratic legitimacy has not been legally established. Moreover, OÉT has the right to hear the report of this body on an annual basis, which constitutes a competence of a public power as well. According to earlier precedents, the concept of the rule of law in Article 2 (1) of the Consti-

27 Redundancies due to economic reasons affecting a large group of employees in order to promote employment with the consent of the national tripartite council.

28 LC. Section 17. (1) a).

29 Decision of the Hungarian Constititional Court No.40/2005 (X.19).

tution requires the state to enact laws whereby the status, structure, (transparent) operation, competence and legitimacy of the organisations exercising public power is granted.[30] The Constitutional Court came to the conclusion that the legal status and the operation of the OÉT does not fulfil this requirement it therefore obliged the Parliament to adopt the appropriate legal basis until the 31 March 2006.

The Parliament has adopted two statutes one on the National Interest Reconciliation Council (OÉT) and another one on the above described sectoral dialogue in December 2006. The bill on the OÉT based the legitimacy of the national level institution mostly on the representativeness of its member organisations. However, László Sólyom, the President of the Hungarian Republic refused to sign the two statues and submitted the draft laws to the Constitutional Court for a review of constitutionality. In this, the President emphasised that the OÉT is an organisation for interest-conciliation which exercises executive powers. Beyond the above-mentioned arguments of the Constitutional Court, he highlighted the fact that the OÉT lacks also democratic legitimacy to take part in the process of legislation. He referred to an earlier decision of the Constitutional Court, where it ruled that the social partners' right of consent – basically a right to veto – in the public administration and their involvement in public norm-setting, constitutes also an exercise of public power.[31] The exercise of public power requires, however, either direct of indirect democratic legitimacy. On the other hand, the decision taken in the OÉT can influence the interest of non-member citizens as well. Therefore legitimacy can only be granted when the organisation which is not directly elected has as its members the "overwhelming majority of the electorate". Since the majority of the Hungarian workforce and the employers is not organised, this cannot be the basis for the legitimacy of the OÉT. The president highlighted, however, that this problem could be solved by granting only consultative functions to the OÉT without giving it any veto power, for example, in legislation.

III. Implementation of the Directives on Restructurings in Central and Eastern Europe

By the time of enlargement, all the new Member States had implemented the directives on the transfer of undertakings,[32] collective redun-

---

30 Decision of the Constitutional Court No.56/1991 (XI. 8.) AB.

31 Decision of the Constitutional Court No.39/1997 (VII. 1.) AB.

32 Council Directive 2001/23/EC of 12 March 2001 on the approximation of the laws of the Member States relating to the safeguarding of employees' rights in the event of transfers of undertakings, businesses or parts of undertakings or businesses, OJ L 82 of 22 March 2001, pp. 16-20.

dancies[33] and the insolvency[34] of the employer. Except for *Estonia* and *Lithuania*, the directive on European Works Councils[35] was successfully implemented in all countries before March 2004. Regarding the directives whose deadline for implementation expired after 1 May 2004, the data shows greater divergence. Most of the new Member States implemented the Directive 2001/86 on the involvement of employees in the European company[36] already before accession but it took effect only after the enlargement. The implementation of the framework directive on information and consultation[37] resulted instead in an intense debate in *Estonia* and *Poland*, since its transposition led to fundamental changes in their existing system of industrial relations. In the end, both counties were late with the implementation.

In the old Member States, the introduction of the directive on the transfer of undertakings and collective redundancies took place in the late 1970s due to the increased competition on the single market, which resulted in mass lay-offs, mergers, acquisitions and great deal of business reorganisation. In contrast, in *Hungary*, the negative consequences of privatisation in the early 1990s pushed the legislator and the courts towards the view that they would have to introduce special regulation in this field (Kiss, 1995). Generally, the rights deriving from the directive were perceived as a minimum floor of labour rights, which the employers were not allowed to undermine. Privatisation and the business transfers generated by it often resulted in the mass termination of employment relationships. Since the Hungarian Labour Code did not acknowledge the automatic transfer of employment relationships, acquired rights based on the former employment were totally neglected. Given the lack of substantive statutory provisions, the recognition of the

33 Council Directive 98/59/EC of 20 July 1998 on the approximation of the laws of the Member States relating to collective redundancies, OJ L 225 of 12 August 1998, pp. 16-21.

34 Council Directive 80/987/EEC [OJ L 283 of 28 October 1980, pp. 23-27] on the protection of employees in the event of the insolvency of their employer, as amended by the Directive 87/164 [OJ L 66 of 11 March 1987, page 11] and revised by the Directive 2002/74 [OJ L 270 of 8 October 2002, pp. 10-13].

35 Council Directive 94/45/EC of 22 September 1994 on the establishment of a European Works Council or a procedure in Community-scale undertakings for the purposes of informing and consulting employees, OJ L 254 of 30 September 1994, pp. 64-72.

36 Council Directive 2001/86/EC of 8 October 2001 supplementing the statute for a European company with regard to the involvement of the employees, OJ L294 of 10 November 2001, pp. 22-32].

37 Directive 2002/14/EC of the European Parliament and of the Council of 11 March 2002 establishing a general framework for informing and consulting employees in the European Community, OJ L 80 of 23 March 2002, pp. 29-34.

compulsory transfer principle by the Supreme Court was a good example of the new regulatory concept of the Labour Code, in which the legislator was looking for the balance of interests between the employers and the employees. The rules of the directive on the transfer of undertakings offered the Court an attractive solution to protect the rights of the employees. However, given the lack of any legal rules in the Labour Code, the Supreme Court published a so-called Resolution of the Labour Collegium,[38] and established several rules for the transfer of undertakings through the interpretation of existing rules. Several cases brought before the courts from the beginning of 1993 formed the basis for an intense debate on the acceptable practice, which was then followed by an interesting discussion in the academic literature, involving almost all scholars in Hungarian labour law (Radnay, 2004; Kollonay Lehoczky, 2004; Berke, 2001).

The most general problem with the legislation on the transfer of undertakings is the lack of meaningful information and consultation procedures. According to a strict interpretation of the law, the employer fulfils his obligations when he informs and consults the employees' representatives and then totally neglects their view (consultation similar to information). Consultation develops to a meaningful dialogue between the representatives and the employer in cases where trade unions are strong, and the personal relationship between the management and the representatives is also important (Neumann, 2004).

Generally, the position of trade unions is weak during the consultations about collective redundancies for several reasons. The employer is not required for instance to draw up a legally binding social plan when it is enforcing dismissals. However, if the employer is contemplating to carry out collective redundancies – fifteen days before he takes his decision – he is obliged to begin consultations with the representatives of the employees. In Hungarian law the employer must consult first of all the works council or in the absence of a works council the representative trade union and an *ad hoc* committee established from the representatives of the employees. The employer has to pursue the consultation until he takes a decision and until the conclusion of an agreement.[39] The employer is obliged to disclose information in advance to the representatives. The substantive requirements follow the rules in the directive on collective redundancies. As a result, consultations must cover the possible ways of avoiding collective redundancies, the criteria

---

[38] Resolutions as binding decisions have been published by the Supreme Court in order to guarantee consistent interpretation of the law and it was only binding on the Supreme Court itself.

[39] Section 94/B (1) of the Labour Code.

for the selection of the workers to be made redundant, means for mitigating the consequences and reducing the number of employees affected. If the employer and the representatives reach an agreement during the course of consultation, it must be notified in writing and sent to the competent employment centre. However, the legal status and as a result the enforceability of this agreement is not clear (Bankó *et al.*, 2006: 372). The Labour Code does not give any guidance on the principle for the selection of employees, therefore the employer may take into consideration other aspects than the social circumstances of the affected workers (Prugberger, 1999: 279).

EU enlargement is a serious test for the functioning of the directive on *European Works Councils*. The ETUI estimates that there are some 737 companies with existing EWCs, and that 505 (about two-thirds) of them operate in one or more of the new Member States (Hall and Marginson, 2004). The operation of these Councils relies on the industrial relation structures in these countries. If there was previously no representation, the companies were obliged to promote the building-up of the necessary structures. Nevertheless, in some cases foreign companies were reluctant to involve the representatives from the new Member States as well. It was expected that the number of those companies falling under the directive with headquarters in the new Member States would increase only gradually before the enlargement (Nagy, 1998). The ETUI reckons that there are no more than 35 such companies, of which twelve have their headquarters in Hungary, ten in Poland and seven in the Czech Republic. Examples of such companies include Gorenje (Slovenia), Magyar Olaj és Gázipari Rt. and the OTP Bank (Hungary) and, in Lithuania, VP Market (Hall and Marginson, 2004). Therefore the discussions have focused on elaborating and eliminating the theoretical and practical problems of company level representation. In some of the respected countries this has paved the way for substantial reforms in the industrial relations system, whereas in others the workers representatives had to be prepared to be able to adapt to the new methods of dealing with problems at transnational level.

The directive 2001/86 on employee involvement in the *European Company (Societas Europea)* aims to facilitate a greater respect of employee interests where and when strategic decisions on restructurings are taken. The representation of workers in the highest organs of a company is a common feature in the majority of the new Member States. Worker-board level representation is acknowledged in seven of the ten countries. In the *Czech Republic*, *Hungary*, the *Republic of Slovakia* and *Slovenia* these rights exist for both private and state-owned companies, whereas in *Malta* and *Poland* board-level representation is limited to state-owned and privatised companies (ETUI-REHS, 2005: 1).

IV. The Role of the Right to Information and Consultation in Reforming Industrial Relations in the New Member States

The framework directive 2002/14 on information and consultation (framework directive) is part of a new concept for regulating the labour law consequences of business restructurings in the EU, where emphasis is placed on anticipation and on the management of the negative consequences (EC, 2005a). According to the preamble of the directive, better social dialogue has the potential to cure the low-trust nature of the employment relationships. This is important to improve risk anticipation and it can in the long run contribute to the adoption of a rather *a priori* approach to change.[40]

The implementation of the directive had far-reaching consequences in the new Member States. This section aims to highlight these changes and the problems during the transposition process. The directives on restructurings, as explored in the previous section, have already legitimised the role of the social partners in the decision-making of the employer about corporate restructurings through providing rights to information and consultation. For this dialogue to be meaningful, the disclosure of information by the employer must be enforced effectively. The Commission has emphasised the importance of establishing the link between the different levels of social dialogue, especially between the company level and the more centralised levels (EC, 2002). Efficient information and consultation procedures enable the different levels of workers representation to be linked and contribute to the development of solid industrial relations. Therefore, the Commission has proposed the revision and consolidation of the information and consultation procedures in the different directives (EC, 2005b). Moreover, as the example of the new Member States and the UK[41] shows, implementation and effective enforcement of the rights to information and consultation can contribute to substantive changes in their system of industrial relations without directly imposing a particular model on them.

The implementation of the directive has triggered the most substantial changes in those countries where only a single channel industrial relations system existed before transposition. In the early 1990s only Hungary and Slovenia have introduced a dual channel system of indus-

---

40 See the seventh and thirteenth recital of the framework directive.

41 As to the implementation of the directive in the UK (see Lorber, 2006: 231-258; Lorber, 2003: 297-319).

trial relations.[42] The idea of the directive was to lay down a general legislative framework for implementing the right to information and consultation of the employees, basically securing this right to the representatives of the workers. Although the framework directive does not require the Member States to provide a specific mechanism for employee representation, according to an earlier decision of the ECJ they are required to put in place the necessary arrangements for designating the employee representatives who must be informed and consulted.[43] Information therefore presupposes worker representation (Morin, 2005). The framework directive on information and consultation have made it clear that direct consultation of the employees is only admissible under Community law if the employees have generally free recourse to collective representation.[44] Therefore in those countries where there was no general statutory system of information and consultation on business, employment and restructuring issues it was necessary to establish legal guaranties for the designation of the relevant institutional structures. It is interesting to note that six of the Central and Eastern European countries introduced for the purposes of information and consultation some form of general and elected representation of the employees at the company level.[45]

In 2001, in the Czech Republic, the institution of works councils was introduced in order to comply with the European directives and to guarantee all employees with the general statutory right to information and consultation. Nevertheless, the election of works councils is only allowed in those undertakings where there is no operating trade union. According to the fundamental provisions on the information and consultation procedure, the undertaking has to inform employees and consult with them directly, unless there is a trade union organisation or a works council.[46] If subsequently a trade union will be set up and a plant level collective agreement will be concluded then the works council ceases to

---

42 On a detailed introduction and comparison of industrial relations in eight Central and Eastern European countries see Kohl and Hans-Wolfgang, 2004).

43 ECJ, Case C-382/92, *Commission v UK*, [1994] ECR I-02435, para. 18-26.

44 Sixth recital of the directive.

45 The first country was the Czech Republic in 2001, then Latvia in 2002, the Slovak Republic in 2003, Lithuania in 2004, and the last country was Poland in 2006. In Estonia, the implementation measure of the framework directive as of 1st February 2007 requires election of representatives for non-unionised workers in all workplaces employing at least 30 employees for information and consultation purposes. In the former system the employer was not obliged to inform and consult the employees if there was not any workplace representation at the company (Kallaste, 2007).

46 Section 276 of the Act No.262/2006 on the Labour Code. The English translation of the Czech Labour Code is available at the website of the Ministry of Labour and Social Affairs (www.mpsv.cz/files/clanky/3221/labour_code.pdf).

exist. Consequently, the co-existence of works councils and trade unions is not allowed. This system of interest representation has been called the "Czech model" (Kohl and Platzer, 2004).

In several western European countries collective bargaining is carried out by trade unions mostly at sectoral, industrial and national levels. Therefore, the establishment of the works councils has filled in a gap in collective interest representation at the company level. In contrast, the co-existence of trade unions and elected representatives at work place level can be problematic for the following reasons in CEE. Parallel competences on same issues have generated competition between trade unions and works councils. Competition between co-existing institutions at workplace level can be problematic in Central and Eastern Europe, since this level has also been occupied before by trade unions. The establishment of works councils meant in these countries that the trade unions have lost part of their competences and their influence in the workplaces. Nevertheless, it is important to note that the role of trade unions is basically that of interest representation therefore their relationship with the employer includes the possibility of conflicts. On the contrary, the involvement of the employees into the decision-making of the employer requires instead an attitude of co-operation (Nagy, 1998: 42).

In Hungary, both works councils, as the elected representatives of the employees, and trade union organisations basically responsible for collective bargaining, can be organised at the workplace level. Election of works councils is possible at all those employers where there are more than 50 employees or at every site (unit) of the employer fulfilling this requirement. In workplaces with less than 51 but more than 15 employees, representation is solved with the election of one workplace representative.[47] If there is more than one works council at the employer the law stipulates that a central works council must be established. Depending on the number of employees all sites (units) of the employer can proportionately delegate members to this central body.[48] The Labour Code has increased the horizontal interrelationship between trade unions and works councils at the workplace level by subjecting the capacity of trade unions to conclude collective agreements within the undertaking to the result of the works council elections.[49] As result approximately 70% of works councils are run by trade unions (Benyo,

47 Section 43 (1)-(2) of the Labour Code.

48 Section 44 (1)-(3) of the Labour Code.

49 According to the basic rule in Section 33 (2) of the Labour Code a trade union is entitled to conclude a collective agreement if its candidates have obtained at least half of votes in the works council election.

2003). Despite the fundamental principle of the separation of trade unions and woks councils (*Zweispurigkeit der Interessenvertretung*) around two-third of the members of the works councils are members at the same time of a trade union in Germany as well (Junker, 2007: 356). However, it must be noted again that in Germany, this strong interrelationship exists between two institutions operating at different levels and with different legal means. The trade unions can use different forms of industrial action, whereas the works council is obliged to maintain cooperative relations with the employer and to act in *good faith*. In contrast, in Hungary the practical co-existence and the overlapping competences of the two institutions have resulted in a situation where trade unions with the right to strike can also have a leading position in other institutions (works councils) to enhance industrial democracy and with a duty to co-operate with the employer (Tóth, 2002: 143).

In several Central and Eastern European countries, the company level has been identified as the most important level of collective bargaining. In those countries where both trade union representatives and elected representatives can co-exist in the same undertaking, one of the most important questions was how the implementation of the framework directive would influence the allocation of competences between the two institutions. Trade unions opposed any changes which would have possibly led to weakening of their positions within company level bargaining. Taking into account also international labour standards the following problems were discussed generally, in Hungary (Czuglerné, 2004: 77-78):

- Who would decide on the question of the allocation of competences?
- In the case of a dual channel system would it be possible to exclude one of the representative institutions from exercising information and consultation rights, or would it be possible to jointly or separately exercise these rights?
- If union density rates are low is it necessary to involve the representatives of the non-organised employees?
- How far is it appropriate if the law allows direct negotiation between the employer and its employees if there is no representative organisation at the workplace level?
- It was common ground that for full compliance with the directives consisting of information and consultation rights, the institutional framework of national and sectoral social dialogue must be strengthened.

- The legislator had to lay down general statutory requirements for information and consultation specifying the substance, the procedure and timing of social dialogue.

Finally, while implementing the framework directive the legislator increased the powers of the trade unions and expanded the overlapping competences of the two institutions. Except Bulgaria and Slovakia, all the new Member States have ratified the convention No.135 on the workers' representatives (1971). According to Article 5 of this convention, when the co-existence of workers' representation is possible the ILO gives priority to trade unions and emphasises that the existence of elected representatives can not be used to undermine the position of the trade unions.

This reveals that the national legislator was constrained by political and legal pressures when it was deciding on the new settlement of workplace employee representation. This led to some amendments in the Labour Code, where the parties were concentrating rather on reaching a political compromise than the efficiency of the new regulation. For instance, the framework directive on information and consultation emphasises the importance of *timing* in exercising the rights to information and consultation in adapting to the challenges of globalisation.[50] According to the Hungarian Labour Code, the employer is obliged to "consult" the works council about any proposed measures which will likely affect a larger group of employees *before he has taken his decision.*[51] This obligation concerns especially business reorganisation, restructuring, privatisation and modernisation and setting up of an independent organisational unit. Several authors have pointed to the fact that according to the strict interpretation of this rule the employer fulfilled his requirements when he informed and consulted the employees' representatives in writing and then totally neglected their opinion (consultation similar to disclosing information).[52] Consultation meant meaningful dialogue between representatives and the employer in cases, where trade unions were strong, and the personal relationship between

---

50 Ninth recital of the directive "Timely information and consultation is a prerequisite for the success of restructuring and adaptation of undertakings to the new conditions created by globalisation of the economy [...]".

51 Section 65 (3) of the Labour Code.

52 Section 66 of the LC only lays down the procedural requirements regarding works councils by stipulating that the works council has to give its opinion within 15 days about the proposed measure of the employer. If it fails to do so its salience must be regarded as if it had given its assent to the measure. Concerning the employer the law only sets forth that he has to disclose the information about his measure to the works council, since arrival of this information is the start of the deadline mentioned in the former sentence. This procedure is applicable also if the employer consults a trade union on the same issue.

the management and the representatives remains to be important as well (Neumann, 2004; Czuglerné, 2004). In order to ensure that this obligation will be enforced in an undertaking having no works council the legislator established the same obligation vis-à-vis trade unions in 2002.[53] However, the legal consequences of the two procedures are different. If the employer fails to consult the works council then the employee has a right to take the case before the labour court and to claim that the measure of the employer is void.[54] Whereas trade unions[55] has a right to object against an unlawful measure or omission of the employer if it directly concerns the rights of trade unions laid down in the statue.[56] If the subsequent conciliation procedure will not be successful between the representatives and the employer, the trade union can take the case before the court. The court can only confirm that the employer has breached his obligations *vis-à-vis* the trade unions. It can not decide on the validity of the measure itself, but it will be suspended.

A further problem is in practice how the above mentioned general rules on "consultation" about the proposed measures which would likely affect a larger group of the employees relate to the specific provisions on information and consultation on the transfer of undertakings and collective redundancies. This is important because the rules on the duty of the employer to cooperate are different in the two cases. According to the general rules this duty only covers "counselling" the representatives (consultation similar to disclosing information), while the special procedures on restructuring measures as described below are more detailed and the consultation has to be filled with substance. This problem was sold partially with the implementation of the framework directive in the Labour Code in 2005.[57] With this implementation substantive general legal requirements have been established for the first time regarding the content, timing and the procedure of social dialogue in the Code. What is still unsolved is the consistency of available remedies referred to in the previous paragraph.

As regards the substance of the new provisions on information and consultation, the Labour Code stipulates that the consultation must be pursued with a view to conclude an agreement. But the employer is not

---

53 The provision refers to the proposed measures of the employer, but only concerns trade unions which have according to their statues a right to representation by the employer (section 21. (2)).

54 Section 67 of the Labour Code. Considering that the works council is not a legal person, therefore it has only a limited *locus standi* before the court in the cases specified by the law (Supreme Court – Legf. Bír. Mfv.I. 10838/1996/3).

55 But only those which have according to its statute a right to representation.

56 Section 23 (1)-(5) of the LC.

57 Act No.VIII of 2005 amending the Labour Code, Act No.XXII of 1992.

obliged to decide in compliance with the opinion of the works council, thus the final decision remains with the employer. This is reinforced by the provision which sets forth that if the parties are not able to conclude an agreement and the statutory deadlines elapse the employer can simply close the negotiations. This procedure only increases the responsibility of the employer since he can not claim ignorance of the negative consequences of his decision on the employment relationship (Bankó *et al.*, 2006: 239). Recourse to consultation still remains a possibility for the representatives, since they can initiate it within fifteen days following the disclosure of information. During the consultations but at least for seven days following the initiation for consultation the decision of the employer will be suspended.[58] The employer and the representatives can agree on longer time limits. These new substantive legal requirements might contribute to the consolidation of the existing system of labour relations.

However, the question of effective legal sanctions remains a question. Member States have to provide *effective, proportionate and dissuasive* sanctions in the event of employers' failure to inform and consult the employees' representatives.[59] In Hungary the law stipulates that it is mandatory to elect a works council by every employer, or at each independent unit of the employer where the number of employees is more than 50. This rule is a so-called *lex imperfecta*, because there is not any sanction or penalty if the employer fails to comply with this requirement. In this respect the Polish Act of 2006 on the information and consultation of employees sets forth a penalty of restricted liberty or a fine if any person prevents the establishment of a works council or does not provide or hinders information and consultation of the employees.[60]

58 The employer can not carry out his measures before the elapse of these deadlines.

59 ECJ, Case C-382/92, *Commission v UK*, [1994] ECR I-02435, para. 52-58.

60 Article 19 of the Act of 7 April 2006 on information and consultation of employees. The penalty may be imposed on those who (1) prevent the establishment of works council; (2) does not provide information when the number of employees exceeds 50 (which implies that the Act becomes applicable to the employer); (3) does not organise or hinders elections to works councils; (4) does not inform or consult the works council with reference to the matters provided by the Act; (5) discriminate a member of works council in connection with his/her performance of information and consultation proceedings. The act is available on the website of the Polish Ministry of Labour and Social Policy, http://www.mpips.gov.pl/index.php?gid=934 (21 September 2007).

Conclusion

The new approach to labour law harmonisation, allowing more discretion and space for legal experimentalism in regulating the labour market, has facilitated political consensus and coordination between the Member States about several major directives. On the other hand, the more a community measure deviates from the legal culture and the practices of a given Member State, the more space must be left for national discretion. Nevertheless, the practical feasibility of this regulatory concept can be at stake if the necessary institutional structures are weak or non-existent in the Member States. However, the overview of the implementation of different directives has also revealed that an effective legal framework which strengthens the legal position of the social partners can contribute to the slow and gradual consolidation of these institutional structures.

Effective legal measures against the negative social consequences of business relocations, as one of the forms of enterprise restructuring, are currently under scrutiny of the European Court of Justice in the Viking[61] and Laval[62] cases as well. As the Advocate General *Maduro* has observed in the Viking case, relocations have for all countries involved its own costs and benefits.[63] Resent research in Hungary has shown that 40-50% of the return from corporate restructurings will be repatriated in the home Member State. The authors of the article identify as one of the main questions remaining to be answered how this income can be redistributed in the most effective and just way (Hunya and Sass, 2006). Collective representation of workers' interests through different social dialogue procedures can help to avoid the benefits gained from these relocations going to those who have normally better bargaining powers.

Social dialogue within the firm and at sectoral level can enhance the legality of workplace relations and the productivity of the firm as a whole. The case of the new Member States has shown that if the relevant system of industrial relations is not the consequence of an organic and constitutional development then this increases the role of the state in regulating labour relations. This requires, however, a consequent legislative policy which is committed to enhancing the quality of social

---

61 ECJ, Case C-438/05, *Interrnational Transport Workers' Federation and the Finnish Seamen's Union/ Viking Line ABP, OÜ Viking Line Eesti*, 11 December 2007.

62 ECJ, Case C-341/05, *Laval un Partneri Ltd. and Svenska Byggnadsarbetareförbundet and Others*, 18 December 2007.

63 ECJ, Case C-438/05 *The Interrnational Transport Workers' Federation and the Finnish Seamen's Union*, főtanácsnoki indítvány, Miguel Poires Maduro (2007. május 23).

dialogue and to expanding the rights to information and consultation. With the implementation of the European directives major steps have been taken in the new Member States towards more autonomous forms of labour market regulation. However, every European strategy aiming at capacity-building might have its own limits. They themselves can not create the necessary social conditions for the long-term sustainability of these institutional structures. Indeed there is a need to promote the culture of social dialogue in the new Member States. This requires also a change in attitude, such as that social dialogue is built into a concept of partnership approach between the representatives and the employers and collective bargaining is looked at as the best way to reconcile the diverse and conflicting interests of the parties. For this to be achieved wide social recognition of the employers' organisations and trade unions must be strengthened by enabling them to become genuine players in economic life (Czugler, 2004: 214). As we have seen in this chapter, this will take a longer time, however, in all new Member States the most important legislative steps have been taken in order to consolidate the different social dialogue procedures to realise the objectives of the "European Social Model".

References

BANKÓ, Z.-B., GYULA, GYULAVÁRI, T. and KISS, G. (2006), *A Munka Törvénykönyvéről Szóló 1992.* évi XXII. törvény magyarázata I. kötet (Interpretation of the Act No.22/1992 about the Labour Code), Magyar Hivatalos Közlönykiadó.

BARNARD, C. (2006), *EC Employment Law*, Oxford University Press, Oxford.

BENYO, B. (2003), *Employee Participation in Hungary*, International Labour Organisation (ILO), Budapest.

BERCUSSON, B. (2002), "The European Social Model Comes to Britain", *Industrial Law Journal*, Vol. 31, pp. 209-244.

BERCUSSON, B. (2005), "Social and Labour Rights under the EU Constitution", in DE BÚRCA, G. and DE WITTE, B. (eds.), *Social Rights in Europe*, Oxford University Press, Oxford, pp. 169-197.

BERKE, G. (2001), "A munkavállalói jogok védelme a munkáltató személyében bekövetkező változaások esetében", in KISS, G. (ed.), *Az Európai Unió Munkajoga*, Osiris Kiadó, Budapest.

BRONSTEIN, A. (2003), *Labour Law Reform in EU Candidate Countries: Achievements and Challenges*, International Labour Organisation, Geneva.

CASALE, G. (2003), "Evolution and Trends in Industrial Relations in Central and Eastern European Countries", *International Journal of Comparative Labour Law and Industrial Relations*, Vol. 19, pp. 5-32.

CZUGLER, I. J. (2004), "The Prospects of Autonomous Sectoral Dialogue", *Hungary Annales Universitatis Scientiarum Budapestinensis de Rolando Eötvös Nominatae*, Tomus XLV, pp. 211-221.

CZUGLERNÉ, D. I. J. (2004), Az információs és konzultációs jogok szabályozása Magyarországon (Regulation of the right to information and consultation in Hungary) *Liber Amicorum, Studia Stephano Kertész dedicata – Ünnepi dolgozatok Kertész István Tiszteletére* (Essays in Honour of István Kertész) ELTE ÁJK Munkajogi és Szociális Jogi Tanszék, Budapest.

DEAKIN, S. (2006), "Is Regulatory Competition the Future for European Integration?", *Swedish Economic Policy Review*, pp. 71-95.

DEAKIN, S. and REED, H. (2000), "The Contested Meaning of Labour Market Flexibility: Economic Theory and the Discourse of European Integration", in SHAW, J. (ed.), *Social Law and Policy in an Evolving European Union*, Hart Publishing, Oxford, Portland, Oregon, pp. 71-99.

DEAKIN, S. and WILKINSON, F. A. (1999), "Labour Law and Economic Theory: A Reappraisal", in DE GEEST, G., SIEGERS, J. and VAN DEN BERGH, R. (eds.), *Law and Economics and the Labour Market*, Edward Elgar Publishing, Cheltenham, pp. 1-33.

EC (2002), Communication from the Commission "The European Social Dialogue, a Force for Innovation and Change", COM (2002) 341 final of 26 June 2002.

EC (2005a), Communication from the Commission "Anticipating and accompanying restructuring in order to develop employment: the role of the European Union", COM (2005) 120 final of 31 March 2005.

EC (2005b), Communication from the Commission on the Social Agenda, COM (2005) 33 final of 9 February 2005.

ETUI-REHS (2005), *Worker Board-level Representation in the New EU Member Sates: Country Reports on the National Systems and Practices*, Social Development Agency and European Trade Union Institute for Research, Education and Health and Safety, Brussels.

EUROPEAN COUNCIL (2000), Lisbon European Council, *Presidency Conclusions*, 23 and 24 March 2000.

HALL, M. and MARGINSON, P. (2004), "Developments in European Works Councils", *European Industrial Relations Observatory on-line*, available at http://www.eurofound.europa.eu/eiro/2004/11/study/tn0411101s.htm, 15 April 2008.

HEPPLE, B. (2005), *Labour Laws and Global Trade*, Hart Publishing, Oxford.

HUNYA, G. and SASS, M. (2006), "Nyer-e Magyarország a Termeléskihelyezéssel? (Does Hungary Benefit From Relocations?)", *Külgazdaság*, Vol. 1, pp. 33-53.

JUNKER, A. (2007), *Grundkurs Arbeitsrecht München*, Verlag C.H. Beck.

KALLASTE, E. (2007), "New Law Sets out Conditions for Employee Information and Consultation", *European Industrial Relations Observatory On-line*, available at http://www.eurofound.europa.eu/eiro/2007/01/articles/ee0701039i.htm, 15 April 2008.

KISS, G. (1995), A Legfelsőbb Bíróság MK 154. Számú állásfoglalása a munkavállalók jogainak és a vállaltok, üzemek és üzemrészek tulajdonosváltozása esetén történő megóvásáról szóló 77/187 (EGK) számú Irányelvének tükrében Jogtudományi Közlöny, Vol. 10, pp. 437-450.

KISS, G. (2005), *Munkajog*, Osiris, Budapest.

KISS, G. (2007), Új Foglalkoztatási Módszerek a Munkajog Határán – Az Atipikus Foglalkoztatásról és a Szerződési Típusválasztási Kényszer Versus Típusválasztási Szabadság Problematikájáig (New Forms of Employment on the Boundaries of Labour Law – The Atypical Forms of Employment and The Freedom of Contract), Magyar Jog, pp. 1-14.

KOHL, H. and PLATZER, H.-W. (eds.) (2004), *Industrial Relations in Central and Eastern Europe, Transformation and Integration, A Comparison of the Eight New EU Member States*, ETUI, Brussels.

KOLLONAY LEHOCZKY, C. (2004), "European Enlargement: A Comparative View of Hungarian Labour Law", in BERMANN, G. and PISTOR, K. (eds.), *Law and Governance in an Enlarged European Union, Essays in European Law*, Hart Publishing, Oxford and Portland, pp. 209-244.

LORBER, P. (2006), "Implementing the Information and Consultation Directive in Great Britain, A New Voice at Work", *International Journal of Comparative Labour Law and Industrial Relations*, Vol. 22, No.2, pp. 231-258.

LORBER, P. (2003), "National Works Councils: Opening the Door on New Whole Area in United Kingdom Employee Relations", *International Journal of Comparative Labour Law and Industrial Relations*, Vol. 19, No.3, pp. 297-319.

MALMBERG, J. (2003) (ed.), *Effective Enforcement of EC Labour Law*, Kluwer Law International, The Hague, London and New York.

MORIN, M.-L. (2005), "Labour Law and New Forms of Corporate Organisation", *International Labour Review*, Vol. 144, pp. 5-29.

NAGY, L. (1998), Az Európai Üzemi Tanácsok Ürügyén a Hazai Üzemi Tanácsokról (About National Works Councils in Connection with the European Works Councils) Munkaügyi Szemle, No.1, pp. 41-43.

NEUMANN, L. A. P. T. (ed.) (2004), *A munkáltatói jogutódlás esete*, Novotni Alapítvány, Miskolc.

OHLIN REPORT (1956), "Social Aspects of European Economic Co-operation", Report by a Group of Experts, New Series, No.46, International Labour Organisation, Geneva.

PRUGBERGER, T. (1999), "Az üzemi tanácsi és a szakszervezeti érdekvédelem kontraktuális lehetőségei az alapvető individuális munkavállalói jogoknál – különös tekintettel a felmondásra és a létszámleépítésre", *Magyar Jog*, No.46, pp. 274-285.

RADNAY, J. (2004), "A munkáltatói jogutódlás kérdései", *Gazdaság és Jog*, Vol. 2, pp. 17-22.

SCHARPF, F. W. (2002), "The European Social Model: Coping with the Challenges of Diversity", *Journal of Common Market Studies*, No.40, pp. 645-670.

SHANKS, M. (1977), "The Social Policy of the European Communities", *Common Market Law Review*, No.14, pp. 375-383.

TÓTH, A. (2002), "Két Tűz Között: Üzemi Tanácsok, Szakszervezetek és Munkáltatók (Between Hell and Highwater: Works Councils, Trade Unions and Employers)", in KOVÁCH, I. (ed.) *Hatalom és Társadalmi változás – A Posztszocializmus vége (Power and in Changes in the Society – The End of Postscialism)*, Napvilág Kiadó, Budapest, pp. 133-153.

VAŠKOVÁ, R., HÁLA, J. and KROUPA, A. (2005), "Trade Union Officials in the Firm", *European Industrial Relations Observatory on-line*, available at http://www.eurofound.europa.eu/eiro/2005/04/feature/cz0504103f.htm, 15 April 2008.

VAUGHAN-WHITEHEAD, D. (2003), *EU Enlargement Versus Social Europe? The Uncertain Future of the European Social Model*, Edward Elgar Publishing, Cheltenham.

WEISS, M. (2006), "Industrial Relations and EU Enlargement", in CRAIG, J.D.R. and LYNK, S. M. (eds.), *Globalization and the Future of Labour Law*, Cambridge University Press, Cambridge, pp. 169-190.

ZEITLIN, J. (2005), "Social Europe and Experimentalist Governance: Towards a New Constitutional Compromise?", in DE BÚRCA, G. (ed.), *EU Law and the Welfare State. In Search of Solidarity*, Oxford University Press, Oxford, pp. 213-242.

Part II

Firms Relocation and Social Treatment of Restructuring in the EU New Member States

Production Relocation

Impacts on Home, Host and Cross-border Industrial Relations

Guglielmo MEARDI and Michael FICHTER

Associate Professor of Industrial Relations at the University of Warwick and Senior Lecturer and Researcher in the Center for Labor Studies at the Freie Universität Berlin

Introduction

The EU enlargement of 2004, by reshaping the EU as a labour market and as a product market, is putting social regulation at the EU and national levels to the test. In particular, the impact on the ways in which employee representatives, including European Works Councils and trade unions, deal with both real and threatened relocation is hard to foresee. Media and political actors can be loud on "social dumping" and "relocations", but both these concepts have rarely been rigorously defined by researchers. In most cases these ideas require the use of counterfactuals and are therefore not suitable for empirical research. The chapter will try to map out the context before taking a more in-depth look at three exemplary aspects of this development: the manner in which relocation can affect the German model of industrial relations; the contours of industrial relations at new (relocated) production sites in Central and Eastern Europe (CEE); and the role of the European Works Council.

The chapter, on the basis of case-study research, will show that the enlargement impact in terms of industrial relations is greater than the simple aggregate impact on employment, and that it is at the same time highly varied depending on country, sector and company specificities.[1]

1 The authors are grateful to Christoph Dörrenbächer, András Tóth, Lászlo Neumann, Marcin Frybes, Miroslav Stanojević and Paul Marginson for their co-operation on the empirical research. Paul Marginson has made a fundamental contribution to the first

I. Production Relocation: Dimensions and Potentials

Despite widespread fears of, and attention to, the potential employment consequences of relocation amongst the EU-15 the available evidence suggests that relocation in its strictest sense, when productive activity is directly transferred eastwards from a location in the old Member States to one in the new, is not widespread. Of the job losses arising from company restructurings across Europe documented by the European Monitoring Centre on Change, around 5% are attributed to relocation over the period from 2003 up until the end of 2005 (Pedersini, 2005). Even if the EMCC, given its methodology based on press reports, probably grossly underestimates restructuring cases, the proportion of relocations is unlikely to be overestimated, as these are exactly the cases that attract most media interest. An assessment prepared by the European Commission (EC, 2006: 65) cites findings on the employment effects of relocation from selected studies relating to Germany, Austria and the Netherlands. Estimates of job loss between 1990 and 2001 directly attributable to relocation in these countries varied between 0.3 and 2% of total job losses.

We will argue that besides these "direct" relocations, there is also scope for "indirect" relocation. This is where investment projects which might previously have been located in the EU-15 are instead located in one of the new Member States. Because of the dynamic nature of investment decisions, and where to locate them, it is frequently less than clear cut whether an indirect relocation has indeed taken place; hence there are no reliable estimates of their possible magnitude. A further effect on employment comes from the threat of relocation, which frequently has the effect of initiating cost-reducing and/or efficiency-enhancing changes in existing operations in the EU-15 which themselves have employment consequences. Examples include the high profile cases of Siemens in Germany and Bosch in France, over the summer of 2004. Again there are no reliable estimates of the scale of such "threat" effects available. In addition there is also the issue of international outsourcing of production to independent suppliers in other countries (Galgóczi *et al.*, 2005), but this – not being within the scope of EWC activity – will not be addressed in this chapter.

Given the variety of situations, we argue for using a contingent approach to uncover the circumstances under which relocations – direct and indirect – and the threat of relocation are more (or less) likely to occur and affect industrial relations.

---

section of the article. The research was made possible by grants from the VW Stiftung and from the ESRC.

A first distinction is between market- and efficiency-oriented motivations for foreign direct investment (FDI), in which the potential for relocation largely arises under the latter. An important part of inward investment into the new Member States is "market seeking" in nature, motivated by the opportunity of opening up new markets for products and services. Such investment by its nature is market expanding, and the largest share involves service activities, which by their nature need to be produced close to the point of consumption. The scope for relocation is minimal. In contrast, efficiency-oriented FDI is motivated by considerations of comparative labour costs and/or labour quality and/or labour productivity, in which companies are looking to take advantage of superior unit labour cost conditions in the new Member States as compared to those prevailing in the EU-15. Given significant differences in labour costs, the presence of workforces with established skills and qualifications, and rising labour productivity amongst the new Member States (Marginson and Meardi, 2006), the resulting scope for relocation is potentially extensive.

Second, amongst FDI into the new Member States which is efficiency seeking in nature a crucial distinction has been drawn between outward processing activity based almost exclusively on the search for cheap labour and investment in which the emphasis is on labour quality, flexibility and productivity as well as costs. Since the mid-1990s there has been a shift from the former to the latter, but both still coexist in the new EU Member States (Tholen and Hemmer, 2005). The recent, high-quality wave of efficiency-seeking investment involves the reconfiguration of production networks in Europe: a more complex reorganisation of activities across different locations than the direct relocations associated with the first wave of efficiency-oriented FDI. As both Galgóczi *et al.* (2005) and Pedersini (2005) recognise, it becomes more difficult to assess the employment impact, either overall or at specific locations. Given the role of human capital, employer commitment to the workforce (including job security and scope for social dialogue and compromise) tends to be stronger.

Third (and not unrelated), the nature of these international production networks and the role of new and acquired sites in the new Member States within the network is likely to have a bearing on the scope for relocation. Expansion and relocation bring with them the need to continually adjust the "value chains" within a new internal international division of labour in which different activities are segmented across borders, depending on skills and cost factors (Kaplinsky, 2001).

A fourth consideration is the extent to which location decisions of companies are autonomous, or are driven by those of major customers. In some sectors, such as automotive components, the location decisions of powerful customers who demand just-in-time delivery effectively require suppliers to follow them to new locations, while in other sectors; companies have greater discretion over the choice of which locations to supply their customers from.

Fifth, the potential for relocation is far from being bounded by the enlarged borders of the EU; relocation has a global as well as intra-European dimension in which some production activities (not all low skilled) are moving to Asia or to extra-EU European countries. The extent to which there is scope for extra-EU relocation would seem likely to vary between and within sectors, according to factors such as technology, skill requirements and the need for proximity to the market.

II. Relocation: An Option for German Enterprises?

Over the past several years, the issue of production relocation from Germany to lower cost sites in Central and Eastern Europe has repeatedly been in the news, reflecting the contentious nature of the political and economic conflicts it has generated. In an academic context as well, there has been a broad discussion of this phenomenon and its potential and existing ramifications for *Standort* Germany. While there is no doubt that there has been a steady and considerable decline in industrial employment in Germany over the past thirty years (Statistisches Bundesamt 2006), there is no data which distinctively shows the extent to which this decline can be attributed to production relocation to foreign countries. Indeed, there has been virtually no discussion of the kinds of changes and developments which such relocation processes have had on the former or remaining company sites in Germany while proceeding and after their culmination.

As recently completed research shows, relocation is a strategic option (and necessity) not only for large multinationals, but also for small and medium-sized enterprises (SMEs). Based on empirical case studies, we will show how relocation is undermining the core of German labour relations – and thus the German model of production – through the elimination of production jobs which have been held by the core workforce, the backbone of union membership and works council mandates.

Production relocation beyond the borders of the home country has become a widespread phenomenon, even beyond the widening circle of multinational "global players". As such, it should be regarded and analysed as an instrument of business restructuring, most likely to be turned to as a strategic option for meeting the challenges of globalisation. Of note is the fact that production relocation is no longer a strategic option open only to large enterprises which are usually categorised as multinationals. Indeed, enormous advances in technology, transportation and (tele) communications have made relocation an affordable and viable option under certain conditions for SMEs as well.

Since 1990, the countries of Central and Eastern Europe have developed rapidly into one of those options. To be sure, prior to 1989 some investment in production facilities had taken place, but on a very restricted scale. Following the collapse of the Soviet bloc and the initialisation of a "dual" transformation process (Offe, 1995) to political democracies and market economies, foreign direct investment in production and services expanded rapidly. The CEE countries, especially those closest to the European Union which quickly became to be regarded as candidates for membership, had the advantage of geographic proximity. Moreover, for companies looking to invest in production, a low-wage workforce with basic tacit knowledge of industrial processes and exhibiting high skill and education levels was available.

According to research carried out by the German Fraunhofer Institute for Systems and Innovation Research (*Systemtechnik und Innovationsforschung*) and published by Kinkel *et al.* in 2004, the CEE region and in particular the eight countries which joined the European Union in 2004 advanced to the top of the list for German FDI. Some 45% of all enterprises surveyed relocated production to the CEE region, whereas Asia with a quota of 29% was second on the list. (Kinkel *et al.*, 2004: 10-14) As for the reasons behind the decision to relocate, 85% of all enterprises named production costs as the primary motivation with market entry a distant second (42.3%).

While the Fraunhofer survey provides interesting data on the structure and evolvement of production relocation to the CEE region during the past few years, it should be recognised that it does not cover the issue completely. Nevertheless, the results are indicative of the relevance of relocation as a strategic restructuring option for German enterprises, both large and small.

Having established the relevance of production relocation to the CEE region for German-based enterprises, the remaining of this section will present findings from empirical research on the impact of such relocations on labour relations (Dörrenbächer *et. al.*, 2003; Fichter *et al.*, 2005). The research involved first case studies of production relocation to Hungary, a leading recipient of German FDI in the 1990s (interviews at some fifteen enterprises followed by in-depth case studies at five enterprises), and then twelve comparative case studies of German and US-owned automotive component companies operating in Poland, Hungary and Slovenia, carried out in 2003-20005.

A. Relocation and Labour Relations. Insights from Case Studies

In regard to the policies of the sample firms in transferring the German production model (in its company-specific forms) to their Hungarian subsidiaries, we found no verification for our hypothesis that labour relations are an integral element of the German production model. Labour relations, training and wage determination at the Hungarian subsidiary showed little resemblance to their counterpart in Germany. Indeed, management made no effort to affect a transfer, assuming that its production system would function without attempting to replicate the home country employee relationships. To put it more bluntly, German companies escaped from the highly institutionalised environment of labour relations and happily accommodated themselves to the comparatively unregulated Hungarian environment.

The second wave of recent research has shown that even this binding may not be found in large German enterprises if they are highly internationalised. Moreover, a comparison with US-owned companies revealed that industrial relations are hardly affected by the country of origin (Fichter *et al.*, 2005: 13).

Several other studies on production relocation and employment relations in the CEE countries have also found corroborating evidence for this phenomenon. While the case study research conducted by Kluge and Voss (2003) showed that it could not be taken for granted that German multinationals would take their company culture of labour relations with them to other countries, there is some evidence that "in terms of labour relations and policies", at least large corporations and stock companies are "bound to the institutions that shaped the German 'production regime'" (Bluhm, 2001: 170).

B. Effects on Employment at Home Country Sites

What is also of interest is the impact of relocation on the subsequent practice of the German production model at those home country sites directly affected by the process. In comparison to the large body of litreature on "forward diffusion" (Ferner and Varul, 2000) and the impact of home-country practices on foreign subsidiaries, there is virtually no research available on post-relocation developments in the home country. In his study of "reverse diffusion", e.g. the practice of introducing employment practices from foreign operations to home country sites, Edwards (2000) touched partly on this issue in seeking to determine the kind of multinational corporation where reverse diffusion was likely to occur. Using data from ten enterprises, he found evidence of such a practice in only two cases, both of which he categorised as being "globally integrated firms" (Edwards, 2000: 120).[2] Edwards also addresses the question of the potential challenge reverse diffusion may pose for worker representatives in regard to established labour practices (*ibid.* 126). However, his concern is limited to the actual transfer of practices from subsidiaries and as such he does not deal with the key issues of this chapter, e.g., the overall impact of changes wrought by the relocation process itself which are not limited to those which fall under the heading of "reverse diffusion".

C. Loss of Production Jobs – Creation of White-collar Employment

The most immediate and noticeable impact of production transfer is the loss of employment "on the shop floor". Depending on the actual product, the kind of jobs lost varied to some extent in our sample cases. For the most part, unskilled and semi-skilled positions, mostly held by women, were eliminated. This can be illustrated by using data from two of the sample companies. In 1989, the electronics component company ALPHA employed 800 persons at its sole production site in Germany. The first wave of production relocation eliminated 250 jobs, and by 1998 all manufacturing processes except for a small production unit for prototypes and special orders had been relocated to Hungary. In this ten-year period, nearly 600 production jobs were eliminated. At the automotive supply company BETA, relocation began in 1998 and when completed in 2001, all of the 120 production workers employed in 1997 were gone. In both of these cases as well as in all of the other cases from the project sample, company works councils were unable to intervene in the relocation process itself and had to content themselves with negotiations over severance pay combined with some retraining.[3]

Interestingly, however, as production jobs were eliminated, new positions were created so that after completion of relocation, employment at the German site of these and many of the other companies in our sample returned to the pre-transfer level or even increased. In 2001, the ALPHA company had 630 employees at its German site; while at the automotive supply company BETA, total employment was back at 204 by 2002. Skilled white-collar employees such as engineers, technicians, commercial staff and IT specialists had been hired to support the new production arrangement, bolster the marketing strategy and control the increased complexity of internationalised production. Even into later stages of the Hungarian investment, when the subsidiary had taken on

2 This would seem to complement the above cited findings of Fichter *et al.* (2005).

3 In neither of these two companies nor in any of the other companies in our sample did the layoffs lead to labour disputes.

responsibilities only indirectly related to production, the home country site did not experience a new wave of job losses similar to that which had taken place in production. In the sample as a whole, when employment cutbacks did occur in Germany, they were the direct consequence of a poor economic performance by that company (Dörrenbächer *et al.*, 2003).

D. Increasing Reliance on Teamwork

A second observation is in regard to effects of the relocation on work processes. We found strong evidence that teamwork at the German site was intensified, both within the site and – necessarily – with the new production subsidiary. The introduction of such German-Hungarian teams proved to be an experiment in intercultural cooperation, in which the Germans had the advantage of language as well as the initial privilege of greater company-specific and product-related knowledge. But they also had to deal with the uncertainty of the future of their positions in respect to the further growth and development of the subsidiary.

E. Erosion of the System of Workplace Labour Relations

A third observation concerns the status of industrial relations and the role of the works council at the German site from which production was relocated. The "delocalisation" of production (Abraham and Konings 1999: 591), e.g. the relocation of the routine and standardised processes to Hungary and the retention of high value-adding activities in Germany, meant that the core of labour relations at the German site was eliminated. The organisation al density of union membership declined proportional to the loss of production workers and the backbone of support for the role of the works council as the representative of workers' interests was deleted. With the disappearance of a sizeable contingent of production workers, the workforce became inevitably almost fully white-collar. In its new composition, the workforce was more non-union and characterised by strong individual career interests. As a consequence, the coordinates of management-workforce relations were redrawn. New topics appeared on the agenda of the works councils at these sites and at election time, they went through membership shake-ups that reflected this extensive shift from a low-skilled, blue-collar workforce to a high-skilled and heterogeneous white-collar workforce. This did not necessarily mean that works councils became generally irrelevant. Although this was the case at some enterprises, at others, their role was not questioned but was launched on the path of redefinition.

In sum, our research sample showed that the first wave of relocation targets mainly core production processes, eliminating production jobs of which most are low-skilled or unskilled, even in so-called technologically "high road" (Soskice, 1999; Turner *et al.*, 2001) processes. As such, union presence on the shop floor and a strong and rather homogenous interest representation disappeared from the context of workplace labour relations.

In contrast, "second wave" relocations are as straight forward, being much more contingent on particular product developments, specific production processes, customer relations and employee qualifications. As regards the role of company works councils, relocation initiated both a change in membership on the works council and a radical shift in the agenda. In general, the role of the works council as a collective voice of the employees decreased in importance. Although there seems to be some recognition of strategic importance of a company-wide (cross-border) approach, there was very little or no interest in taking concrete steps toward initiating contacts or policies with employees or their workplace representatives at the new subsidiary, or even with the responsible sectoral trade union in the other country. An important cause of this reticence was the language barrier which existed on both ends of the line.

For their part, trade unions seem to be overextended and overtaxed by the widespread incidence of relocation and restructuring, thus concentrating their limited resources on dealing with such cases at large enterprises. As complementary research shows, the impact of such processes on attitudes of union members, whether direct or indirect, can foster right extremist attitudes (Fichter, 2008).

In contrast to the large corporations, the establishment of a European Works Council is not considered to be a strategic option in most SMEs because such enterprises do not reach the employment threshold required by law. Where it is an option, employees in SMEs face such problems as a lack of interest (which may be indicative of an underlying element of internal competitiveness) at the subsidiary level in coordinating and cooperating with employee representatives from the headquarters; the difficulty of initiating and establishing representative selection procedures; a general lack of resources to develop an infrastructure of representation; and, on top of all this, reluctance and even opposition on the part of management.

III. Evidence from Central Europe

While such outcomes from relocation at SMEs in Germany seem rather predictable, we need to return to our argument in favour of a contingent approach when analysing the effects of relocation on employment policies in CEE production sites. As such, this section tests the contingencies hypothesised at the outset of this chapter using the findings of the second phase of research mentioned, on the automotive component sector in Hungary, Poland and Slovenia. As the study was primarily plant-focussed, the findings refer to the industrial relations integration of specific plants and cannot always be generalised to the whole of the corporations.

The automotive component sector is particularly interesting for a discussion of relocations for a number of reasons: it is regionalised rather than globalised (90% of production sold in the EU is produced in the EU); both labour skills and labour costs are important (lower capital intensity than car assembly), and human resources in the new EU Member States are comparable to the western European, while much cheaper; foreign investment in this sector is purely efficiency-seeking (90% of production in Central Europe is re-exported), more so than final car assembly.

Table 1: Relocation Threats and EWC Responses

Contingent factor	Level	Implications for EWC responses to relocations	Empirical evidence from case studies
FDI motivation (efficiency v market)	Sector	Seriousness of threat	Automotive component sector: strong efficiency motivation, strong threats
Human resources consideration (skills v cost priority)	Sector, sub-sector	Potential for social compromise, dialogue	Three companies focusing primarily on labour costs: frequent direct relocation threats Seven companies with high but not primary labour cost motivation: frequent indirect relocation threats Two companies with little labour cost focus: relocations only a remote threat
International configuration of production (standardisation v segmentation/segregation)	Sub-sector, company	Degree of competition and of international integration/socialisation	Most operationally integrated companies have strongest cross-border employee representative networks.
Location decision (autonomous v dictated by customers)	Sub-sector	Level of response (company or sector/political)	Two companies with little location autonomy: relocation not an issue for plant/company level IR
Extension of product market (EU v global)	Sector, sub-sector	Suitability of European response	Plants affected by extra-EU competition: employee representative have little interest in co-operating with western counterparts.

Of the five contingencies we introduced above, the first (efficiency v market-orientation) is basically constant within the sector, and therefore is excluded from the analysis. The other four factors, together with the effects on relocation threats and industrial relations responses, all appear to be relevant, as summarised in Table 1.

Overall, across the case studies the examples of direct cost-driven relocations are relatively rare: three among twelve companies, and of these one was from Poland to Western Europe, for broader efficiency reasons than just labour costs. However, relocations as a threat and coercive comparisons are a daily reality in most plants. In the most integrated companies, it is usual for production teams to have open displays with their weekly production and quality results compared to those of the other company plants.

The intensity of inter-site competition affects employees differently, though, depending on the role of labour costs in investment motivation. In none of the case studies are labour costs the only motivation. However, labour costs have played a primary role in three cases, and an important one – beside others – in another seven. In the former, relocation are an explicit issue in two cases (if not on all production lines) and an indirect issue in the third, where inter-site competition occurs in the form of contest for attracting future investment projects.

Competition for the new investment exists in five among the seven companies where labour costs are important, but beside other considerations such as quality and flexibility, while actual incidents of relocations are rare (and in one case from the East to the West). In the other two relocation threats are rather remote or very indirect. Finally, there are two cases where labour costs were a secondary consideration in comparison to quality, development and flexibility. As expected, here relocations are only remotely threatening.

The second important issue is location autonomy. Most of the case studies come from rather autonomous producers of easily transportable components, and they have sufficient market power to have an own location strategy. Only for two of them was location choice based on client choices. As expected, relocations in these situations are decoupled from employment relations considerations: in one case they are not an issue, and in the other they are only within regional boundaries, in competition with neighbouring countries but not with Western Europe. The situation can be obviously very different in the large number of smaller, often second- or third- tier suppliers, which are not covered by our research.

The third important company-level contingency relates to the degree of vertical integration and standardisation. The process of outsourcing and fragmentation in the automotive industry has been particularly fast since the mid-1990s, and combined with the parallel process of internationalisation, causing strains on sector-level arrangements and allowing diversification of employment policies for different segments of the value chain, often located in different countries (Faust *et al.*, 2004).

Vertically integrated or standardised companies relying on continuous transfer of semi-products, technology and information between different sites, indirectly encourage stricter standardisation of work organisation and a degree of industrial relations harmonisation. The continuous flow of information and contacts, and the requirement for highly standardised production imply that employment practices cannot be divergent. Research on the eastward extension of the EWC (Meardi, 2004; Voß, 2006) has shown that these are the cases where avoiding big cultural or employment conditions gaps between sites is in the employer interest, for the sake of joint projects and common understanding of productive issues. More generally, multinationals' recent concern with business techniques such as programme management, benchmarking, performance measurement may lead to more general mutual learning between stakeholders, and encourage "global strategies" of "local players" (Kristensen and Zeitlin, 2005). The situation is different in plants working on specific products or semi-products, often allocated to them on the basis of cost considerations, with little integration with other sites. Here, cross-border dialogue has less space to develop.

The company with the strongest operational integration is also the one with the strongest employee-side network of co-operation and information sharing in the sample. The causal link is demonstrated by the developments in another, similar large company: here a network did emerge, but only after the Hungarian subsidiary had been substantially upgraded. By contrast, plants that are entirely responsible for specific products, and while they are in competition with some other sites, cross-border co-operation is occasional, and mutual knowledge limited to little more than anecdotes, stereotypes. For instance even in a company covered by a long-established EWC, we found that the 500-employee Polish plant in 2004 was still not represented in it, and the German works councillors did not see their integration as a relevant issue.

A final factor affecting both the extent of relocation threats and the forms of employee responses is competition with low-cost sites east of the EU and in Asia. Its emergence coincided with the already mentioned process of transition from "first" to "second-wave" FDI at the end of the 1990s, and today, its importance is still growing. In a Hungarian subsidiary, for instance, relocation of part of the production to Romania in 2003, which at the time was not yet an EU Member State, came as a shock and effectively blocked any further improvements in the climate of labour relations.

In these cases where competition comes from outside the EU, EU-level institutions such as the EWCs are not fit to the purpose of negotiating relocation threats in a coordinated way, The extension of EWCs to Romania is beginning to develop (2007), and there are attempts to include Turkish and Ukrainian sites. But Asian sites are unlikely to be represented in any employee forum. As a result, employee representatives on EWCs at Hungarian plants facing Chinese competition show little interest in this body as their informational needs and strategic options are in the East rather than the West.

A. Union Strategies

While in aggregate terms the significance of relocation threats is more limited than media reports seem to suggest, in those situations where the threat is real the answers by trade unions are of variable nature and intensity.

Removing from the analysis the three case studies where the relocation threat is currently only remote, we are left with nine cases where the capacity for cross-border employee reactions and arrangements varies sharply. Four different scenarios are particularly clear.

One extreme, if isolated, case, which may be labelled as "pro-active" strategy, is detected in the Polish plant of a large German company: here there has been an early union engagement in internationalising company-level industrial relations, through the European Works Council and a number of other international projects which translate into daily contacts through specific international teams on both works council and management sides. The main strategy is an attempt at exporting the German model rather than defending it at home, and to enforce a spirit of "fair competition" between sites. An international negotiation of wages is however still explicitly ruled out, allowing for different pay policies in different countries.

A variation of this strategy, which we can call "organising", occurred in two Hungarian plants where a similar union engagement took place, but more slowly and initially resisted by management. Company-specific factors that allowed consensual expansion of western solutions were missing, and therefore some preliminary "organising" effort was required. In these cases the chances of union success are affected by the market situation.

An opposite, more defensive strategy from German unions is detected in two companies (US and German owned) operating in Poland. In the German one, for instance, the *Gesamtsbetriebsrat* chair defended

German arrangements rather than proposing their extension eastwards, arguing that "fifty years of union experience cannot be acquired in ten years" (our interview.) A similar argument is used about production, to defend German employment: "in terms of productivity you can't compare people who have 200 years of industrial experience with people who have nearly no industrial experience" (*ibid.*). The German union has had some success through local strategies: it has negotiated restructuring in several German sites and obtained (through a mix of resistance, mobilisation, expertise and political exchange involving local authorities) some social guarantees, but could not avoid a continuous cost competition from Central Europe and cuts of hundreds of jobs directly due to relocations eastwards. The European Works Council is active but in a rather "reactive" way, with no negotiation role. In spite of business similarities with the two previous case studies, the different level of vertical integration and of geographic competition has meant that EU-level cross-border employee co-operation has had much less space to develop. The company, in spite of its business being definitely global, has an adaptive approach in industrial relations, which in turn promotes local union strategies rather than co-ordination. German disinterest mentioned above is mirrored by similar – and equally misinformed – views among Polish staff about their German counterparts. Defensive views in this case lead to a scenario of weak or missing cross-border links.

A fourth scenario is that of competition and diffidence. In a US company with a large Hungarian plant there are experiences of tensions between western and eastern employee representatives. Here, inter-site competition exists not only on employment and relocations (including white-collar workers), but also through "coercive comparisons" on employment conditions, with for instance management trying to introduce "Polish practices" in an Italian plant against local union resistance. Diffidence among western trade unions towards their eastern counterparts is strong, with questions raised as to whether "they are really unions'. Europeanisation through the EWC had worked well within Western Europe, but is struggling to cope with the new geography of production, including the company decision to relocate their European headquarters from Spain to Hungary and the increasing direct competition from Chinese subsidiaries.

Finally, the rather specific situation of three Slovenian plants is worth referring to as it does not fit with the above-mentioned scenarios. Here, trade unions are relatively strong and production is integrated in European networks with multiple cross-borders contacts, but cross-border links are still rather weak. The reason may be similar to the one that has discouraged Scandinavian unions from Europeanisation for some time. Labour strength in Slovenia is rooted in the national industry and in national-level arrangements. Unlike other new EU Member States from central Europe, union density and influence is weaker in multinational companies than in domestic ones. The path towards Europeanisation may be then perceived as a risky undermining and departure from the traditional and safer national arrangements.

Overall, the contingencies identified above explain the variety of union reactions even within the same trade union in the same country (e.g. IG Metall), in spite of the apparently common institutional and ideological background (e.g. two similar-size German companies in Poland). Unions in vertically integrated companies with product markets closely overlapping with EU boundaries will deal with Europeanisation better than others. Also, direct inter-site cost competition and location autonomy will often lead to an "organising" approach. Other, more autonomous and development-oriented sites may lead to strategies of local "competitive solidarity", including risks of concession bargaining. A problem with these situations is that such strategies tend to be path-dependent and keep being followed even when their efficacy is declining, preventing the development of more courageous – but initially risky – lines, as seen in the above-mentioned case of the defensive *Gesamtsbetriebsrat*.

IV. The Most Visible EWCs in Central and Eastern Europe[4]

To date, few EWCs have ever "made the news" through high-profile activity, and none of them involved the new Member States in a prominent way. As long as there is no systematic research on the issue, a closer look at those well-known EWCs that include sites from the new Member States is a good starting point before moving in "uncharted territory".

The most famous case of EWC mobilisation against restructuring remains that of the so-called "Euro-strike" at Renault in 1997. In that case, while Renault had an important site in Novo Mesto, Slovenia, which eventually was the net winner of restructuring through relocation of production and job creation, the mobilisation was geographically concentrated in the West and more precisely in Belgium and France. The Slovenian plant was hardly mentioned. Slovenian employee representatives did express solidarity with their western counterparts but they did not go on strike as solidarity strikes are forbidden by their regula-

4 We are grateful to the editors of *Transfer* for allowing to publish this section, which in an earlier version has been published in Meardi (2007).

tions (an issue which we will deal with again in the conclusion). It is overall questionable whether the Slovenian employees would have felt the urge to mobilise in support of their richer western colleagues, and potentially against their own immediate interests. That event occurred well before EU enlargement, and cases from after 2004 complement it by showing how practice can be changing.

Two other cases of EWC mobilisation in the automotive sector (a prominent sector for industrial relations in general and for international developments in particular) have taken place more recently: Ford and General Motors. While Ford is nearly absent from the new Member States, General Motors – while still keeping their overwhelming majority of employees in western Europe – includes an important factory in Gliwice, Poland, which is quite large (3,000 employees) and was ranked in 2005, by the corporate benchmarking system, as the best GM factory in Europe. During the restructuring of 2004, 10,000 job cuts were threatened in the western sites (mostly in Sweden and Germany), while 2,000 additional jobs were promised for the Polish plant. The EWC mobilisation has been portrayed by many as at least partly (some intra-site competition emerged during the agreement implementation) a success (e.g. Bartmann and Blum-Greenen, 2006; Da Costa and Rehfeldt, 2006). The Solidarity union representing the Polish workforce took part in the mobilisation through the distribution of leaflets and the display of union flags at the gates. There was no strike, however, as meeting the requirements of Polish labour law for a legal strike (notably, a long notice and a ballot) was deemed impossible (our interview with a Solidarity EWC representative). More concerning than the lack of strike was that in the previous months, soon after Polish EU accession, Solidarity had agreed to a pay cut in order to secure the transfer of the Zafira model assembly line, with one thousand jobs, to the factory. Given the overall situation in the company, this case may be labelled as "social dumping" in so far as it involved an intentional lowering of social standards directly aiming at affecting the investment location decision process (94% of Gliwice production is for export and therefore directly in competition with plants abroad). Indeed this was how the event was perceived among the German employees of the Rüsselsheim factory, where the line had been located previously. Politically, the issue was made even more sensitive by the fact that this American investment was included in the overall transaction of the Polish government purchase of F-16 military airplanes from the US, which had made Poland collide with France and Germany. Some informal diffidence among western EWC delegates towards their Polish colleagues was anecdotally reported at the time (our interviews).

Two years later, in 2006, the GM EWC mobilised again against the threatened closure of the plant of Azambuja in Portugal. In this case the concerns by the Polish representatives appeared more convinced: the employees under threat were clearly not the most expensive in Europe, and indeed were earning wages that Polish employees hope to achieve shortly. The impression was, therefore, that if the Portuguese are under threat today, the Poles themselves may be tomorrow (our interview). The threat of redundancies was not unknown to the Polish employees: GM had cut 400 jobs during the economic slow-down of 2002. Gliwice had also lost, at the beginning of 2006, the competition with Saragossa for the new model Meriva. Polish participation in the day of action of the 13th of June was appreciated from the West as more convinced and determined than in 2004. Still there was no strike in Poland for the same legal reason as two years earlier.

A different situation, which despite less dramatic events and weaker media interest has been seen as an important experience, is that of another large US corporation, General Electric (Pulignano *et al.*, 2005). Its Power Controls division has had an effective EWC since 1999. It has been very active, although with dubious success, in managing restructuring across western sites in seven western European countries, but did not include any of the Central and Eastern European plants. Its Lighting division, concentrated mostly in Hungary and Poland, with only small operations in UK and Italy, did not have a EWC. In 2004, the enlargement of the EU coincided with a major restructuring process in the corporation, which merged the two divisions. Given the larger size of its Lighting sites, the Hungarian workforce alone would now constitute more than 50% of the total GE workforce in the EU. Different industrial relation traditions existed between GE Power Controls and GE Lightings, as an effect of both geographic differences between East and West, and divisional differences. GE Lightings, which is directly exposed to Chinese competition and gives more weight to cost considerations, displays a "leaner" and more flexible productive organisation, and lacks some of the collective bargaining traditions of Power Controls in western Europe.

Following the announcement of reorganisation and considering the legal consequences of EU enlargement, the EWC of GE Lighting (whose members represent only sites in the EU-15) reached an agreement on a new EWC for the amalgamated corporation. The agreement was signed on 28 April, 2004, three days before EU enlargement, and then presented to the Hungarian and Polish representatives, who had not been informed of the negotiations, as a *fait accompli.* The Hungarian representatives protested for having been allocated only three out of eleven EWC members, and none of the three seats in the select committee, in spite of a clear majority in the workforce. The ensuing negotiations led to an increase of the Hungarian contingent to five and the inclusion of one Hungarian in the select committee. Meanwhile, the EWC (with a majority of western European members), with the support of the European Metalworker Federation and the involvement of the European Parliament, had started a campaign for the improvement of information and consultation with regard to restructuring. The dispute over the seats may have exacerbated the Hungarian representatives' mistrust in the motives behind such a campaign. They criticised it as a protectionist measure (employment is falling in the western GE sites, but is increasing in the eastern ones) and initially, refused to sign the EWC petitions. The case shows how micro-organisational rivalries (such as on the composition of the EWC, which is only of relative importance given its lack of decision-making power), combined with deep segmentations (different productions dominate in the East as compared to the West) may hamper the development of the EWC into an effective supra-national body.

Finally, an exceptional case of EWC including the new Member States is that of Volkswagen. A pioneer in European and global employee representation, this company also saw a very early extension of the EWC to its Central Eastern European plants well before EU enlargement. Such extension went further, with the effort at exporting much of the Volkswagen home model of industrial relations, including elements such as high union density, joint committees and working time flexibility negotiations (Müller *et al.*, 2004). In many regards, it may be said that VW plants in the Czech Republic, Slovakia and Poland in many regards conform more to the German model of industrial relations than to their own national ones. However, this is rooted in the company-specific system of corporate governance. By special agreement, foreign investment decisions by the company require works council approval: the possibility of the company playing different national workforces against each others is therefore prevented. In spite of increasing competitive pressure and some concession bargaining in the German plants, direct cross-national competition has not occurred and, by contrast, EWC cross-border information is of very high – and possibly unique – quality.

These three cases summarise difficulties and potentials of the EWC in the new Member States: consultation and harmonisation (VW), mobilisation (GM), diffidence (GE). The situation is dynamic, and GM shows how the gradual experience of competitive threats may strengthen co-operation overtime (according to game theory, it would be a classic case of reiterate game as against single.) It remains to be explained which scenario is more likely in the many other, less visible situations.

Conclusion

The chapter has shown that regardless the comforting data on the limited aggregate effects of relocations, in both Germany and at EU level industrial relations in manufacturing have been hit by very serious threats. Direct relocations in the narrow sense may be relatively rare, but competition over investment projects is nearly constant and relocation threats are frequent. The industrial relations effects are therefore independent from the employment effects: the actors are affected by threats as well as by actual incidence of relocations. The forms of representation and negotiation are also under pressure, as best seen in the changing contours of employee representation in German plants.

Relocations are not only a consequence of macroeconomic readjustment, but are also an organisation al issue that varies from company to company and from union to union. In particular, it is apparent that the amount of information and communication enjoyed by employee representatives is varied, and that in most cases increasing it would affect the dynamics of negotiations and the power balance, for instance by allowing to distinguish more clearly between real threats and "bluffs".

At the same time, company-level factors such as operational integration, labour cost considerations, location autonomy determine to a large extent the nature of relocation threats and the space available for social dialogue over it. The empirical evidence from Central Europe suggests that it would be misleading to search for best general solutions, as different company situations call for different responses. Whether to rely on social dialogue or on organizing, on local strategies or on European responses is largely dependent on company-level contingencies.

The overall picture with regard to union policy on restructuring and relocations is therefore of a serious, growing difficulty. There are however two faces of it. On one side, the evidence shows that German companies do not automatically transfer social dialogue – neither do they need it, because up to now the German companies transferring their organisational and technological pillars but not the social one have been economically very successful. This fact could foster pessimism as to future developments. The second finding (especially from the more recent case studies) is nonetheless that in some, if few, cases social dialogue has emerged over time, whether through union organising, or networking, or company choices. In these cases plants have kept being successful as well. So, in conclusion, the social negotiation of change in the enlarged EU is not automatic – but it is not impossible either. But it must be constructed and strategically pursued.

References

ABRAHAM, F. and KONINGS, J. (1999), "Does the Opening of Central and Eastern Europe Threaten Employment in the West?", *The World Economy*, Vol. 22, No.4, pp. 585-601.

BARTMANN, M. and BLUM-GREENEN, S. (2006), "Ein betrieblicher Lichtblick. Die Suche nach neuen Regeln für die Standortskonkurrenz bei General Motors Europe", *Mitbestimmung*, No.5, pp. 32-35.

BLUHM, K. (2001), "Exporting or Abandoning the 'German Model'"?: Labour Policies of German Manufacturing Firms in Central Europe", *European Journal of Industrial Relations*, Vol. 7, No.2, pp. 153-173.

CARLEY, M. and HALL, M. (2006), "European Works Councils and Transnational Restructuring", Report for the European Foundation for the Improvement of Living and Working Conditions, Dublin.

DA COSTA, I. and REHFELDT, U. (2006), "European and World Works Councils in the Automobile Sector: Union Strategies between Europeanization and Globalisation", Paper for the IREC Conference, Ljubljana, September 2006.

DÖRRENBÄCHER, C., FICHTER, M., NEUMANN, L. and TÓTH, A., (2003), "Exogenous Influences in Path Dependent Transformation Processes – The Effects of German Foreign Direct Investment on Work Organisation and Labor Relations in Hungary", Final Report, Berlin (http://www.polwiss.fu-berlin.de/tu/english/research.html).

EDWARDS, T. and ZHANG, M. (2005), "Multinationals and National Systems of Employment Relations: Innovators or Adapters?", unpublished paper.

EDWARDS, T. (2000), "Multinationals, International Integration and Employment Practice in Domestic Plants", *Industrial Relations Journal*, Vol. 31, No.2, pp. 115-129.

EC (2006), "Enlargement, Two Years After: An Economic Evaluation" *Occasional Paper*, No.24, Directorate-General for Economic and Social Affairs, Commission of the European Communities, Brussels, May 2006.

FAUST, M., VOSKAMP, U. and WITTKE, V. (eds.) (2004), *European Industrial Restructuring in a Global Economy: Fragmentation and Relocation of Value Chains*, SOFI, Göttingen.

FERNER, A. and VARUL, M. (2000), "Vanguard Subsidiaries and the Diffusion of New Practices: A Case Study of German Multinationals", *British Journal of Industrial Relations*, Vol. 38, No.1, pp. 115-140.

FICHTER, M. (2008), "German Trade Unions and Right Extremism: Understanding Membership Attitudes", *European Journal of Industrial Relations*, Vol. 14, No.1, pp. 65-84.

FICHTER, M., MEARDI, G., FRYBES, M., MARGINSON, P., STANOJEVIĆ, M. and TÓTH, A. (2005), "Varieties of Multinationals. Embedding Foreign Investors in Central Europe", Paper for the 7th ESA Conference, Toruń, 9-12 September 2005.

GALGÓCZI, B., KEUNE, M. and WATT, A. (2005), "Relocation: Challenges for Trade Unions", *Discussion Paper, DP 2005*.01, ETUI-REHS, Brussels.

KÄDTLER J. and SPERLING H.J. (2002), "After Globalisation and Financialisation: Logics of Bargaining in the German Automotive Industry", *Competition & Change*, Vol. 6, No.2, pp. 149-68.

KAPLINSKY, R. (2001), "The Value of Value Chains: Spreading the Gains from Globalisation", *IDS Working Paper*, No.110, Institute of Development Studies, University of Sussex, Brighton.

KINKEL, S., LAY, G. and MALOCA, M. (2004), "Produktionsverlagerungen ins Ausland und Rückverlagerungen. Ergebnisse aus der Erhebung "Innovationen in der Produktion" des Fraunhofer-Instituts für Systemtechnik und Innovationsforschung", *Bericht zum Forschungsauftrag* No.8/04 an das Bundesministerium der Finanzen, Karlsruhe.

KLUGE, N. and VOSS, E. (2003), "Managementstile und Arbeitnehmerbeteiligung bei ausländischen Unternehmen in Polen", Tschechien und Ungarn, *WSI-Mitteilungen*, Vol. 56, No.1, pp. 66-69.

KRISTENSEN, P. and ZEITLIN, J. (2005), *Local Players in Global Games: The Strategic Constitution of a Multinational Corporation*, Oxford University Press, Oxford.

MARGINSON, P. (2000), "Multinational Companies: Innovators or Adaptors?", in Rainbird, H. (ed.), *Training in the Workplace*, Macmillan, Basingstoke, pp. 81-100.

MARGINSON, P. and MEARDI, G. (2006), "EU Enlargement & the FDI Channel of Industrial Relations Transfer", *Industrial Relations Journal*, Vol. 37, No.2, pp. 92-110.

MEARDI, G. (2004), "Short Circuits in Multinational Plants. The Extension of European Works Councils to Poland", *European Journal of Industrial Relations*, Vol. 10, No.2, pp. 161-78.

MEARDI, G. (2007), "Restructuring in an Enlarged Europe: Challenges and Experiences", *Transfer*, Vol. 13, No.2, pp. 253-266.

MÜLLER, T., PLATZER, H.-W. and RUEB, S. (2004), *Globale Arbeitsbeziehungen in globalen Konzernen?*, VS Verlag, Wiesbaden.

OFFE, C. (1995), "Designing Institutions for East European Transitions", in HAUSNER, J., JESSOP, B. and NIELSEN, K. (eds.), *Strategic Choice and Path-dependency in Post-socialism. Institutional Dynamics in the Transformation Process*, Edward Elgar Publishing, Aldershot, pp. 47-66.

PEDERSINI, R. (2005), "Relocation of Production and Industrial Relations", *European Industrial Relations Observatory online*, available at http://www.eurofound.europa.eu/eiro/2005/11/study/tn0511101s.htm, 15 April 2008.

PULIGNANO, V., MEARDI, G. and TÓTH, A. (2005), "EWC and Organisational Change: The Case of General Electric", *European Works Councils Bulletin*, No.58, pp. 10-13.

SOSKICE, D. (1999), "Divergent Production Regimes: Coordinated and Uncoordinated Market Economies in the 1980s and 1990s", in KITSCHELT, H., LANGE, P., MARKS, G. and STEPHENS, J. D. (eds.), *Continuity and Change in*

Contemporary Capitalism, Cambridge University Press, Cambridge, pp. 101-134.

STATISTISCHES BUNDESAMT (2006), "Erwerbstätige nach Wirtschaftsbereichen. Deutschland – Ergebnisse des Mikrozensus", available at http://www.destatis.de/indicators/d/lrerw05ad.htm, 12 November 2006.

THOLEN, J. and HEMMER, E. (2005), "The Effects of Direct Investments by German Companies in Central and Eastern Europe: Scopes, Motives, Strategies, Jobs", *IAW Forschungsbericht*, No.8, IAW, University of Bremen, April 2005.

TURNER, L., WEVER, K., and FICHTER, M. (2001), "Perils of the High and Low Roads", in WEVER, K. (ed.), *Labor, Business, and Change in Germany and the United States*, W.E. Upjohn, Kalamazoo, pp. 123-156.

VOß, E. (2006), "Overstreched: European Works Councils Experience in New EU Member States", Report for the European Foundation for the Improvement of Living and Working Conditions, Dublin.

Strategies of MNEs in Hungary

Yordanka CHOBANOVA

Senior Fellow, Economic programme,
at the Center for the Study of Democracy, Sofia

Introduction

Foreign Direct Investment (FDI) spillovers depend on the local absorptive capacities of the host country as they allow domestic actors to capture the knowledge of the MNEs (Narula and Marin, 2003). The wider technology gaps between foreign companies and domestic companies the fewer backward linkages and lower technological content in the inputs sourced locally (Lall and Narula, 2006). Local actors cannot benefit from innovations if they do not possess a minimum level of scientific and technical knowledge (Perez and Soete, 1988).

This study uses the *Systems of Innovation (SI)* approach and the *International Business (IB)* literature in order to explain the embeddedness of food MNEs in Hungary. SI gives a macro level view as it stresses the role *of institutions and economic actors* for the embededness of FDI, while IB literature explains that phenomenon from a micro-level perspective using firm strategies and investment motives.

The concept of "systems of innovation" as suggested by scholars like Freeman (1987, 2001), Nelson (1993), Lundvall (1992), Edquist (1997), Narula (2002) is a new approach that has emerged only during the last decade. It reflects the significance of knowledge for country competitiveness. "SI is simply at the centre of modern thinking about innovation and its relation to economic growth, competitiveness, and employment" (Edquist, 2002: 225). As Edquist argues, the strongest asset of SI approach is that it encompasses all the important factors that influence the development, diffusion, and use of innovations as well as the relations between these factors. Even more important, it focuses not only on the elements of the system, but also on the interactions among these elements. In the centre of this system are the firms. However, firms do not innovate in isolation but in interaction with other *organisation al actors* (other firms, universities, standard-setting agencies, etc.) and this interaction is shaped by (and shapes) the framework of existing institutions and rules (laws, norms, technical standards, etc.). Briefly, innovations emerge in systems where organisation al actors and institutional rules are important elements (Edquist, 2002: 226-227).

In other words, these *external* for the MNEs factors play a crucial role in shaping their strategies. An economy with a strong knowledge capacity has greater chances to attract and keep FDI. Yet, whether or not a certain MNE would embed in the host economy is very much a decision internal to the company. The *internal* for the company determinants, which influence its level of embeddedness in the host economy, include 1) the entry strategies and entry modes of MNEs in CEE, and 2) their business strategies.

The entry strategy in a given market can say a lot about the plans of the company in a certain economy. Scholars (Dunning, 1993; White and Poynter, 1984) have identified four main motives for investment: 1) market seeking; 2) resource seeking; 3) efficiency seeking and 4) strategic asset seeking. The relative importance of each is a function of the stage of economic development which itself is a function of the quality of its absorptive capacity. Companies following asset-seeking strategy have the highest willingness to lock in a certain economy.

As far as food MNEs are concerned they followed market-seeking strategies when they penetrated CEE market. In general, food companies have been interested in the extension of production into a new country or region. As Meyer and Tran (2006: 3) outline "the main attraction of emerging economies is their high economic growth and the corresponding expectation of rapidly increasing demand of consumer goods".

The major entry modes popular among Western firms for CEE were exporting, forming a joint venture with a local partner, acquiring a local firm in the course of the privatisation process and greenfield investments. When the privatisation of state-owned companies began in the early and mid 1990s, the sale of large national companies offered a unique opportunity for established foreign companies to expand their market position and for new entrants to become major players in the market. For packaged food MNEs, the most common entry mode in CEE was acquisitions of plants through privatisation. Chocolate, dairy products and beer are traditional, culturally embedded products. This fact made local producers attractive takeover candidates for foreign companies, and major players such as Nestlé, Unilever, Kraft Foods and Interbrew (now InBev) seized the opportunity offered by the privatisation process to establish a presence in the region.

Apart from entry strategies and entry modes, the other important factor that illustrates MNE willingness to embed or not in a certain economy is its business strategy. Hence, the question is, "What strategies drive food MNEs and how do they affect Hungarian subsidiaries?"

Seeking efficiency in continuously globalizing markets becomes a condition for worldwide competitiveness. Only those enterprises that manage to organise their international business activities within global networks have chances to attain durable worldwide competitiveness (Bartlett and Ghoshal, 1989). The search for synergies between different business units leads to many restructuring operations. Those activities that do not correspond to a targeted profitability or return on investment ratio calculated on a mid-term or long-term basis are considered outlying activities and are sold off as soon as possible. Duplication of a number of functions by these hundreds of subsidiaries and dozens of divisions that composed these giant multi-product multinationals (e.g., Unilever, Nestlé, Sara Lee Corp.) reduced the firms' profitability and economic efficiency.

Host governments influence the globalisation plans of MNEs through trade policies, technical standards and marketing regulations. Measures like high import tariffs and quotas, non-tariff barriers, export subsidies, local content requirements, currency and capital flow restrictions, and requirements on technology transfer affect globalisation strategies of the MNEs. The easing of government restrictions, Yip (1989: 38) argues, "can set off a rush for expanded market participation".

EU membership is an example of such easing of government restrictions. Are the outcomes an expanded market participation and concentration of production? Meyer and Jensen (2003) analyse the effect of EU membership on the corporate strategies of FDI in CEE. They confirm the argument that the removal of trade barriers and the consequent economic integration facilitates the access of western European business to CEE. As trade barriers do not exist any more "operations across Europe will be integrated to a higher degree, which in turn may lead to centralisation of production facilities and therefore closure of peripheral operations" (Meyer and Jensen, 2003: 295). Eden (2001) arrives at the same conclusion, arguing that regional integration leads to improved economies of scale and scope, increased efficiency through the rationalisation and reallocation of firms' activities, and improved interregional linkages. Benito *et al.* (2003: 447) present similar findings, namely that "regional integration promotes the widening of markets, and because "insiders" have easier access to the larger market they are, all else being equal, in a better position than "outsiders" to exploit economies of scale as well as economies of scope".

To summarise, the combination of IB literature and SI approach allows for better understanding of MNEs behaviour in Hungary and more precisely of the forces, which determine the embeddedness of food MNEs in the country. SI approach stresses the importance of national innovation system to attract and to embed FDI by giving special attention to the role of national institutions and government. IB literature sheds a light over the factors, which shape the business strategies of the companies.

The remaining part of the chapter is organised as follows. The *first section* stresses the efforts of the national government to embed FDI through broad policy measures and programmes, which on one side promote linkages between foreign companies and local suppliers, and on the other side, enforce more intensive academia-industry relationships. In this sense, a number of elements of the national innovation system are analysed. The *second section* gives a recent picture of the Hungarian food industry and underlines the challenges the industry faces since EU accession. The *third section* discusses the cases of Unilever, Nestlé and InBev and constitutes the principal empirical contribution of the chapter. The final section concludes.

I. Governmental Policies to Encourage Embeddedness

A. Broad Policy Measures

One of the major actors responsible for competitiveness and development of a country is the *government.* Until EU accession in 2004 the role of Hungarian governments has been very significant in FDI promotion through the introduction of different trade and investment policies to facilitate the linkages between Multinationals and domestic suppliers. These have been high import tariffs; rules of origin; local content requirements; join venture requirements (this was a major policy aim already during the 1980s and a large number of Joint Ventures were established); export performance requirements; fiscal, financial and other initiatives. Trade barriers had a positive influence on local sourcing. For instance, heavy duty was levied on the import of food products into Hungary. In 1997, the rates for industrial products and agricultural and processed food products were 8.2% and 37.1% respectively. Average MFN tariffs were relatively high for imports of agricultural products and prepared food. There was no preferential access for EU and EFTA countries in these areas (WTO, 1998, TPR/S/40). This protectionist policy required foreign investors to look for domestic suppliers in order to reduce production costs and to be more competitive. The representatives of Nestlé, Unilever and InBev all underlined in face-to-face interviews that these measures encouraged their affiliates to cooperate with local suppliers. In short, although raw material sourcing is highly dependent on the global strategy of the mother company and the place of the foreign affiliate in the global production network, in the beginning of 1990s the MNEs in Hungary were "forced" by the government to source many products locally because of the high import barriers.

B. Fiscal Measures to Encourage Innovations

The purchase from domestic companies, however, depends not only on the protection barriers the government introduces but also on the product quality they offer. To increase their competitiveness local firms have to increase efficiency by using modern production facilities, information and communication technologies. A dynamic innovation policy can be important in this respect. Since May 2002, Hungary follows a National Development Plan, also called the Community Support Framework (CSF) document, which sets as a priority the competitiveness of the country through innovation. One of the major challenges in this respect is to overcome the lack of finance. Tax incentives have been introduced to stimulate firms spending more on R&D. Another step forward was the creation of the "Research and Technology Innovation Fund" aimed at creating a stable and reliable financial ground for research, technological development and innovation activities.

The Government established a Research and Technology Innovation Fund, a unique initiative for CEE, to promote demand driven innovation and the knowledge based competitiveness of companies. The Fund is financed by mandatory contributions of all companies registered in Hungary, matched yearly by the government budget. The so-called innovation contribution, based on the percent of the (adjusted) net turnover, for medium size and large companies has grown from 0.2% in 2004 to 0.3% by 2006.

In Hungary, the government has been encouraging R&D since 1997 through fiscal measures related to R&D. These have been R&D tax allowances of 20%. Their rate has jumped in 2000 from 20% to 100%, while the special 300% rule is applicable from 2004. Since 2004, Hungary has used several fiscal measures to stimulate R&D, the most important of which:

- 100% RTD (Research and Technology and Development) corporate tax allowance (also available for subcontracted R&D activities if partner is public/non-profit research site);
- 300% RTD tax allowance if the company lab is located at a university or public research institute;
- In case of SME's, there is a special IPR tax allowance. The emerging costs of getting and maintaining of the patents, utility

model and design in the area of Hungary can be deducted from the corporate income, supposing these costs can not be regarded direct costs of fundamental research, applied research and technological development;
- Others.

Mr. Balogh, Director[1] Innovation Department, Ministry of Economy and Transport, explained that the new fiscal measures have a great impact on the knowledge institutions, local and foreign companies. The higher corporate tax allowance and the mandatory innovation contribution to the Innovation Fund motivate MNEs to cooperate with local universities and research institutes over certain projects. "Instead of paying the Fund's contribution or carrying out own intramural R&D, many companies prefer to buy R&D services from any public or non-profit R&D institution", Mr. Balogh clarified. This led to increase in company's spending for R&D – the share of the business sector in financing Gross Expenditure on R&D (GERD) increased by 2.3 percentage points (rising to 39.4% from 37.1% in 2004).[2] As result of this policy development, research institutes hold much greater funds and undertake more innovative projects. Figure 1 illustrates the strength of linkages between MNEs and local innovative actors. One could see that there is a very strong link between the MNEs and their subsidiaries as they are integrated in the global production network of the mother company. The mandatory contributions to the Innovation Fund contributed for stronger linkages between research institutions and industry (domestic and foreign companies). In addition, the programmes, which the government initiated to support SMEs through different financial measures turned local companies into competitive suppliers to MNEs. Hungary is the only CEE country, where government, business and academia are interconnected. Although the linkages between academia and business are still very fragile, there is a good potential for development in this direction.

---

1 Interview with Mr. Tamas Balogh, Director, Innovation Department, Ministry of Economy and Transport, Republic of Hungary, Budapest, January 2006.

2 *TrendChart Newsletter*, September 2006, Hungary: 2005 R&D statistics published, available at http://www.trendchart.org/tc_article.cfm?ID=3452&NEWSID=19, last accessed May 2007.

Figure 1: MNEs, Domestic Suppliers, the Linkages between the Different Actors of the Hungarian Innovation System

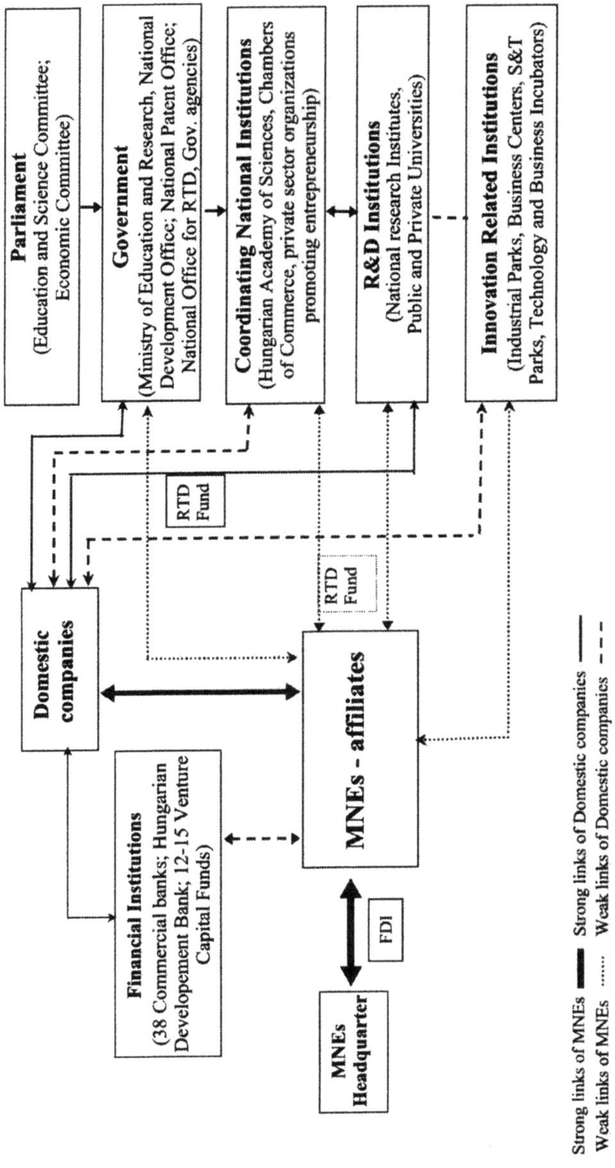

Source: The author, based on European Trend Chart Country Reports, Hungary.

Apart from fiscal measures, further schemes are designed to contribute to enhancing competitiveness via specifically targeting academia-industry relationships, usually by supporting joint development of new products, services and processes. Co-operative Research Centres (CRCs) are being established jointly by higher education organisations, R&D institutes and companies in order to target-oriented RTD co-operation for strategic purposes. One such a programme has been "Regional Knowledge Centres at Universities" which aimed at fostering the creation of research and technological innovation centres at universities in close co-operation with businesses.[3]

C. Programmes Encouraging Linkage Creation

There are two basic approaches to promote linkages. One involves *encouraging linkages* between foreign and local supplier companies *in general*, regardless of the industries involved. The positive effects of this relationship lies in technology transfer, shared information, training provided and giving financial support to supplier companies. The other approach goes further in that it involves the establishment of a linkage promotion programme for *a specific industry*.

As far as the first approach is concerned, an important role in this process of linkage formation is undertaken by the supporting meso-institutions such as chambers of commerce, business associations or providers of business development services. "Without this kind of institutional support, domestic firms may be unable to get a required quality certificate, training or capital needed to become competitive. Moreover, the costs incurred for foreign affiliates may simply be too high for them to get engaged in supplier development activities" (*WIR01:173*). The Agricultural Marketing Centre (AMC), a public benefit company of the Ministry of Agriculture and Regional Development, for example, is an important meso-institution, which contributes for the promotion and upgrading of Hungarian producers. Created in 1997, this institution has launched a project to identify and protect the origins of certain Hungarian products. As result, eleven Hungarian agricultural foodstuffs have been patented with a geography-related trade name (origin labelling and geographical marking) and are on the national register of protected product origin; ten of them have made submissions to the European Union origin protection system for the purpose of recognition and will gain a European market label.[4]

---

3 Trendchart, "Country Report Hungary 2005", available at http://trendchart.cordis.lu/reports/documents/Country_Report_Hungary_2005.pdf, page 34.

4 AMC CD-rom (2005), Collection of Hungary's traditional and Local Agricultural Products.

Mr. Jozsef Urban,[5] project manager, explained that AMC also assists the marketing of Hungarian products with publications, market research, event organisation, participation on international exhibitions and markets. It is enough to enter the building and talk to the people there to feel the professionalism of AMC. The agency experts are open and provide foreign clients a great variety of professionally prepared marketing materials. The agency focuses predominantly on promoting domestic producers. However, AMC does not include in its priority tasks the development and strengthening of the links MNEs – local suppliers. In general, the cooperation between local and foreign companies is not a persistent policy for any agricultural or food authority. Striking are the examples of the National Association of Food Processing Companies and the Hungarian Agricultural Chamber which do not even communicate with MNEs.[6] As an outcome, MNEs consider the role of food meso-institutions not powerful enough to influence their decision to work with local suppliers.

The other approach to increase competitiveness of local firms is by the *establishment of a specific linkage promotion programme* dedicated to increasing and deepening linkages between foreign affiliates and domestic firms.

In Hungary, a linkage promotion programme was introduced already in 1997 under the name Supplier Target Programme. The firms involved were representatives of the automobile industry. The programme aimed at promoting the most promising way of positive FDI spillover effects – the establishment of local supplier ties. However, as Laszlo Kallay[7] from the Ministry of Economy explained, the programme happened to be ineffective. He clarified that Multinational companies were not interested to collaborate with local firms; their first priority was to increase efficiency, not to think for the local development. In this sense, it happened to be quite difficult to promote linkage creation when MNEs were not motivated to participate in this initiative. However, later on, some basic principles of the programme were reconsidered and it was re-launched in 2000 under the name Integrator Supplier Target

---

5 Interview with Mr. Jozsef Urban, Project Manager, Marketing Department, AMC, Budapest (Hungary), April 2005.

6 The Food Association and Hungarian Agricultural Chamber have been absolutely non-cooperative and non-willing to talk about their activities, although I have made many efforts to approach them, including offering to talk to them with a Hungarian interpreter, as nobody there spoke anything, but Hungarian. Later on, after several interviews with foreign producers became clear that these institutions are not recognised as dynamic and efficient organisation s by the food companies.

7 Interview with Laszlo Kallay, Ministry of Economy and Transport, Budapest (Hungary), April 2005.

Programme (ISTP). The basic idea of the new Programme was not to create new linkages, but to develop further the already existing supplier networks in a local cluster. The development of business clusters was also supported by the Széchenyi Plan.[8] The primary purpose was to increase local suppliers' share from the current 10-20% to 30-40%. In the centre of the project was the core company, the Integrator. The Integrator firm was the primary partner of the state agent. The chosen Integrators were Suzuki, General Electric, AUDI, OPEL and Rába. This time the programme seemed to be effective. Training and advising of SMEs, qualification and auditing of supplier members of the programme contributed for the success of the programme. In addition, long-term finance for necessary investments in supplier firms has also been assured; this included both loans and equity participation (venture capital function) (Bacskai *et al.*, 2005).

In short, since mid-1990s Hungary has a policy of strengthening the competitiveness by broad policy measure, fiscal measures for R&D and promotion programmes. Some of the institutions, which promote innovation and technical development, include Hungarian Patent Office, Hungarian Centre for Productivity, Hungarian Innovation Association, The National Office of Research and Technology (NORT).[9] These institutions have been responsible for the improvement of innovation capabilities of SMEs and promotion of the establishment and development of innovative entities among them (Bacskai *et al.*, 2002). Different support programmes for SMEs have been launched since the mid 1990s and include many incentives to encourage the creation of science and technology parks. Local governments and/or agents received payments in order to create industrial parks, industrial clusters, incubator houses as all these contribute to the transfer of know-how from MNEs to domestic enterprises (Szanyi, 2001). All the above mentioned innovation institutions have conducted consultation and training activities and

---

8 The Széchenyi Plan is a medium term development programme of the Hungarian economy for the period 2001-2006. The objectives of the programme are to maintain economic growth, to improve the international competitiveness of the Hungarian economy. It stimulates five major areas: housing; bridge and highway construction; development of the small and medium-sized enterprise sector; tourism; and innovation and R&D (particularly in the field of information technology).

9 NORT devises R&D and innovation programme, manages international R&D cooperation in bilateral and multilateral relations as well as supervises the network of Hungarian science and technology attachés. NORT's activities are guided by the Research and Technological Innovation Council. This 15-strong committee is appointed by the Prime Minister. This body makes the major strategic decisions: what sort of RTDI policy schemes should be launched by NORT, and how much funding to be earmarked for the EU Structural Funds as well as those launched by NORT, and funded by national sources specific schemes.

identified possible financial resources to increase the competitiveness of the local economy. The Hungarian Innovation Association, for instance, has been involved in the legislation process and actively participated in the elaboration of legislation and concepts related to R&D and innovation, by cooperating with other ministries, chambers and organisation s. The question that arises now is, "Have the all above mentioned governmental measures been sufficient to embed MNEs in the local economy and to motivate them to internationalise their R&D centres in Hungary?" Next section traces the answer by presenting the development of Hungarian food industry and showing how deep the linkages between the MNEs and the domestic companies have been after the entrance of the country into EU.

II. Food Industry in Hungary

A. Overview

This section will make a short review of the Hungarian food industry, in order to introduce the reader with the importance and competitiveness of the sector and make him understand in what context MNEs operate. I also analyse the development of agriculture in order to show its potential to supply the food industry. By focusing on the consumer market, I reveal the significant contribution of MNEs for its development and underline that MNEs managed to become important players on it by being market leaders. The knowledge of the Hungarian food industry and consumer market will contribute for the better understanding of the strategies of MNEs in the local market and in the region.

In 2005, the agriculture and food industry contributed 6.8% to the gross domestic product (GDP) of Hungary, the share of food industry being 3.5%. Food processing industry is a traditional for the Hungarian economy and has a strategic role in domestic food supply and export. It occupies second place within the processing industry, which consists of 14 branches. Food industry remains one of the most important sectors in the economy, giving up to 14% of industrial production according to the Hungarian Investment and Trade Development Agency (ITDH).[10] The industry operates with domestic raw materials, purchasing 75% of the agricultural output. About one fifth of the industry's products are sold abroad. The food, drink and tobacco products group represents 6% of

[10] Hungarian Investment and Trade Development Agency (ITDH) (http://www.itdh.hu/itdh/nid/foodprocessing).

Hungary's total exports and 3.5% of imports. The trade balance has remained positive over a long period.[11]

The Food industry is a big employer. Although, during the years the number of workers has decreased it still remains significant. In 2004, it employed close to 120,000 people, which is about 4% of employed Hungarians.

The value of the products of the food and drink industry of the 25-member European Union totals close to 670 billion euro, of which the share of Hungarian products is 1.3%. The production of the Hungarian food industry is approximately identical with that of Portugal, Sweden, Finland, the Czech Republic and Austria. In Hungary, the share of agricultural products, which end primarily in processing, amounts to 66%.[12]

Food manufacturers in Hungary are extremely diversified. There are approximately 8,000 enterprises involved in the food industry, 79% of which are micro-enterprises with less than ten people, 19.8% are small and medium enterprises, while large enterprises with more than 250 employees make up only 1.2%. Considering the shares from production and export, however, the proportion is the other way around; the large companies have a share in 64% of production and 72% of exports. Large multinational companies are strongly represented in some branches of the industry, like vegetable oil and margarine industry, confectionary industry, brewing and tobacco industry. FDI contributed for factories' modernisation and increase in the production efficiency. The inflow of foreign capital also helped develop competition and marketing in the food-processing sector, which was previously structured in such a way that production units served their own local areas and often the Soviet market, free from any real competition (Hastenberg, 1999). Investments in the food processing industry increased the competitiveness of the sector by raising market adaptability, productivity, and the speed of concentration. The priority has been to conform to EU standards in quality, food safety, animal protection, hygiene and environmental protection.

The productivity of the industry, however, is still modest. A transformation of the production structure, increase of utilisation of capacity,

---

11 Ministry of Agriculture and Rural Development, Hungary (2005) The Hungarian Agriculture and Food Industry in Figures, Department of International Relations, available at http://www.fvm.hu/doc/upload/200601/stat_2005_angol.pdf, last accessed May 2007, page 37.

12 *Ibid.*, pp. 37-39.

and greater specialisation remain important tasks.[13] The food processing industry depends on a well-developed agricultural production sector capable of delivering large volumes of high quality raw products. This is critical if Hungary is to compete with other nations in the EU. Small volumes of raw products supplied on an inconsistent basis will not allow for the development of a food processing industry that meets the quality and efficiency standards of EU competition.

B. Consumer Market

The modernisation of food industry changed the trends in Hungary's consumer market.

It is increasingly converging to the consumption patterns of Western European countries. Still 38% of the population is considered to have traditional eating habits, but there are more and more "modern consumers". These are Hungarians typically between the ages of 25 and 29, which reside in urban areas and come from higher income backgrounds.[14] As Hungarians increasingly lead busier lifestyles, the demand for processed foods, which are predominantly offered, by food MNEs is also growing. These include breakfast cereals, dairy products, frozen foods, ice cream and frozen yoghurt, snacks, nuts, and alcoholic beverages.

For 2004, Hungarians gave about 25% of their income on food and beverages. This number has been decreasing in recent years and trending toward that of high-income countries where consumers typically spend 10% of their income on food. At the same time, 31% of total food expenditure goes toward food for consumption outside of the home.

The domestic retail food sector underwent significant changes. The key drivers for change were the demand for foreign branded goods with which Hungarian consumers were increasingly familiar through the media and foreign travel. In addition, big hypermarkets offer high comfort as they propose great variety of products and in some cases at the cheapest possible price (Lidl, for example). Food MNEs also prefer working with western retail chains as most of them are global partners with whom they have long-term relations. In addition, retailers stipulate a quality standard, which is very important for the work of the food

---

13 Ministry of Agriculture and Regional Development, Hungary Future of Food Industry in the CEE and NIS, Expert Papers, Technology Foresight Summit Budapest,
27-29 March 2003.

14 Government of Canada, Marketing Report: Agri-Food Past, Present & Future Report Hungary, November 2005 (http://atn-riae.agr.ca/europe/4079_e.pdf), last accessed May 2007.

processors. By introducing consumers to new varieties or products of higher quality with a longer shelf life, retail chains are increasingly shifting consumer demand towards healthier foods.

Hungary has been one of the most important expansion markets for western retail groups since the early 1990s, and many of the continent's big names are present in the country, although a few local players are still holding their own. By the end of 2005, the competition had become stronger between hypermarkets and discounters. In 2005, Tesco was the most progressive chain, opening almost twenty new outlets, while the new discount chain Lidl had more than fifty outlets by the end of 2005. The discount channel Plus changed its strategy, and, like Lidl, offered fewer branded and more private label products (Euromonitor International, 2006).

The Market leader is Metspa, a joint venture between Germany's Metro group and the Austrian Spar business, with sales of €1.6 billion in 2002, according to a recent list compiled by M+M. But Hungarian-owned CBA Kereskedelmi and Co-op Hungary are not far behind, with sales of €1.4 billion and €1.23 billion respectively, just ahead of British market leader Tesco with €1.15 billion.[15]

53% of the retail grocery sector in Hungary was controlled by international retail chains in 2003.[16] The changing environment of retail distribution is positively affecting food sales – hypermarkets and supermarkets enjoy substantial market power. In fact, about 35% of households in Hungary already shop in hypermarkets (11% of the consumers buy their food from supermarkets).[17] The increasing presence of retail chains reinforces the position of hypermarkets as families decide to carry out one large weekend shop (Euromonitor International, 2005).

The Hungarian consumer groups are becoming more segmented as the income gap between the wealthy and poor grows. Due to this difference, consumer demand for cheap food products and expensive luxury items increases. The cheapest food is offered by discounters, 21% of

---

15 Food and Drink Europe.Com, Lidl Planning Hungarian Rollout, 7 January 2004, available at http://www.foodanddrinkeurope.com/news/ng.asp?id=48848-lidl-planning-hungarian, last accessed May 2007.

16 Government of Canada, Marketing Report: Agri-Food Past, Present & Future Report Hungary, November 2005 (http://atn-riae.agr.ca/europe/4079_e.pdf), last accessed May 2007.

17 GFK Marketing Agency, The results of the project "Shopping Monitor Central and Eastern Europe", 7 February 2006, available at http://www.gfk.at/de/default.aspx?path=/de/press/releases/reader.aspx&msg=943&lng=EN&ctr=204, last accessed May 2007.

Hungarian shoppers choose the low-price format.[18] In Hungary, Tesco's hypermarkets are the most popular, taking 18% of shoppers. Not surprisingly, the penetration of private labels is also increasing. Private labels are already well established in Hungary with 68% of shoppers saying that they buy them on a regular basis. A very big challenge for the Hungarian producers was the entrance of the Lidl chain into the discount market. This was the most important event in Hungarian retail trade in 2004 as the chain offers 20% lower prices than the EU average. Lidl is characterised with a lot of private label and exclusive brands in its selection, and imports many of the products in its portfolio thus being a tense competitor to local manufacturers. However, the flood of cheap retailers on the Hungarian market is just a piece of all the challenges, which the local food industry faces.

C. EU Impact on MNEs

In May 2004, Hungary joined the EU. This had a significant impact on food industry as it faced more intense competition. The relatively safe and protected Hungarian market could no longer exist. EU membership resulted in large restructurings in the local economy.

In economic terms, the sector is practically integrated in the EU's food industry. According to ITDH, 50% of the investments in the sector are from EU investors, and 80% of the export goes to other EU countries. Since 2001, the trade turnover of organisation s classified as belonging to the food industry has grown annually, in 2004, by 3%. A decisive percentage of exports were aimed at the inner-European Union market where market expansion could be reached as result of accession to the EU. The proportion of imported raw and processed foods from the European Union Member States is significant. ITDH reports that because of accession, this proportion is growing faster than that of exports.

EU membership facilitated MNEs to follow their global strategies oriented towards increased competitiveness. The accession of ten countries to the EU on May 1 meant that export quotas, customs levies and export subsidies are lifted between existing and new Member States. The null tariff barriers since 2004 allowed MNEs to import products from all over Europe. It was no longer possible to force the companies to source locally; there was a global supply chain. MNEs do economies of scales thanks to concentration of production, e.g. the different products from the global portfolio are manufactured in different countries and the products are exported to the others. The standardised products,

[18] CEE FoodIndustry.com, "Central Europe: Hypermarkets Poised for Rapid Growth", 24 February 2004, available at http://www.cee-foodindustry.com/news/ng.asp?n=50123-central-europe-hypermarkets, last accessed May 2007.

e.g. the global brands can be imported easily from one EU country to another. To increase competitiveness MNEs put efforts to optimise productivity and reduce costs, which often results in plant closures. As the government cannot be protectionist any more and the competition from EU firms is tougher, MNEs started to pull out of Hungary.

A good example is Kraft Foods – the leading manufacturer of confectionery on the Hungarian market. The number one market share did not stop the company from relocating confectionery production to Bratislava to reduce costs. The company has also been the third largest producer of coffee on the Hungarian market, but relocating production to Vienna, Austria seemed more efficient. The company closed down its only production facility in Hungary in the first half of 2004 with the loss of 320 jobs. The management justified the closure of the Hungarian plant with its four-pillar plan for "sustainable growth". The plan emphasises investment in brand development, whilst trying to reduce costs for the company's overall structure. Although Kraft Foods does not have any more production facilities, in Hungary, the company confirmed that its existing lines of Kraft products would continue to be sold on the local market and that for the most part the products would be imported from the Vienna and Bratislava plants. Even the fact that company was market leader did not stop the management to close the plant and the Hungarian government could not do anything to react to this.

Another example is Unilever, which closed its margarine and salad dressing plant in Budapest. Unilever relocated production to plants in Katowice in Poland, Pratau in Germany and Nelahozeves in Czech Republic. The company dismissed 200 workers at the plant, which closed in 2006.[19] Unilever wanted to cut operation costs to serve better its largest central European markets in Poland and Germany from closer locations. The company will continue to operate three other plants in Hungary, which make instant soup and ice cream.

The story of the margarine factory is interesting. It was acquired in 1992. The company was owned by Unilever before it was nationalised in 1948, and it produced under the license of Unilever afterwards. In short, Unilever had very strong links with this specific factory. The plant was producing the local margarine brand Delma and the global brand Rama solely for the Hungarian market. After the acquisition, the company invested heavily in new equipment in order to increase production capacity and the quality of the products. The Budapest-based plant turned into one of the best Unilever plants (Hastenberg, 1999).

---

19 *Népszabadság*, 24 January 2006.

Despite this rich history of Unilever's margarine plant Unilever is going to close it in mid-2006 and move its production to other countries. This is in line with the global restructuring of the company aiming to increase efficiency and has been facilitated by the entrance of Hungary into the EU.

Before EU entry one would certainly claim that the two above-mentioned companies have been embedded in the local economy – they invested heavily; they were market leaders and they sourced many products locally. In addition, as seen from the previous section, the Hungarian government has done a lot to improve its innovation system. It was EU entrance, which led to the questioning of their embededness in the Hungarian economy.

The next section presents the actions of Unilever, InBev and Nestlé in Hungary. The interviews with the management staff of these companies reveal the strategies, which dictate their operations. Business managers have been directly asked about their relations with local suppliers, research institutes and universities, and retailers.

III. Unilever, Nestlé and InBev

A. Unilever, Hungary

Unilever started its expansion into the central and east European marketplace in the early 1990s. Unilever Magyarország Kft was established in 1991 and entered into the ice cream and the margarine and detergent business through acquisitions, rapidly becoming a dominant player in the Hungarian consumer marketplace.[20] In addition to its well-known international brands, Unilever acquired a wide range of domestic brands, which have subsequently been integrated into its portfolio. Unilever Hungary boasts several manufacturing facilities in Hungary, as well as a research and development centre in Nyírbátor in Eastern Hungary.

Mr. Hans Buss[21] the former vice-chairman of Unilever Hungary and East Central Europe was contacted to discuss Unilever's policies. Mr. Buss was directly involved in the negotiations for CEE acquisitions and he mentioned that Unilever was interested in Central and Eastern European markets since 1988. The first negotiation about a joint-venture with a Hungarian Company took place in February 1988. In mid-1991, Unilever started to build the Hungarian business in Foods, Ice Cream,

---

20 *Budapest Sun*, 9-15 June 2005.

21 Interview with Mr. Hans Buss, former Vice-chairman of Unilever Hungary and South Central Europe, Budapest, Hungary, January 2006.

Frozen Products, Detergents and Personal Care. The company introduced its global brands; however, it kept strong local brands, for example: Delma, Biopon, Amodent, Baba. It produces or distributes margarines (Rama, Delma, Flora), dehydrated stocks (Knorr), mustards, ketchups, mayonnaises, teas (Lipton), ice creams (Carte d'Or, Magnum, Vienetta, Cornetto), cleaning supplies (Biopon, Domestos, CIF), soaps, shampoos and body care products (Baba, Dove, Sunsilk, Signal, Amodent). Since 1992 Unilever is a market leader in the fast moving consumer goods in Hungary – margarines, tea-based drinks, ice creams, domestic cleaning products and tooth-care products. Since 1996, Unilever Hungary developed the countries of former Yugoslavia, Bulgaria and Albania.

According to Mr. Buss the major factors, which explain the higher level of embeddedness of Unilever subsidiaries in Hungary and Czech Republic compared to Bulgaria and Romania, are: the stage of economic development, the legislative framework of the country, transparency in the privatisation schemes in early 1990s.

In comparison, in Bulgaria and Romania the move to the market economy came later; the privatisation schemes were not clear and the legislative framework was not developed. In these circumstances, the risk to invest in these countries was rather high. "If you are not sure that you will get your money back when you invest, you simply do not go on for this", Mr. Buss said. "We were in negotiation process for acquisition of some Bulgarian and Romanian factories, however, the uncertainty was high". In Romania Unilever bought a detergent company later on; in Bulgaria, Kaliakra, the margarine company. The Bulgarian subsidiary is relatively small and is governed by the Unilever Romania. In 1997, because of the political and financial crisis in Bulgaria, Unilever closed its operation and then came back to Bulgaria in 1998.

How did Unilever decide which local companies to acquire? Mr. Buss explained that Unilever has a very clearly defined strategy in which markets to enter. First, their strategy was to pick-up the best companies, no matter big or small. Second, speed dictated their approach as the competitive advantage of being the first mover was crucial. Third, Unilever's idea was to buy local well-known products, which could become strong brands.

Unilever has one operation in each of the countries in CEE, but in some countries, there could be more than one factory: e.g. Unilever Hungary runs four factories[22] with approximately 1500 employees.

---

[22] Since June 2006 Hungary subsidiary would run three factories.

The strategy of Unilever is not to produce all brands everywhere that is why in each country they are specialised in different products depending on the facilities of a certain country (in Bulgaria – margarine; in Romania – detergent business; in the Czech republic mainly food business, in Hungary – food, ice cream detergents, personal care). All countries enrich their portfolios with global brands by importing them from where the products are manufactured.

As regards the backward integration of Unilever, this is a permanently changing process, Mr. Buss underlined. Back in *1992, Unilever had very strong backward integration with local suppliers*. More than 90% of the raw materials, e.g. sunflower and rape were locally sourced. The rationale was that governments limited imports into each country by high import regimes and Unilever was very much forced to work locally. Packing suppliers were also locals, although many of them were later purchased by Unilever's Western packing suppliers, which came to Hungary together with Unilever. In any case, local packing suppliers benefited because they got Unilever's know-how in packing and introduced western quality standards. When Unilever acquired a factory there was a network of suppliers and they used it, however they also developed new suppliers themselves and many western suppliers also came. Nowadays, Unilever *goes in a direction of globalisation of its sourcing networks*. Mr. Buss pointed that all CEE countries are fully integrated in Unilever's global networks.

Unilever worked closely with a number Hungarian Universities and business schools for recruitment of young trainees and qualified staff. The student organisation s AIESEC and IAESTE did a survey, asking who the most preferred employer is and the results showed that Unilever could score number one in several years of the mid 1990s. The strategy of Unilever was to train its managers and the best of them were to be trained abroad. In Hungary and in the Czech Republic, Romania, Unilever has internal R&D centres responsible for some categories of products. Unilever has its own network of R&D centres. It has market research everywhere, while basic research is done only in home countries with personnel from all over the world. Unilever contributed to the local development also by introducing standards to consumer goods. However, Mr. Buss considered management development as the strongest contribution of his company to the Hungarian economy. He underlined that this was much more than helping suppliers to upgrade. Unilever came with an "army" of expatriates to train youngsters and to help for the creation of one integrated Unilever. Of course, technology investments were also an important benefit for Hungary.

In the beginning of 1990s Unilever used predominantly local retailers; others, were simply not existing. In addition: "Local retailers did not know too much about the integrated supply chain and we tried to develop them. They had no capital and limited know-how", Mr. Buss mentioned. Since 1994 Western retail chains entered the Hungarian market and this situation changed.

Nowadays, Unilever distributes partly directly to the mainly large size retailers and partly through its concessionaire distributors to small size retailers. Distributors sell two thirds of the overall production of the company. "Unilever itself is also engaged into a kind of retailing. Under the name Algida Express ice creams and other deep frozen products are distributed directly to the consumers on the street from vans in regular, scheduled journeys".[23]

Concerning domestic competitors "Unilever does not have such as most of them disappeared or occupy the low-market niches in Hungary", said Mr. Buss. Unilever works with the local branch associations and governmental institutions. Mainly their cooperation aims at creating a favourable legislative framework. The associations, which have been of particular importance for Hungary and Unilever, were the Branded Association and the Food and Detergent Association.

Mr. Antoine De-Saint-Affrique,[24] Chairman of Hungary, Croatia, Slovenia until 2005, enriched the picture about the strategy of Unilever in Hungary. When asked whether Unilever had a regional investment strategy plan, which pre-determined the level of investment in a certain country, he confirmed that there was such a plan. However, he added, this plan was influenced by the level of development of the country. "The more developed a country was the more investments it attracted", said Mr. Affrique. This explains why Unilever invested much more in Hungary than in Bulgaria and Romania.

The duration of the partnership mattered. Unilever had good relationship with Hungary since the 1970s (different brands of Unilever were produced under brand licenses – Rama margarine, for example). Otherwise, Unilever, invested heavily in Hungary in the beginning of 1990s.

The basic reason to invest in Hungary, first and foremost was the strong opportunities the company saw in the local market. Secondly, the company was attracted by the proximity of the Western and Central European markets. The stable political and economic situation also had an impact over the decision; the legal context of the country mattered.

---

23 Hungarian Competition Authority, available at http://www.gvh.hu/index.php?id=4021&l=e, last accessed October 2006.

24 Interview with Mr. Antoine De-Saint-Affrique, Chairman for Hungary, Croatia, Slovenia, Budapest (Hungary), October 2004.

Then, the strategic decisions of Unilever were influenced by the production performance of the sector, the low labour costs, etc.

Unilever produces for the local market, mainly, but also for export – to Eastern and Western Europe, it exports ice-cream and detergents. In 2004, Mr. Affrique was asked, "Is it possible to close a plant in Hungary?" He said the following: "One should distinguish between two things: a) to shut down totally all activities of the subsidiary and b) a closure of a product line or reduction of the production in general. What concerns the first, it is quite difficult a subsidiary to be shut down completely. It can happen under some force major circumstances like a war (as in the case of ex-Yugoslavia, or political instability etc.). Concerning the second option, to close a plant, this might happen at some point as Unilever *has a global supply chain strategy* and a certain product can be imported from somewhere instead of being produced in Hungary". Two years later, it became clear that this moment had arrived as Unilever closed its Hungarian margarine plant.

As far as retailers are concerned, Mr. Affrique said that it is a must for Unilever to work both with local and foreign retailers. In Hungary, for example COOP is an extremely mobile and strong local retail chain with which Unilever has good relationship. The subsidiary tries to find a good balance between the two types of retailers local and foreign.

Unilever cooperates with universities and professional schools as it needs a qualified labour force and there should not appear a vacuum for a labor supply. Does Unilever receive help from the local branch associations, business centres, or agencies for regional development? – Mr. Affrique pointed, "Unilever is on one side a MNE, but on the other side is a local company". Hence, they work within the national legacy and with the local authorities. No specific support or relations have been underlined.

Unilever Hungary uses a mix of local and western banks, but they do not use them for credits – this is a decision taken on at the level of headquarters. The strategy of Unilever towards suppliers is a balance of global and local suppliers according to the interest of the company. Global suppliers are related to logistic services, telecommunications, packaging. Local suppliers they use to provide them with raw materials, packaging, and some services.

Unilever's strategy towards local competitors is to compete with them in different ways. There is no such a thing as a "small" competitor. Local competitors deserve a lot of attention. In Croatia and Slovenia, Unilever has distribution agreements with some of its competitors. The Hungarian subsidiary is independent from the headquarters in its everyday decisions, but is *dependent on global decisions*.

B. InBev, Hungary B.

In Hungary, only a few local brewers owned by large international holdings are active. Currently, there are four big beer producers on the Hungarian market – Borsodi Brewery (InBev), Brau Union Hungarian Breweries (Heineken Group), Dreher Breweries (SAB), Pecs Brewery (Ottakringer group, Vienna). In addition to introducing new products, brewers add innovative forms of packaging for their traditional beer products from year to year. Beer produced in Hungary is traditionally of excellent quality.[25]

Mr. Feher,[26] Communications Director explained, "Beer is expensive to transport as it contains water and is heavy". Therefore, for breweries it is clear that if they want a certain market they had to buy an enterprise there. When Interbrew (since 2004 InBev) was in the process of negotiation to buy a Hungarian brewery a spontaneous privatisation was undertaken, e.g. there was still no privatisation agency. Heineken was also negotiating for Borsodi but while Interbrew was interested to buy good local brands, Heineken only sought good facilities. This contributed to Interbrew achieving ownership of Bersodi in 1991, as its strategy included the retention of local brands. This acquisition led to significant changes in the life of the brewery, as privatisation gave new momentum to the procedures aiming at the improvement of quality, technologies and products. Yet, "buying a local brand is a risky business", Mr. Feher admitted, as the brewery might face market difficulties if there are economic or political changes.

The success of InBev in Hungary motivated the HQ (headquarters) to start a process of acquisitions on a broader scale in CEE. Since 1991, InBev bought companies in Romania, the Czech Republic, Poland, and Russia. In Bulgaria, following the same strategy to keep local brands, Interbrew bought several breweries as they were quite cheap, however, they could not maintain the brand portfolio and lost market share.

In Hungary InBev owns one factory Borsod Sörgyár Rt. with 550 employees and an office in Budapest where sales managers are situated. InBev had also a malt plant, which was sold in 2004. Borsodi is one of Hungary's largest breweries, which started producing beer and malt in 1973, in the suburbs of Bõcs, a settlement located in the vicinity of Miskolc.

---

25 Association of Hungarian Brewers, "Annual Report 2004" available at http://www.merlin.hu/referenciak/mssz/2004eves.pdf, last accessed May 2007.

26 Interview with Mr. Imre Feher, Communications Director, InBev, Budapest (Hungary), 2006.

Hungary and Czech Republic are rather mature markets. Borsodi is a market leader in Hungary; however, its advantage over the second ranked company is just 2-3%.

In the socialist times, all breweries had well defined regions in Hungary where they operated. There was no competition among the breweries about regional markets. Borsodi was responsible for the Eastern part of Hungary and served this market. After the privatisation process in the early 1990s all breweries became competitors as they were fighting for the largest possible share of Hungarian market. Borsodi Sörgyár Rt. managed to stay one of the biggest players on the market and has further strengthened its position on the Hungarian beer market by offering a wide choice of brands to beer drinkers. The principal brand of the brewery is "Borsodi Sör" the biggest selling beer brand in Hungary. In order to maintain and improve the market position of this best-known and most popular brand, "Borsodi", the factory pursues intense marketing communication activities. The brewery regularly participates in the organizing and sponsoring of various sport events (both mass events and professional competitions) and music. In addition to "Borsodi Sör", other members of the Borsodi family are "Borsodi Barna" (a brown beer), "Borsodi Póló" (an alcohol free beer), and the new brand "Borsodi Bivaly" ("The Buffalo of Borsodi") introduced to the market in 2003. "Borsodi Bivaly" is a lager with an alcohol content of 6.5% ABV (the result of domestic research and development), that created a new segment in the Hungarian market of sales.

Borsodi cooperates with Miskols University for market research projects. The University also has a post-graduate programme where Borsodi's personnel are trained. The other university with which Borsodi cooperates is Kerteszeti Egyetem (Food and Agricultural University), Budapest, which prepares food engineers.

During the spring of 2003, Borsodi Sörgyár introduced an innovative product, a new Hungarian premium brand called "Borostyán" ("Amber"). In the wide range of products offered by the brewery there is another popular premium brand of the Hungarian market – this, the global brand Stella Artois and "Stella Artois NA", an alcohol free beer. This is one of the dynamically developing brands of the premium segment of Hungarian beer market that has significantly expanded its position during the last years. Among the product of the brewery there are "Holsten", the "light" American "Rolling Rock", the traditional "Kinizsi" beer and the favourites of connoisseur beer drinkers, the imported "Staropramen", "Leffe", and "Hoegaarden" beers.

In Hungary, there is a strong Czech beer culture and that is why Borsodi decided to import Staropramen, Mr. Feher explained. In addition, there is a strong Czech film culture, every year there is a festival of the

Czech cinema and Czech companies subsidised the marketing of Staropramen. HQ agreed to import Staropramen in Hungary but they were sceptical about import of the beer in the CEE region as a whole as this could have been non-profitable. The company also offers the global brands Brahma and Beck's, the latter brewed in Hungary. The key factors of the company success are the long-term strategic planning, the consequent brand construction, and the permanently *excellent quality*, the *European level of productiveness*, the *outstanding cost efficiency* and the *innovating practices* of the company.[27] InBev's results are due to its quick-to-respond attitude and its flexibility, with which it reacts to consumer and market demands, as well as its product and packaging innovations, which enable it to act as a trend-setter in the Hungarian beer market.

At the beginning of the 1990s, when Interbrew bought the Borsodi plant the beer was low quality and very cheap. The main consumers were low class people working in heavy industry. When they were laid off and hence became unemployed the consumption of beer considerably decreased. At the same time, the price of beer also went up and this additionally shrank the beer market. Hungarians used to consume over 100 litres of beer *per capita*; however, the average beer consumption *per capita* decreased and now (2006) is around 72 litres. "Approaching the over 100 litres *per capita* beer consumption characterizing 1970s and 1980s no longer seems to be a realistic target," said Mr. Feher. He pointed that there was very high levels of competition from wine producers. Wine consumption became trendy in Hungary and took a bigger and bigger market share. There are many good private wineries and many people prefer drinking high quality wine, which is considered very healthy. In addition, many Parliament members have wineries and the excise on the wine is very low (for years there was no excise duty on wine production at all). As many of the beer consumers are mainly low income people, a strong factor contributing to the decrease of beer consumption is the so called "junk wine" – a beverage made of chemicals and very cheap with 12% alcohol. It is a beverage, which has been produced illegally and has attracted clients with low-incomes. Put it differently, 30% of beer market has gone and there is no perspective that it shall be recovered. Borsodi has 3 ml Hl productive capacity but sold 2.26 million hectolitres of beer in 2004, which is 1.3% less than in 2003. The company's net sales returns decreased by 4.6% compared to 2003 because of a strong competition from low-price imported beer. In contrast to earlier years, the company's before-tax profit underwent a

[27] Association of Hungarian Brewers, "Annual Report 2003" available at http://www.merlin.hu/referenciak/mssz/2003eves.pdf, last accessed May 2007.

drastic fall of 45%, decreasing to HUF 4 billion in 2004, for which the recent flood of cheap, imported beers accounted.[28]

In response to customer demand and following international tendencies, brewers in Hungary have successfully increased the share of beer sold in aluminium cans on the market.[29] As a rather adverse development in the years before 2004, the gradual saturation of the consumer market was coupled by a significant, if not dramatic increase in the level of the most important taxes in the sector: consumer tax and excise tax. Since 1990s, the excise duty increased gradually Mr. Feher explained. In 2006 excise for 0.5l bottle for example is 25 HUF; VAT in 2006 is 20% (used to be 25% in 2004). Although VAT decreased, the excise increased and so the price of the beer did not go down. Put it differently, there is around a 50% tax burden over beer.

Until 2004, the Hungarian beer market had been closed. Hungary's accession to the European Union brought about fundamental changes in the situation of the brewers on the Hungarian market. As of May 2004 all import restrictions and levies on beer produced in other EU Member States were lifted and even import duties to non-EU members decreased significantly (Hungary faces competition from Croatia). This resulted in an excessive volume of cheap canned beer being dumped on the Hungarian market, which had a significant negative impact on the local brewers' positions. Another reason for the flood of canned beer in Hungary was that in January 2004 the German Bundestag introduced environmental law according to which producers had to pay a deposit fee of 0.25 cents on a beer can in a drive to reduce garbage. The legislation in one sense proved to be dramatically successful; the German beer market had to switch from cans to renewable packaging. However, this left German brewers with underused canning lines and desperate for new markets. In Hungary, beer had good prices and beers in can were considered premium. This motivated German beer producers to export their can production to Hungary in order to get rid of the stock they had. "In Hungary multinational retailers are very strong and a German producer can easily sell its production because retailers were interested to sell cheap products", the communication manager of InBev clarified. "Moreover, beer is one of the so-called attractive products as it invites customers to enter the supermarket. This additionally motivated retail chains to have cheap beers". By June 2004, the Hungarian market was flooded with cans. It was physically impossible for InBev (Borsodi) to produce a beer in a can at this price. However, the company reacted to

28 Association of Hungarian Brewers, "Annual Report 2004" available at http://www.merlin.hu/referenciak/mssz/2004eves.pdf, last accessed May 2007.

29 *Ibid.*

this market challenge and now the situation is not the same. Borsodi worked with the Government over a new environmental legislation promoting renewable packing. The law is in power since January 2005 and puts limitations on can production. If a certain producer exceeds its quota (ratio) then he has to pay a penalty tax. This is also valid for retailers. This way producers and retail chains are no longer motivated to sell unlimited quantities of cheap beer in cans. However, it should be taken into consideration that for the beer business, price has become more and more crucial factor. Retailers introduce their own private label beers to satisfy low-income market niche. And, even though the beer, which they distribute is often of lower quality, it still attracts many clients.

As far as the governance of the company is concerned, Borsodi has always been governed by local managers. At the first years of investment there were 2-3 foreign managers, but as the operation process was going smoothly the governance was transferred to locals. However, since 2005, the policies of InBev have changed and from January 2006 Borsodi will have again a foreigner as an executive director. This is a result of the global strategic reorganisation of InBev since December 2005. In the past, the HQ did not intervene locally as far as market share was growing. Now the situation has changed and the HQ uses more centralised approach. In any case, marketing activities for Borsodi beers are local; for Stella Artois, they are global.

Borsodi gets also centralised orders, which suppliers use, to determine at what price and under what conditions to work with them. Purchasing of malt is also centralised after the sale of the malt plant to InBev's global suppliers and hence the HQ negotiates with them. Packaging activities are centralised. IT issues are also centrally negotiated. Energy supply is local. Some years ago, back in 2001 for example, Hungarian brewers including Interbrew paid special attention to purchasing input materials locally (agricultural materials, packaging materials, chemicals, fuels and electricity), and were thus considered to be major drivers of raw material and energy demand in Hungary.[30]

Since 2004, following two major events, Interbrew became the global world leader InBev, and Hungary entered EU the picture is a little bit different. Borsodi turned into a highly centralised subsidiary completely integrated in the global supply chain of the mother company. The suppliers are centrally approved, the executive director is a foreigner, every activity is reported to the HQ and all decisions are concentrated on regional or global level (the only exception are sales issues).

30 Association of Hungarian Brewers, "Annual Report 2001" available at http://www.merlin.hu/referenciak/mssz/2001eves.pdf, last accessed May 2007.

C. Nestlé, Hungary

Nestlé Hungary runs five factories in Hungary in Szerencs, Diósgyôr, Bük, Kékkút and Törökbálint. Nestlé entered the Hungarian market in 1991 acquiring two chocolate factories in Szerencs and Diósgyôr. Initially, there were three confectionary companies in Hungary – Budapest Chocolate Company; Győri biscuits (privatised by Danone) and Szerencs Company. Nestlé bought the last one. Since 1992, Nestlé has permanently enriched its businesses. In 1998, Nestlé group acquired pet food company Jupiter in Bük close to the Austrian border. Moreover, Nestlé has chosen Budapest as a location of its CEE pet food headquarters. The reasons were: 1) the company had good traditions in Hungary; 2) the production of pet-food in Hungary was relatively cheaper compared to Western Europe; 3) before 2004, there existed a "custom curtain" between CEE and WE, and therefore many products had to be produced locally. In 2000, Nestlé acquired water business in Kékkút, and in 2003, further extended its activities into ice-cream business in Törökbálint. The group has between 1500 and 2000 employees as they use seasonal workers also mainly in the Ice Cream and Water Businesses.

In Hungary, the company is present on the market with instant coffee, chocolate and confectionery, culinary products, cocoa powders, breakfast cereals, infant nutrition, pet food, mineral water, ice cream and frozen foods.

Mr. Kapus[31] explained that Nestlé Hungary enriches its portfolio with imports of products from neighbouring countries like confectionary products from the Czech Republic; Kit-Kat from Bulgaria; chocolate waffles from Romania. Hungary normally exports beverages to the other CEE markets. In short, in line with the global restructuring of Nestlé, every country is specialised in the production of certain products.

The high volume of investment of Nestlé in Hungary Mr. Kapus justifies with the early openness of the Hungarian economy. The entrepreneurship in Hungary has been encouraged since 1980s when many foreign companies started to collaborate with local companies either by creating co-packing agreements with them or by licensing agreements. Nestlé had a licensing agreement with Szerencs plant and later on, the group acquired the same company as they already had good business partnership relations. In short, Nestlé bought plants, which previously produced Nestlé's products, and at the same time these products were a core priority for Nestlé. In any case, in early 1990s, Hungary had a competitive advantage over all countries from the region as it had well

31 Interview with Mr. Kapus, HR Manager, Nestlé, Budapest (Hungary), 2006.

trained workers and semi-workers who had good willingness to work and management cadres who spoke foreign languages. In addition, it had a relatively advanced financial system and reasonable infrastructure. Hungarian customers were used to Western products; probably they purchased the highest quantity of "western" goods among the CEE countries. The Nestlé Group is the biggest food company in the world and its products have been well known in Hungary even before the company decided to be among the first foreign investors in the country.

In the early 1990s customs barriers were very high, so MNEs had to buy local companies if they wanted to be present at a certain market. After CEFTA (Central European Free Trade Agreement), the circumstances changed and so did Nestlé. It introduced a regional strategy, the essence of which was a specialisation of different countries in different products and the importation of all other products from the portfolio from neighbouring CEE countries.

In the late 1990s, Nestlé closed one plant, Zamat, which used to be a grind roasted coffee factory. The rationale behind the closure was that this was not a core business; some of Zamat's activities like the production of Nesquick were transferred to Szerencs. In the first years of investment Nestlé had to restructure the newly acquired plants as they had very low efficiency levels and very wide product ranges. In Szerencs, for example 1600 people worked, producing less than 10,000 t. of products. Now there work 350 people producing 25,000 t. This change may be attributed to the replacement of the handmade production of chocolate and sugar products with automated beverages.

Nestlé's supply is organised on global scale. There is the so-called Euro purchasing team, which is responsible for the whole Europe, for example, the purchasing of different types of packaging materials such as boxes, bottles, etc. The Hungarian purchasing manager is responsible for the purchases for the Czech Republic and Poland. There is a global tendency of standardisation of packaging materials.

To illustrate better the global supply chain of Nestlé, let us take for example the production of beverages. The raw materials are cocoa or coffees, which are imported from Germany or Spain. The jars come from Poland and the filling is made in Hungary and the production uses only the best suppliers in the region.

The production of Nesquick presents another example of the production chain. The raw materials are sugar and cocoa powder. Cocoa powder is imported from the Czech Republic. The sugar is imported from abroad, as the *next door* sugar company does not cover Nestlé's criteria – the highest quality at the lowest possible price. According to this principle Nestlé chooses suppliers – no matter local or global. The foreign supplier charges lower prices and carry better quality products. These lower prices abroad are a result of long-term contracts for world-wide supplies in large quantities. This enables Nestlé group to buy raw materials and semi-manufactured articles at very favourable prices. Nestlé makes use of such networks of approved suppliers for worldwide supplies. Besides this, Hungarian local suppliers generally cannot offer the large quantities involved, so they have little chance of becoming an approved supplier.

Nestlé distributes its products through local and foreign retail chains. The company works with the local retailers such as COOP, CBA; and multinational chains such as TESCO or AUCHAN and METRO. The foreign chains have greater market share and hence they sell most of Nestlé's products. Nestlé pursues a "wherever, whenever, however" distribution strategy, specifically designed to find alternative distribution channels to the food retailers for products such as pet food, ice cream and bottled water. There is a special team in Nestlé Hungary, which is responsible for alternative channels of distribution such as corner shops or petrol stations.

Nestlé collaborates with Technical University Budapest and Budapest University of Economics. However, the company does not have any special contracts with them as every year the company employs very few of the graduates of these universities. However, the company stays in touch with the younger generation, as it is the basic consumer of Nestlé's products.

"Different governments have different attitude to Nestlé", Mr. Kapus said. The previous government, which was conservative, rather supported the local small and medium entrepreneurs, while the present social-liberal government recognised better the role of the MNEs.

EU membership further increased competition. The salaries grew up 3-4%, and energy prices went up, however, the prices of the food products could not grow more then 0.5 – 1%, which meant that Nestlé had to be more and more efficient. Efficiency improvement is crucial for Nestlé's success on the Hungarian market. However, Nestlé Hungária Kft. posted record sales growth in 2004, achieving exceptional progress. The company made more than 70 billion HUF in net sales, a 20.5% increase compared to 2003. This growth, achieved in a competitive environment shows the success of the company's business policy and its growing role in supplying Central and Eastern Europe with its products.

Conclusion

This chapter presented the efforts of the Hungarian Government to increase competitiveness of domestic enterprises and embed Multinational companies in the local economy. In order to root foreign companies, the government was applying broad policy measures such as high tariffs and customs duties, rules of origin, joint-venture requirements, etc. Since 1997, it started to introduce programmes that encourage linkage creation in general and programmes that encourage the further development of the already existing links between suppliers and foreign companies. Moreover, since mid-1990s Hungary has been working to improve its innovation system. The greatest effort has been undertaken following Hungary's entrance into EU in 2004 when a 200% rule was introduced for Business Expenditures for Research and Development. This measure serves as a tool to motivate foreign and domestic companies to cooperate with the research institutes and universities for R&D services: they have either to pay contributions to the Innovation Fund or to invest in R&D and for every forint invested to get two forints back. Despite all these efforts undertaken by the government, it seems that food Multinationals are not "locked" in the host economy. When Hungary entered EU in 2004 and all the protectionist measures were removed, food multinationals commenced intense processes of restructurings in line with their global growth strategies. The strong competition forced them to go for regional optimisation plans. MNEs relocated activities all over CEE and Western Europe and fully integrated their CEE subsidiaries into their global supply chains.

The chapter revealed that food MNEs did not collaborate with the local institutes and research centres. None of the three companies had a research centre in Hungary and did not plan to open any. MNEs cooperated with universities only to recruit personnel, but did not have any other projects related to common scientific projects, the training of students, PhDs, etc. Therefore, more efforts are needed from the government to strengthen the partnerships between food companies and local knowledge institutions, so that the local economy benefits further from the knowledge and know-how of the foreign investors.

References

BACSKAI, T. *et al.* (eds.) (2005), "State of Small and Medium Sized Business in Hungary", *Annual Report 2005*, Hungarian Institute for Economic Analysis, Hungary.

BACSKAI, T. *et al.* (eds.) (2002), "State of Small and Medium Sized Business in Hungary", *Annual Report 2002*, Hungarian Institute for Economic Analysis, Hungary.

BARTLETT, C. A. and GHOSHAL, S. (1989), *Managing Across Borders: The Transnational Solution*, Harvard Business School Press, Boston, MA.

BENITO, G. R. G., GROGAARD, B. and NARULA, R. (2003), "Environmental Influences on MNE Subsidiary Roles: Economic Integration and the Nordic Countries", *Journal of International Business Studies*, No.34, pp. 443-456.

BIACS PETER, A. (2003), Deputy State Secretary, Ministry of Agriculture and Regional Development, Hungary Future of Food Industry in the CEE and NIS, Expert Papers, Technology Foresight Summit Budapest, 27-29 March 2003 (http://www.unido.org/file-storage/download/?file_id=10567).

DUNNING, J. H. (1993), *Multinational Enterprises and the Global Economy*, Addison Wesley, Wokingham, Berkshire.

EDEN, L. (2001), "Regional Integration and Foreign Direct Investment: Theory and Lessons from NAFTA", in KOTABE, M., AULAKH, P. and PHATAK, A. (eds.), *The Challenge of International Business Research*, Edward Elgar Publishing, London.

EDQUIST, C. (2002), "Innovation Policy – A Systemic Approach", in ARCHIBUGI, D. and LUNDVALL, B.-Å. (eds.), *The Globalizing Learning Economy*, Oxford University Press, Oxford, pp. 219-239.

EDQUIST, C. (1997), *Systems of Innovation: Institutions and Organisations*, Pinter, London.

EUROMONITOR INTERNATIONAL (2005), *Packaged Food in Hungary*, January 2005.

EUROMONITOR INTERNATIONAL (2006), *Packaged Food in Hungary*, May 2006.

FREEMAN, C. and LOUCA, F. (2001), *As Time Goes By*, Oxford University Press, Oxford.

FREEMAN, C. (1987), *Technology Policy and Economic Performance: Lessons from Japan*, Pinter, London.

HASTENBERG, J. (1999), *Foreign Direct Investment in Hungary: The Effects on the Modernization of the Manufacturing Industry and the Demand for Labor*, Faculty of Geographical Sciences, Utrecht University.

LUNDVALL, B- Å. (ed.) (1992), *National Systems of Innovations*, Pinter, London.

MEYER, K. E. and TRAN, Y. T. T. (2006), "Market Penetration and Acquisition Strategies for Emerging Economies", *Long Range Planning*, Vol. 39, No.2 (in press).

MEYER, K. E. and JENSEN, C. (2003), "Foreign Investor Strategies in View of EU Enlargement", in STUTING, H.-J., DOROW, W., BLASZEJEWSKI, S. and CLAASEN, F. (eds.), *Change Management in Transformation Economies: Integrating Strategy, Structure and Culture*, Palgrave, London, pp. 291-308.

NARULA, R. and MARIN, A. (2003), "FDI Spillovers, Absorptive Capacities and Human Capital Development: Evidence from Argentina", *MERIT Infonomics Research Memorandum Series*, No.2003-16, Maastricht, July 2003.

NARULA, R. (2002), "Innovation Systems and 'Inertia' in R&D Location: Norwegian Firms and the Role of Systemic Lock-in", *Research Policy*, No.31, pp. 795-816.

NELSON, R. (1993), *National Innovation Systems: A Comparative Analysis*, University Press, Oxford and New York.

LALL, S. and NARULA, R. (2006), *Understanding FDI-Assisted Economic Development*, Routledge, London.

PEREZ, C. and SOETE, L. (1988), "Catching-up in Technology: Entry Barriers and Windows of Opportunities", in DOSI, G., FREEMAN, C., NELSON, R., SILVERBERG, G. and SOETE, L. (eds.), *Technical Change and Economic Theory*, Francis Pinter, London, pp. 458-479.

SZANYI, M. (2001), *Policy Consequences of FDI, Linkage Promotion Opportunities in Hungary*, UNICE/EBRD, Geneva.

UNCTAD (2001), World Investment Report 2001 – Promoting Linkages, United Nations, New York and Geneva.

WHITE, R. E. and POYNTER, T. A. (1984), "Strategies for Foreign Owned Subsidiaries in Canada", *Business Quarterly*, Summer, pp. 59-69.

WTO (1998), "Trade Policy Review – Hungary", Report by the Secretariat, WT/TPR/S/40, World Trade Organisation, Geneva, 7-8 July 1998.

YIP, G. S., (1989), "Global Strategy. In a World of Nations?", *Sloan Management Review*, Vol. 31, No.1 (1989: Fall).

Managing Mass Dissimissals and High Unemployment – Employment Policies and Unemployment Compensation in Poland after 1989

Catherine SPIESER

Researcher in the Department of Social and Political Science of the European University Institute (Florence)

Introduction

The issue of unemployment, for all its relevance and supposed salience, has long been left in the background of economic and political transformations taking place in Central and Eastern Europe, by policy-makers and researchers alike, especially in the countries considered to perform best on the path of economic reform. In the early years of "transition", unemployment was commonly depicted as an inevitable short-term side-effect, a mechanical consequence of liberalising economic activities, a problem that would solve itself on its own when output recovers and national economies start growing again. It took some years for domestic policy-makers and international experts alike to realise the scope and long-lasting character of the unemployment crisis. The idea of short-term transitional unemployment became clearly discredited as the unemployment rate exceeded 20% fifteen years after the fall of the communism, in the first country to recover economic growth: Poland. From the emergency measures of the early 1990s to the emergence of more encompassing labour market policies, the chapter assesses the content and impact of the public policy response to rising unemployment in the context of socio-economic transformations. The empirical part is based on the Polish case and deals primarily with the consequences of the first generation of firm restructuring associated with privatisation, in other words, the job destructions generated by the closure of loss-making state-owned units or their transformations into profitable private firms. It assumes that, by and large, the current level of unemployment, whether openly observable as such, or hidden in a high level of inactivity, is the unavoidable by-product of the process of building a market economy on the remains of a communist economic system.

Firm Restructuring in Post-communist Transformations

In a market economy, firm restructuring encompasses the variety of solutions adopted by enterprises in need of continually adaptating to market trends and pressure in order to maintain or regain a competitive advantage (EMCC, 2006). As a process of adaptation to changing demand and market conditions, it implies the strategic reorganisation of production and resources within the firm, but also around it. Firm restructuring can involve a reorientation of activities on a given product, a change in strategy, a change in the kind of production, a re-location of activities to a different place, downsizing or outsourcing, innovation. All these solutions, if they allow the firm to recover competitiveness, imply an adjustment of production factors which, in the case of labour, ranges from the internal reorganisation of work to mass layoffs. Restructuring is a process in which firms are the dominant, but not the only actor since they are embedded in an institutional environment that simultaneously constraints and enables them, thereby influencing the range of well-functioning solutions (Hall and Soskice, 2002). This is particularly relevant as far as the organisation of work, hiring and firing are concerned and in the case of large-scale economic transformations likely to lead to significant job destructions, and thereby calling for a public policy response to alleviate the social cost of restructuring. The meaning of enterprise restructuring in the post-communist context goes beyond this. Following the collapse of the communist economic system based on central planning, shortages and bargaining, the process of enterprise restructuring was particularly complex in Central and Eastern Europe, to the point that it would perhaps be more justified to speak about the restructuring of the whole economy since the concept first refers to the transformation of state-owned enterprises which were in a situation of monopoly, and therefore, to a radical change of economic system. Before 1989, the economy was dominated by large, state-owned industrial groups and a strong emphasis was put on heavy industry at the expense of services and consumer goods production. Prices were fixed, transactions and production targets were governed by a central administration, financial budget constraints were soft and payments or credits not always enforced (Kornai, 1992). In view of building a viable, competitive, market economy with free market transactions, prices determined by offer and demand and open borders, large state-owned firms were split into smaller entities and privatised when viable, while unprofitable industries went out of business. A sectoral reorientation of activity, away from heavy industry and towards consumer-oriented industries or services led some economic sectors to disappear and plants and mines to close down, including in geographic areas where they represented a quasi-monopolistic employer. The focus in this chapter is on the consequences of this first generation of restructuring, which is embedded in systemic change.

Employment Restructuring, Job Destruction and the Mitigation Role of Policies

While successful restructuring of many entities was a key factor for them to recover competitiveness and for the country to recover growth, the process no doubt imposed a significant cost on workers, particularly on certain categories of workers. In turn, the rise of unemployment triggered expectations of government action to address this new social problem and a demand for adequate policies to be put in place.

Under the pressure of hardening budget constraints, large-scale enterprise restructuring in Central and Eastern Europe in the 1990s first and foremost implied an adjustment of the size, wages and skills of the workforce. The main factor of unemployment is the elimination of a general situation of labour hoarding[1] characteristic of the pre-1989 command economy (Mickiewicz, 2005: 92). Downsizing the workforce was a priority if privatised firms were to become viable players in open market competition. In fact, this applied to all types of firms, from state-owned ones to private ones, and workforce reductions took place regardless of the type of ownership: in some cases, dismissals took place before privatisation, in other cases afterwards; often this was a process spread over several years. Some industries were hit particularly badly by changing market conditions. As an example, employment in manufacturing has decreased almost every year in the period 1992-2002, with only two exceptions in 1995 and 1997. Similarly, some regions are more affected than others and, given their variety of productive specialisation prior to 1989 and varying growth performance after 1989, the employment and unemployment situations are widely differentiated across areas. Given the limited capacity of the regional administrations to deal with these issues, this does not, however, lessen the need for the central state administration to develop national employment policies.

The consequences of workforce reductions can be alleviated by various measures falling into two broad categories: either immediate, but often short term, emergency public policy measures or more comprehensive social and labour market policies, built over a lengthier period

[1] Employment above the efficiency level, labour hoarding was estimated to reach up to 20% of the workforce at the end of the 1980s (Mickiewicz, 2005: 84).

of time. In large firms or specific sectors, restructuring can also be managed at a decentralised level: it then becomes a negotiated process involving cooperation between various actors in designing and implementing a restructuring plan that they agree upon. The chapter investigates both aspects of the policy response and shows that the consequences of job loss were only partially mitigated by social policy and labour market policy measures.

Individual ad hoc *Measures or the Emergence of a Policy for Socio-economic Change?*

Clearly, in the Polish context, policies for labour market adjustment could at best accompany rapid change, while anticipation was out of reach. The systemic dimension of post-communist transformations, at least in the first decade, is again worth recalling here. Three fundamental levels of decision-making in the political system have been radically redefined: the social and cultural boundaries of citizenship, marking the borders of the polity; rules, procedures and rights that make up the constitutional and institutional framework of the "regime"; and ultimately, "who gets what, when and how in terms of both political power and economic resources" (Offe, 1991: 505). The policy response to economic transformations is thus designed within a new market economy paradigm, as a result of "radical changes in the overarching terms of the policy discourse associated with a 'paradigm shift'" (Hall, 1993: 279). This naturally also takes place on a background of a shift of paradigm in Western Europe as Keynesian demand-side policies are gradually being replaced by supply-side policies, with consequences on welfare systems (Frege, 1997; Hemerijck *et al.*, 2006: 264-266; Avgadic and Crouch, 2006: 200).

In this context, building employment and social policies is a complex process involving three successive steps: in a first step, securing a change of paradigm calls for emergency measures compensating immediate losers; in a second step it is necessary to build new institutions to turn policy principles into concrete policies, and finally, reform and adjustment within established social policy institutions may place in the medium term (Offe, 1993; Orenstein, 1995). Emergency measures are *ad hoc* or discretionary measures "intended to cope with pressing transition-induced social problems such as rising unemployment" (Orenstein, 1995: 179); they aim to alleviate transition costs in order to secure the regime change, or paradigmatic change. Only once this is resolved, "governments may construct new social policy institutions that fit the demands of the new economic system" (*ibid.*). In a third step, policies can be refined – in other words, reformed. An argument frequently met is that Polish social policy has long been a composite sum of emergency and *ad hoc* measures, rather than a genuine social policy, let alone the foundation for a welfare state (Orenstein, 1995). The empirical investigation is guided by a re-examination of this argument, and seeks to trace the emergence of a new policy area concerns with changes on the labour market.

The chapter starts with some background and conceptual considerations to map an analytical frame (I), before proceeding with an empirical study of policies for unemployment (II), policies for employment (III) and finally two cases of negotiated restructuring process (IV).

I. The Shrinking State in Search of a New Role in the Face of Rising Unemployment

This section sets the framework for investigating the role of public policies in times of economic, social and political transformations.

A. The Re-commodification of Labour and the Rapid Rise of Unemployment

Far from being an objective reality, employment and unemployment are shaped by labour law and statistical definitions (Zimmerman, 2001; Baxandall, 2002); they should therefore not be considered as abstract phenomena or in isolation from those. In the communist system, employment was universal and little differentiated; the concept of unemployment was rarely used as an analytical category and non-existent as a category of public intervention. While it existed at a marginal level in the form of frictional unemployment (the gap between one's job and the successive one, when one changes jobs), the stock of unemployment was never high (few people remained without a job for a long time). Frictional unemployment was estimated as not exceeding half a percentage point in Poland.

When setting the conditions of eligibility for unemployment compensation, the laws of 1989 introduced an initially broad definition of unemployment, which was subsequently fine-tuned. While the first proposal for an unemployment benefit scheme in 1990 assumed a moderate increase in the number of unemployed (300,000), more than one million people became unemployed in that year alone,[2] when "the labour market switched in a matter of months from excess demand to excess supply" (Rashid *et al.*, 2005: 84). The registered unemployment rate thus jumped from quasi nil prior to 1989, to 11% in 1991, and

2 Registered unemployment jumped from 55,000 people (0.2%) to 1,125,000 (6.1%) in twelve months (Rashid *et al.*, 2005: 84).

16.4% in 1993.[3] Since unemployment registration varies with changes in the legal definition and the rights and benefits granted to the unemployed, the labour force survey[4] often provides a better indicator of unemployment as a mismatch of labour offer and demand and unemployment as an economic phenomenon (Table 1). It shows that unemployment increased steadily except in the period 1996-1998 when the economy recovered growth. Meanwhile, real wages declined and the trend did not entirely reverse when growth upturned.

Table 1: Employment and Unemployment in Poland (% of Active Population)

	1992	1993	1994	1995	1996	1997	1998	1999	2000	2001	2002	2003	2004	2005
Unemployment rate (LFS)	13.7	14.9	13.9	13.1	11.5	10.2	10.6	15.3	16	18.5	19.7	19.6	19	18.9
Employment rate (LFS)	53.3	52.1	51	50.7	51.2	51.5	51	48	47.4	45.5	44.1	44	44.3	44.1

Source: Labour force survey, all data fourth quarter except 2005, Q1.

As underlined above, unemployment was in large part[5] a direct consequence of labour shedding resulting from enterprise restructuring. It grew to a high level out an unfortunate combination of uncertain economic conditions, adjustment to changing demand, changes in the governance of work, and inadequate human capital. After more than forty years of "command economy" in which everybody had a constitutional right to work and unemployment had been made illegal (Mlonek, 1999), in 1989 the first democratically elected government had a task to restore some market mechanisms in the allocation of jobs and workforce. The *Dismissal Act* of 1989 thus authorised workforce reduction under certain conditions. The *Employment Act* of 1989, revised in 1991, provided a basis for new labour market governance and institutions compatible with a capitalist market economy. It instituted a network of public employment offices; tripartite employment councils; an unem-

3 Ministry of Economy and Labour (available at www.praca.gov.pl, downloaded August 2004).

4 The labour force survey asks a representative sample of the working age population about their work situation in the week preceding the realisation of the survey. It has been sometimes objected that respondents still tend to extrapolate their answers from their administrative status rather than their actual working hours. Yet such behaviour is not generalised and therefore remains less of a bias than the changes of definitions and benefit eligibility that account to a larger extent for the fluctuations of registered employment.

5 However, it is worth noting the relatively high level of youth unemployment (which to a certain extent also touches graduates of higher education). This shows that the Polish labour market is affected not only by job destructions in declining economic sectors, but also by a low level of job creation in the growing private sector, especially between 1997 and 2001 (Szylko-Skoczny, 2004: 32).

ployment compensation scheme; and a dedicated Labour Fund to finance labour market programmes.

1. An Inevitably "Shrinking" State

The process of privatisation of state-owned enterprises is no doubt the most striking aspect of the state withdrawal from productive activity. It led to a firm decrease in public sector employment and a rising share of private sector employment.

Table 2: Employment by Ownership Sector (End of Year)

% of total	1995	1996	1997	1998	1999	2000	2001
Private	61.4	63.6	67.9	69.4	71.3	72.2	73.2
Public	38.6	36.4	32.1	30.6	28.7	27.8	26.8

Source: GUS, as in Golinowska *et al.* (2003: 18).

What makes Poland an interesting case, however, is that the state remained much bigger than one might have expected for a country embarking on a liberal reform path, and than in other Central European countries. Although the state was expected to shrink significantly in terms of scope and expenditures after 1989, this is not exactly what happened in Poland in the first decade. The share of social expenditure in GDP grew significantly between 1990 and 1992 (Table 3), partly as a result of costly unemployment benefit schemes, partly as a result of growing pension expenditures, which, alongside with other cash transfers, were rising considerably also in real terms (Rutkowski, 1998). Public social expenditure then stabilised at a level close to the EU-15 average (23% of GDP in 2001), several percentage points higher than Hungary, the Czech Republic or Slovakia. This clearly suggests that some kinds of social measures were actively implemented.

Table 3: Public Social Expenditure in Selected Countries

% of GDP	1990	1991	1992	1993	1994	1995	1996	1997	1998	1999	2000	2001	Av. 92-96*	Av 97-01
CZ	17.0	18.3	18.7	19.2	19.2	18.9	18.8	19.7	19.5	19.8	20.3	20.1	19.0	19.9
HU										20.8	20.0	20.1		20.3
PL	15.5	22.1	26.2	25.6	24.4	23.8	23.9	23.3	22.0	22.2	21.9	23.0	24.8	22.5
SK						19.2	19.1	18.7	19.0	18.9	18.3	17.9	19.2	18.5
UK	18.6	19.5	21.1	23.1	23.7	23.2	23.0	22.8	22.0	21.5	21.2	21.7	22.8	21.8
US	13.0	13.4	14.5	15.2	15.4	15.4	15.5	15.3	14.9	14.5	14.2	14.2	15.2	14.6
FR	25.2	26.6	27.2	28.0	29.5	29.3	29.2	29.4	29.4	29.0	28.9	28.3	28.6	29.0
DK	29.5	29.3	30.2	30.7	32.3	33.1	32.4	31.7	30.7	30.2	29.8	28.9	31.7	30.3
EU-15	23.4	24.4	25.6	26.5	26.2	25.6	25.6	24.8	24.3	24.2	23.7	24.0	25.9	24.2

* Average for the four-year period

Source: OECD SOCX database (2004). The last two columns represent yearly average for the period.

Similarly, there is no evidence of a quick downsizing of the number of employees in the government sector. During the first decade, while privatisation resulted in decreasing public sector employment, employment in state administration increased markedly,[6] with a share of the general government sector in employment still exceeding 18% in 1997[7] (Ekiert, 2001: 17-18).

2. Contrasting Views on Appropriate Economic and Social Policies in Emerging Capitalism

Beyond these macro-economic indicators, which can be misleading, it is essential to examine what public policies and related programmes actually do (Esping-Andersen, 1990), and in particular, what social categories they single out by providing them various kinds of support. What is the possible scope of policies accompanying restructuring in the context of post-communist transformations? An efficient state in emerging capitalism ideally combines three kinds of capacities (Bruszt, 2001: 53-54). Firstly, it enables economic actors to operate in a predictable policy environment. Secondly, state institutions remain exempt from capture by powerful private groups seeking to redistribute wealth and opportunities to themselves. Finally, it is able "to regulate relations among economic actors in a balanced way and prevent the misuse of asymmetries in economic and informational power within the market". Accordingly, the normatively desirable role of the state in post-communist political economies is to guarantee three essential freedoms: freedom from the state; freedom of the state (as opposed to state capture by a few, powerful, private interests); and freedom of the market (as opposed to the distortions resulting from corruption) (Bruszt, 2001: 55). In this view, the distributive functions of public policy are secondary in the sense that they can only be fulfilled in a second step, once these freedoms are ensured. Others have argued that a social safety net was essential from the start, and the only possible way was to adopt a universal model of basic unemployment compensation for its relative easiness of implementation (Barr, 1994). This serves also a political objective by helping to win support for reforms inevitably conducive to a rapid rise of unemployment, increased hardship for some in the initial phase: in that sense it falls into the category of emergency measures (Orenstein, 1995: 179).

---

6 State administration employees were fewer than 70,000 in 1989, but the figure rose regularly to reach 171,000 in 1998 (Ekiert, 2001: 17).

7 To be compared with 5.8% in the Czech Republic and 7.2% in Hungary the same year.

In Poland, in the early 1990s, in effect, the priority was to achieve macro-economic stabilisation and address the fiscal crisis. There was a consensus that the instrument for that was Balcerowicz's "shock therapy" plan. Social policy programmes were primarily seen as a burden on the reform process (Ksiezopolski, 1993: 179). The worsening state of government finance, undergoing a severe crisis since the 1980s, implied that stabilisation was a pre-condition to major changes in any other policy area. The strategy of the first post-communist government in 1990 was to build a pluralist democracy and set the basis for a market economy, all the more as there was a clear and broad consensus in this direction, while the ultimate goal of social policy remained controversial and confusion reigned over its definition (Ksiezopolski, 1993). Building a market economy was largely understood as "liberating markets from the state" (Bruszt, 2001) and the urgency lied in state withdrawal from the economy (Balcerowicz, 1995), which included withdrawal from the social "guarantees of communism" without any serious attempt to propose an acceptable alternative system of needs satisfaction (Ksiezopolski, 1993: 180). In 1990-1991, the necessity of a major social policy reform was clearly underestimated and the belief that marketisation on its own would be sufficient to trigger the necessary adjustments was widespread. Some social measures related to unemployment and employment were adopted, but without a new comprehensive policy framework, while many aspects of the universal and generous communist welfare state remained in place well-into the 1990s. This is easily explained: aside the macro-economic trade-off mentioned above, there was a need to find a compromise between, on one hand, the objective of ending financial support to loss-making enterprises and, on the other one, the political pressure to avoid mass lay-offs and large-scale unemployment (Barr, 1994: 147).

Until the mid-1990s, discourses on appropriate policies for Poland were marked by a clear under-evaluation of the severity of the institutional, employment and poverty crises. A wave of strikes in 1992-1993, electoral reversal in 1993 and 1995,[8] and the simultaneous severe deterioration of labour market conditions and public finance, for two different reasons, brought the issue of social policy reform back on the agenda. The shift of emphasis from enforcing market competition to building institutions and state capacity, and the increasing awareness of the salience of the unemployment crisis in several major policy reports and official publications from 1996-1997 onwards provide good evi-

[8] The former communist party won the majority in parliament in 1993 and the presidency in 1995 with A. Kwasniewski, succeeding to the historical Solidarity leader L. Walesa.

dence of a change of view.[9] The idea that building capitalism and democracy was best characterised by continuous and incremental change rather than by a single "big bang" simultaneously gained ground. By the end of the 1990s, a wide consensus was reached on the importance of the state and institutions, on one hand, and the necessity to address the issue of unemployment with a comprehensive programme on the other one. In a nutshell, the state started to be seen as an asset rather than a problem (Ekiert, 2001) and it became more obvious that what was needed was "a 'functional' or 'capable' state, a state which enables society to adjust continuously to a changing international environment" (Fritz, 2004: 2).

3. *Welfare State, Labour Market Policies and Regime of Labour Market Adjustment*

In most European societies, the state does more than just regulating markets; it is also a major welfare provider. Public policies serve distributive functions, whether one considers them an issue of allocative efficiency or a matter of equity. The degree and nature of involvement of the state in the regulation of economic relations, the labour market and welfare issues contributes to defining a limited number of "welfare regimes" (Esping-Andersen, 1990). The objectives of public intervention in the modern welfare state are manifold. They aim both to improve the allocative efficiency of public spending, work and welfare, and to redistribute towards the weak, the vulnerable and the poor, or offer collective protection against certain economic risks (Barr, 2004: 7).

Opening up the concept of regime, welfare policies can be mapped according to two dimensions, the extensiveness of eligibility and the degree of de-commodification (or protection against market risk) that they introduce. Esping-Andersen has built his famous "three worlds of welfare capitalism" on a classical distinction between residual and institutional welfare state previously established by Titmuss (Esping-Andersen, 1990: 20). In a residual welfare state, the state assumes responsibility only when the family or the market fails; it seeks to limit

---

9 In 1997, Golinowska edited a national UNDP report stressing precisely the role of the state (Golinowska and UNDP, 1997) while the Human Development Report published in 2004 dealt specifically with employment. Around the Polish government itself, the socio-economic body composed of academics advising the Prime Minister published a first report concerned with the issue of unemployment in 1995, before addressing labour market reform (2001) and job creation in the economy (2004). At the same time, the Ministry of Economy published the first comprehensive report drafted by governmental services on "Employment in Poland" in 2005. The World Bank published reports on Poland centred on the employment issue in 2001 and 2004; other reports were commissioned by the European Commission (Golinowska *et al.*, 2003), or the Friedrich Ebert Stiftung (Golinowska, 2005).

commitments to marginal and deserving social groups. On the contrary, the institutional welfare state is addressing the entire population, universalistic, and embodies an institutionalised commitment to welfare; therefore it will, in principle, extend welfare commitments to all areas of distribution vital for societal welfare. To locate the CEECs in this conventional analytical perspective, there seem to be a relative consensus among scholars on the following stylised picture: Slovenia excepted,[10] if Central European countries are approximating any of these ideal-types, they are coming closer to the residual or liberal welfare regime (Standing, 1996; Vaughan-Whitehead, 2003).

Policies for the labour market fully belong to the welfare nexus. They are simultaneously economic policies and social policies, since they aim to intervene in the governance of economic activity and influence the market mechanisms that regulate it, but with a normatively defined social equity objective (Barbier, 1998: 383). The idea of un/employment policy (or "labour market policy")[11] as an integrated policy area is primarily an administrative and analytical construction (Barbier, 1998), but nevertheless proves useful to study issues that are located at the intersection of the economic, social and political realm. Since labour market policies encompass a diversity of measures and objectives, they are best defined by their aims and functions. First of all, policies for the labour market construct social categories by defining employment and unemployment, and identifying those categories of people eligible for certain kinds of support, or not. Secondly, they are redistributive in that they have a corrective effect on the market allocation of work and income, seeking, for instance, to alleviate the cost of market adjustment. Third, if the welfare state has become most protective and encompassing in countries where labour was most powerful, this is because welfare policies also had a political aim: to avoid social conflict by granting increased protection to the groups that had the highest level of veto power (Korpi, 1983).

Despite the increasing influence of European instruments, strategies of employment adjustment continue to be constructed nationally and vary from one country to another (Barbier, 1998: 387). Together with

10 Slovenia is closer to a Bismarckian welfare state (Wright *et al.*, 2004). It is also the only country of the region to exhibit a relatively centralised collective bargaining system. Some authors attribute this to the imitation of the structures of social protection and industrial relations of neighbouring Austria, while others emphasise the legacy of Yugoslavian communism, which had a unique tradition of workers' self-management. If the latter is to serve as an explanation for the singular position of Slovenia, it is only in combination with a successful and quick economic recovery that distinguish Slovenia from the other former Yugoslav Republics.

11 I use the terms interchangeably.

other elements of welfare regimes and systems of industrial relations, labour market policies constitute an employment adjustment regime. Governments seek to reach a situation in which unemployment becomes socially and politically acceptable while policies remain economically viable. The cumulative action of successive governments and public authorities allows to trace an "adjustment path", which though not always linear, represents a country's policy trajectory over time.[12]

To unveil the logic of "dealing with" unemployment and restructuring in Poland, it is necessary to examine the content of policies while keeping in mind the political foundations explaining why they were adopted. In the study of fast-changing countries, two principles should guide the empirical investigation. First, we should look at policies in a dynamic perspective and try to map change across time. Secondly, when possible, we should always make an effort to look beyond the formally existing rules, institutions and policies in order to take into account incomplete or diverted implementation when it occurs. Finally, while labour market policies are the main policy tool to accompany job destructions, the role of special measures negotiated in restructuring pacts should not be under-estimated.

4. Labour Market Policies in a European Comparative Perspective

Under the influence of the OECD, labour market policies are increasingly considered in a comparative perspective, by policy-makers and analysts alike, which rendered necessary the development of concepts and tools to make possible the comparison of national policies that are rarely functional equivalents (Barbier, 1998). The concepts of passive active and labour market policies as "de-contextualised" comparison tools are rooted in this context. For the study of the Polish regime of labour market adjustment, the typology of passive and active policies provides a useful starting point (Table 4).

---

12 The idea of successive governments acting in a cumulative manner, independently of majority turnovers, is justified by the fact that all of them operates in the perspective of a change of paradigm and seek to build policies for, or adapt them to, emerging capitalism. While this can be realised in a top-down manner by pushing through encompassing, one-off radical reforms, as often occurs with macro-economic stabilisation plans, the adaptation of social and employment policies tends to be more gradual. In that sense, incremental, low level changes in the instruments or the goals of policies, departing from a given historical path and occurring both repeatedly and in a relatively consistent manner across policy sectors, also come to constitute "[…] a major shift in social policy orientation", (Palier, 2005: 128) These changes are typically " […] slow-moving, incremental and only 'cumulatively transformative'" (*ibid.*, 129).

Table 4: Typology of Labour Market Policies

	Passive Labour Market Policies	Active Labour Market Policiexs	
		"Nice" (social-democratic) activation	"Nasty" (liberal) activation
Aim	Alleviating the effects of losing a job	Facilitating return to employment	Ensuring that the beneficiaries are deserving (and facilitating return to employment)
Measures	Unemployment compensation Severance payments Early retirement	Vocational training Public employment service Measures for young labour market entrants Subsidies for hiring certain categories of people	Monitoring job seekers' activity and job search Obligation to taking up any job Benefit cuts targeting the "inactive" unemployed
Logic	Income support (compensation)	Social investment	Workfare

Passive and active policies can be pursued simultaneously. Most European countries have traditionally pursued a mix of both. However, since the mid-1990s, an increasing emphasis has been put on active policies and on the idea of "activation". The normative emphasis on activation as "good practice" in employment and social policy and "value for money" came from two different sources, Scandinavian countries on one hand, and the US and the UK on the other one, before being diffused in the rest of Europe by the OECD and the processes linked to the European Employment Strategy and the Lisbon Strategy. Activation consists in "the introduction of an increased and explicit linkage between on the one hand, social protection, and on the other hand, labour market participation and labour market programmes." (Barbier and Ludwig-Mayerhofer, 2004: 425-426).

There are, however, many "worlds of activation" and significant variations in their modalities of implementation and implications. Activation can thus be oriented towards a liberal social policy or a universalistic one (Barbier and Ludwig-Mayerhofer, 2004: 427). Building on dichotomies established by others, Clegg makes a useful distinction between "nice", market-correcting activation on the one hand, and "nasty", market-enforcing activation, on the other (Clegg, 2005: 52-54). These two kinds differ much more radically than as a matter of nuance: they reflect different aims and functions and are inspired by opposed values. The fact that, for long, activation policies have been more market-correcting than market-enforcing explains their rapid development in states with institutionalised commitments to social rights: active labour market policies, in their "nice", supply-side version, originated in Scandinavian countries (*ibid.*, 54). However, later reforms of labour market policies, there as well, have started to fundamentally differ from earlier ones, although the emphasis on skill and human capital development remain greater than elsewhere (*ibid.*, 55).

These ideas about "good" policies, through various channels,[13] have spread to Poland where, to some degree, they were taken up by policy-makers. What remains to be explored is what these ideas have become in practice, once adapted to the local context and integrated in national policies. The following sections present empirical material on the development of labour market policies in Poland, before turning to two examples of restructuring pacts, which can rely on similar measures or extraordinary ones. The policy response to unemployment is threefold: policies aiming to manage unemployment (2), policies facilitating (re-)employment (3) and policies aiming to overcome the barriers to restructuring thanks to a negotiated pact (4).

II. Policies Aiming to Manage Unemployment

The core measure allowing for enterprise restructuring was the institutionalisation of unemployment, combined with special – more generous – compensation for the actors most likely to oppose socio-economic reforms, aiming to satisfy them at least temporarily.

A. *Alleviating the Individual Loss of Income: Introduction and Gradual Restriction of the Universal Unemployment Benefit*

From the beginning, the government reaction included both passive and active labour market policies, but the first clearly prevailed. The *Law on Employment*, subsequently revised as *Law on Employment and Unemployment in 1991*, established policies for unemployment benefits, employment services, and limited active labour programmes[14] (Kabaj, 1996; Rashid *et al.*, 2005: 84). They were financed by the Labour Fund, with a budget heavily relying on state subsidies (up to three-quarters of the total), and to a much lesser extent on social contributions.

13 Already as a country in the process of acceding to the EU, Poland was encouraged to "[...] modify the language and operation of welfare arrangements" (Wright *et al.*, 2004: 512). The requirements to comply with the European Employment Strategy and the Lisbon Strategy have become even stronger for Poland as a new EU Member State.

14 Small business loans, loans to employers for creating jobs, training, public service employment, and wage subsidy programmes.

Initially, in 1989, the unemployed were entitled to obtain a benefit starting seven days after the date of registration as unemployed, providing that the labour office had failed to offer them a job or training (Gardawski, 2002). The level of benefit was calculated on the basis of the last remuneration and length of unemployment, with a starting level of 70% during the first three months, subsequently falling to a lower rate, but unlimited in time (*ibid.*). In practice, the benefit could not be lower than the minimum wage nor higher than the average wage. In the context of the time, when a significant rise of unemployment was expected, this was a generous and costly scheme, which would quickly become unsustainable. More strikingly, the law gave preferential status to young graduates entering the labour market by granting them special unemployment benefit which could reach up to 200% of the minimum wage, even if they had no previous employment history (MPiPS, 1995: 9; Gardawski, 2002). It is highly likely the initial generosity of the scheme aimed to achieve a peaceful institutionalisation of unemployment in Poland: "The government, seeking to gain social acceptance for its far-reaching reforms, was more interested in a temporary solution" (Gardawski, 2002: 2).

Quite logically, from 1991 onwards, the conditions of eligibility and length of the unemployment benefit were subject to an increasing number of restrictions. The scheme had turned to be rather costly, given the number of unemployed persons, and it was foreseen that it would quickly become unaffordable if eligibility was not contained in a restricted period of time. A 12-month limit was introduced, with the possibility of extending the benefit to 18 months in total for people with a long employment history. The level of the benefit was linked to the local unemployment situation. Both the lower and upper limit of the benefit amount were lowered drastically: it could be as low as 33% of the average wage but not higher than the minimum wage. Restrictions on the benefit for unemployed graduates were also introduced in parallel. The relation between the benefit entitlement and the last wage was completely eliminated in 1992: the unemployment benefit became a flat 36% of average wage.

As a result of the limited length of the unemployment benefit, with many unemployed staying in unemployment, the number of beneficiaries declined mechanically over the years to become a marginal proportion of the unemployed, falling to below 20% in 2005.[15] Most people stopped being eligible for benefits over time. The long-term unemployed, who make nearly half of the unemployed after 2002, are likely

[15] The ratio falls to around 10% for women. This may suggest that they have a different coping strategy and are less inclined to claim benefits.

to be covered by basic forms of social assistance, but unlikely to receive any other form of income replacement.[16] As table 5 shows, the "generosity" of the unemployment benefit was thus only very temporary.

Table 5: Coverage of the Employment Benefit

	1990	1991	1992	1993	1994	1995	1996	1997	1998	1999	2000	2001	2002	2003	2004
Registered unemployment rate, %	6.1	11.4	13.6	16.4	16	14.9	13.2	10.3	10.4	13.1	15.1	19.4	20	20	19.1
Unemployed persons, thousands	1,126	2,156	2,509	2,890	2,838	2,629	2,359	1,826	1,831	2,350	2,703	3,115	3,217	3,176	3,000
of which:															
Previously employed			1,965	2,246	2,186	2,075	1,968	1,478	1,417	1,793	2,059	2,376	2,450	2,411	2,291
Previously not employed			544	644	652	554	392	348	415	557	643	739	767	764	708
Entitled to benefit	892	1,703	1,312	1,394	1,423	1,549	1,224	557	420	554	549	624	539	478	426
Entitled to unemployment benefit, % of unemployed	79	79	52	48	50	59	52	30	23	24	20	20	17	15	14

Source: all data end of year, Ministry of Economy (download, 2005). Figures rounded to the nearest thousand.

1. *Easing Exit and Making Unemployment Invisible: Early Retirement, or Exit from Work and the Labour Market at Once*

Like in Western Europe in the past, early retirement was another widely-used policy to ease exit of employment while reducing the visibility and alleviating the effects of unemployment. Granted as a privilege in pre-1989 Poland, early retirement became a mechanism for employment adjustment afterwards, initially building on the same rules. After 1990, the pension system continued to allow a long list of professions to retire earlier with full pension rights (Czepulis-Rutkowska, 1999: 152). Social plans accompanying firm restructuring made extensive use of measures allowing to peacefully get rid of redundant workers

16 As Gardawski (2002) notes, in 2000, the average *annual* subsistence allowance paid by the social services barely amounted to *one month* of the average wage.

and put them on the two kinds of inactivity pensions available: old-age retirement and disability. In 1991, a regulation targeting people who would be unable to find new employment allowed those who had been working for 35 (women) or 40 years (men) to retire with full rights regardless of age if they had been made redundant (Czepulis-Rutkowska, 1999: 152). An additional, pre-retirement benefit, financed on the labour fund, was later created to bridge the period between becoming unemployed and the legal retirement age, targeting especially the long-term unemployed (Czepulis-Rutkowska, 1998: 196).

Early retirement allowed up to 3% of the workforce to move from employment to inactivity in the peak years, in 1991 and in 2000-2002 as a result of the acceleration of privatisation and restructuring of former state-owned industrial giants. Evidence of the scope of early retirement in practice is provided by several indicators which capture the people moving from work or unemployment to retirement before the legal retirement age. The number of people retiring significantly exceeded those reaching retirement age in several given years. In 1991 and 1992, around 40% of all pensioners had not yet reached the legal retirement age (Golinowska, 1994: 33-35; Orenstein, 1995: 191). In 1996 again, 39.5% of all men and 28% of women who retired had not yet reached retirement age.[17] In 1999, one third of the male workers who retired were below 60, the percentage decreasing to one fourth in 2001. In 1999, still more than 10% of men who received an old-age pension were below 60.[18] While the number of employed people fell by 14% between 1989 and 1996, the number of pensioners of all kinds[19] rose simultaneously by 34%. Pensions clearly played the role of an additional unemployment benefit scheme. In the year 2003, out of around one million people who had lost their job, remained without work and were receiving some kind of benefit accordingly (less than 30% of the total), slightly more than half were receiving a pre-retirement benefit, while less than half were receiving a proper unemployment benefit.[20]

III. Policies Aiming to Facilitate Employment: Social Investment for Who?

The introduction of active labour market policies (ALMP) and the idea of activation in the CEECs is often linked to the pressure exerted

17 ZUS, quoted by Müller (1999: 101).

18 ZUS figures.

19 Including those receiving a disability benefit.

20 Ministry of Economy and Labour data, August 2004.

by external players like international financial institutions,[21] the European Union[22] or the OECD,[23] which can be either as an objective government constraint in the case of policy-based lending or legal approximation required to join the EU, or simply as an instrument of justification. In Poland, as a matter of fact, ALMP were set up as early as in 1990-1991, well before constraining international pressure but, in line with a long experience of state organisation of the economy, they initially relied heavily on subsidised employment and public works. If in 1992, business start-up loans and training schemes concerned nearly 60% of the unemployed enrolled in active labour market programmes, this fell below 20% between 1993 and 1996, when the majority of participants were involved in subsidised temporary work (Krynska *et al.*, 1998: 93). The emergence of genuine active labour market programmes took longer than expected.

A. Young Graduates at Stake

In 1995-1997, discourses on appropriate policies began to mention the need to link assistance and individual effort in the specific context of policies for the young unemployed, whose entry into work became a priority. Even though Polish policy-makers were acting in an environment increasingly characterised by comparative policy evaluation and the diffusion of activation policies in Europe, the idea of activation was first promoted for idiosyncratic domestic reasons. It first appeared in a reform of the programme for young graduates adopted in 1995 and coming into force in 1996[24] (MPiPS, 1995), which claimed a number of policy principles: to give priority to work over unemployment (concentrating efforts on first jobs); to favour income from work rather than benefits; activation over social protection; training over inactivity and private sector employment over subsidised work. Until then, the logic of assistance without control had prevailed: benefits were limited in time; their level had been lowered and eligibility criteria narrowed, but they were not conditioned by any particular behaviour with respect to job-seeking or training. This signalled a shift to a logic of social investment

---

21 For instance, the World Bank is providing both policy expertise and conditional lending to government.

22 In the context of pre-accession European law (acquis), policy strategies such as the European Employment Strategy, or structural funds programming already have an impact: while formally candidate countries will have to abide by them explicitly only once they become Member States, it is something that they prepare well before accession.

23 The OECD was the first major promoter of labour market reform and active labour market policies, well before the EU became interested in the subject.

24 Programme "Promoting the Activation of Young Labour Market Entrants".

through training grants and activation and shifted the focus on "people interested in improving their qualification" (MPiPS, 1995), without giving up public intervention and employment subsidy, which, though reduced, continued to exist. Two factors explain why this particular group was first targeted by activation: graduates were entitled to a special kind of unemployment benefit that turned out to be costly, and they faced a higher rate of unemployment,[25] which was considered particularly unjust and inefficient while it was certainly thought that helping the young was a fair and worthy choice in comparison.

For other kinds of unemployed, active labour market policies for long remained marginal. While all labour offices could in theory set up active labour market programmes for categories of unemployed other than those targeted by the centrally-defined national programmes such as *First Job*, for which they received an earmarked transfer from the Labour Fund, in practice they often lacked the both the know-how and the financial resources to do so.

B. The Limited Implementation of ALMP – Imported Ideas without Matching Domestic Resources?

Assuming the measures were more or less appropriate in the Polish context, three major obstacles account for the limited impact of ALMP in practice. The first obstacle lies in the insufficient financial commitment. The resources devoted to labour market policies are subject to significant variation from one year to the next. The financing of the Labour Fund is far from being ensured by contributions alone. It is heavily dependent on *ad hoc* subsidies from the state budget. The share of expenditures allocated to active labour market programmes every year ranges from anywhere between less than 5% in 1992 up to almost one quarter of labour fund expenditures in 1998. By international comparison, this remains a low commitment to ALMP. As a result, only a small fraction of the unemployed benefit from ALMP: in 1994 and 1995 training was offered only to 3-4% of the unemployed, compared to an average ratio of 20% in OECD countries (Kabaj, 1996: 46), a figure that has not changed significantly since, except maybe for the young, thanks to the "First Job" programmes, which involved around 200,000 people in active measures.

25 Roughly twice the average in the mid 1990s, but the situation worsened in the following years. It is likely that the eligibility of graduates for a special unemployment benefit has encouraged them to declare themselves unemployed immediately upon graduating.

Table 6: Expenditures and Revenues of the Labour Fund

	1990	1991	1992	1993	1994	1995	1996
Expenditure on passive policies (unemployment and early retirement benefits)							
% of total	51.1	82	86.3	83.9	83.8	84.8	85.2
Expenditure on active policies							
% of total	32.1	7	4.7	11.1	12.8	11.9	10.7
Resources from the state budget as a share of total revenue							
% of total	72.8	61.4	70.3	61.3	62	63.8	61.1

	1997	1998	1999	2000	2001	2002	2003	2004
Expenditure on passive policies (unemployment and early retirement benefits)								
% of total	77.6	58.7	69.2	82.8	84.8	89	82.6	79.1
Expenditure on active policies								
% of total	17.2	23.8	19.2	11.1	7	5.4	12.8	14.4
Resources from the state budget as a share of total revenue								
% of total	48.5	16.8	12	13.7	31.3	38.7	40.2	14.9

Source: Ministry of Economy.

A second obstacle is the weakness of the employment services that lack the capacity to implement active labour market policies. Building on the early laws on employment and unemployment and the "activation" turn, a number of actions were taken in order to "strengthen the institutional structure of the national and local employment services, including additional staffing, training, and automation of service", with considerable external support and assistance, both bilaterally from a variety of countries and from the World Bank (Rashid *et al.*, 2005: 84). The outcome of these actions is a mixed picture. In 1997, five hundred local labour offices existed across Poland and "the automation of services was well-advanced"; a national labour office with a tripartite governing structure had been established to implement programmes on the basis of the policies defined at the ministry level (Rashid *et al.*, 2005: 84). A few years later, however, the responsibility for the labour offices was decentralised to the regional level and the national office ceased to exist. More importantly, the labour offices never really tackled unemployment as a priority: as in the past, "their primary role had been to act as a local labour exchange and to deal with specialised labour programmes (for disabled people for example). The offices were understaffed and under equipped to deal with rapidly increasing numbers of unemployed". (Rashid *et al.*, 2005: 84). All in all, the Polish labour offices were considered to be lagging behind those of other central European countries in terms of organisation al capacity and work overload (Boeri, 1997: 128).

With a telling survey conducted among managers of labour offices to find out how they really operated, Kabaj identified some of the deficiencies of the employment service (Kabaj, 2000). He shows that labour offices tend to work only for the most active people: "activation interviews" are far from being at the centre of the tasks of advisors, rather, it appears to be a completely marginal activity in their daily timetable, and in the allocation of human resources to these tasks (*ibid.*, 76). Even worse, it is the whole function of labour market intermediation that appears to be marginal in the work of the labour offices, whose time and resources seem to be mostly spent on administration, analysing unemployment figures and writing reports. This is quite a paradoxical development given that their intermediation function is central since the law of 1994. In sum, the structure of the labour offices remains very bureaucratic and dominated by an administrative culture rather than a logic of service provision. The ratio of employment advisors to the number of unemployed registered was often less than 1 to 1,000 (*ibid.*, 80). As a result, if the word "activation" is frequently used by domestic actors, the idea of monitoring job search and implementing a "workfare contract" is very far away.

At the level of regulation at least, the act on *Employment promotion and labour market institutions of 2004* addressed many of the lacunas of the employment services identified in the earlier years as factors of inefficiency. A clear objective of this law was to re-focus the action of the labour market institutions on the promotion of employment instead of the management of unemployment benefits (MEL, 2005: 205 box 21). The act defined better the role of labour market institutions and the services that they are expected to provide and the programme and instruments on which they can rely. Accordingly, the duties of the labour offices relating to the administration of unemployment benefits (namely, the allocation and payment of the benefits) were reduced. Further provisions aim to turn the employment service into a more professional activity and improving the quality of the staff. Some managerial reforms were thus included: the new requirements in terms of qualifications for becoming an employee of the public employment services; the definition of standards for the services provided. At least at the formal level, a clear change of focus thus took place.

C. From ad hoc *Measures to a Comprehensive Policy?*

The third obstacle is the limited capacity of the Polish administration and labour offices to diagnose the situation and design a consistent and comprehensive programme. As the unemployment crisis worsened and Poland embarked on the road of EU accession, the influence of external policy recommendations emphasising the need for adequate (active) labour market programmes increased, and thus the incentives to adopt a more integrated programme of labour market policies gained ground. In

1997, both income support and ALMP were refined. The latter consisted in: retraining that could last up to a year; public works paying salaries up to 75% of average income; intervention works paying six months of wages and social charges for workers hired by firms; micro loans for small business start-up and general employment services. A monitoring process of active labour market programmes was introduced, with a view to inform policy makers and parliament about the results obtained (Rashid *et al.*, 2005: 85). The first National Employment Strategy adopted in 2002 as part of the EU accession requirements focused on labour programmes, improving the employment rate, equality of opportunity, but did not contain any significant innovation. It recognised that unemployment was still very high and that labour participation was dropping. But at the same time, the Labour Fund declined to 1.4% of GDP in 2002. As a consequence, active labour market policies continued in a reduced fashion, thanks to supplementary funding by the World Bank for rural areas (Rashid *et al.*, 2005).

Progressively, but slowly, ALMP became better targeted and better organised. In 2002, the *"First Job" programme for young people* (*Pierwsza Praca*) was launched as "the first national-scale programme for the vocational activation of young people" (Czarzasty, 2004), a coordinated action primarily aimed at facilitating entry into the labour market and improving vocational activation for the 15-24 year olds. It entailed the usual range of measures: an internship scheme; professional training; subsidised private-sector employment through refunds of remuneration. Activation measures *stricto sensu* benefited around 150,000 people during the first year of operation, while a further 600,000 benefited from other measures (Czarzasty, 2004).

The *Law on employment promotion and labour market institutions of 2004* finally extended the target groups and provided the necessary legal basis to develop policies for those over 50, the long-term unemployed, the disabled and single parents. Soon after, the programme "50 +" was launched to increase the employment rate of people over 50, in line with the Lisbon strategy objective, while a fund financed by employers' contributions started to operate to subsidise the employment of the disabled. It may not be incidental that this extension was adopted in the year when Poland joined the EU and became fully part of the European Employment Strategy policy review exercises.

Although, from an outcome viewpoint, external recommendations had a limited impact on the actual outcome of policies that were implemented, they clearly contributed at a cognitive and procedural level to initiate or support the choice of certain options. At a cognitive level, they allowed the terms of the debate on unemployment to be modified, backing up a shift of emphasis from passive to active labour market policies. Activation was guided to a greater extent by policy templates present in the international and European arenas. The reports of the World Bank, which include concrete policy solutions, were often quoted and proved fairly authoritative among the national political and administrative elites. Being less inclining to offer ready-made solutions, the European Employment Strategy called for a comprehensive plan to increase employment and provided some tools for doing so. Adapting to "the language and methodology of Europe" resulted in a shift from the nationally contextualised diagnostic to the adoption of "European methodology", "European concepts" and "European Union principles" as Michal Boni, a former Minister stated (Boni, 2002: 31). In the run-up to EU accession, the obligation to draft National Development Plans and Employment Strategies as required by structural funds implementation and policy review processes, which had to be taken seriously if Poland wanted to be able to use the funds, forced the government to carry out diagnoses, reflect upon comprehensive plans and coordinate with various social and regional actors (Boni, 2002) even if this was done in a very imperfect manner. However, beyond "the common language of activation", as in other countries of the region, "it is certainly not true that there has been convergence at a substantive level" (Wright *et al.*, 2004: 529).

IV. Overcoming Barriers to Restructuring: Negotiated Restructuring Plans and Special Measures in "Strategic Sectors"

While overall the re-commodification of labour and the institutionalisation of unemployment went rather smoothly in Poland (Spieser, 2007), the prospect of massive job destruction triggered protest and opposition in the context of the restructuring of large heavy industry and mining entities. In those sectors, mining especially, workers had a long tradition of organisation coupled with a relatively privileged position related to their workplace; therefore they were particularly reluctant to leave their activity. This section draws on secondary literature and serves to illustrate the decentralised management of restructuring as opposed to centrally-defined public policies.

In these specific cases of large firm restructuring, the conditions of dismissal led to much more intense negotiations. The legal framework of the *Act on Dismissals* adopted back in 1989 had set the conditions of large workforce reductions and measures to protect affected employees (Kabaj, 1996). The employer was obliged to notify the relevant trade unions in advance, stating the reasons for redundancies and the number of people concerned. It also had to inform the local labour office and develop a programme for retraining and the re-employment of the employees sent home. The Ministry of Labour and Social Policy, in consultation with the Ministry of Finance, could suspend a collective dismissal plan for a period up to three months.[26] Finally, dismissed employees would receive redundancy payments of up to a maximum of three months of wage. While restructuring plans were adopted in various cases, in practice, they led to intense negotiations and complex agreements only in the case of declining heavy industry units where the workers exposed to dismissal were strongly mobilised through powerful unions.

The steel and mining sector provide two contrasted illustrations of such a negotiated process of restructuring marked by the power game between business and labour interests at the regional level as well as national level. Key activities of the times gone by, mining and steel production were heavily concentrated in Upper Silesia,[27] with a tradition of strong local trade unions, higher wages and better than average welfare entitlements. Because many have feared social unrest and a contagion at the national level, the mining sector and its Silesian base have enjoyed longer and stronger public support than elsewhere. Consequently, the pace of restructuring has been slow and progress difficult.

In attempting to remedy the stalled situation, dialogue and coordination among the social partners have always come high on the agenda. As early as Spring 1995, representatives of socio-political, professional, local government and economic circles came together to draft a "Regional Contract for the Katowice Voivodship", including a regional social pact in which the actors declared their willingness to cooperate in a programme for restructuring and development in Upper Silesia (Bafoil, 1996). This was followed by a four-year reform plan prepared by the deputy Ministry of Industry Markowski in 1996, taking a narrow sectoral approach and opting for subsidies in the form of social transfers, investment loans and export subsidies. The regional leader of *Solidarnosc* then presented an alternative, more encompassing scenario, calling for a broader perspective, more involvement of the national government and a wider consultation of regional and local actors. The Regional contract tended to reflect the traditional power structure of actors in the region, i.e. the prominence of industrial actors linked to the biggest plants, which made it difficult to envisage innovative solutions. At the end, however, restructuring was negotiated at the sectoral level, for steelworks and mines separately.

---

26 However, this clause was never used although mass lay-offs have affected 600,000 people in the period 1990-1994 (Kabaj, 1996).

27 At the outset of transition, 64 out of Poland's 66 deep coalmines and one of the two major steelworks were located in Upper Silesia. (Blazyca, 2002: 26).

Contrasted Fates and Restructuring Paths

Beyond these common features, the path of restructuring of the steel and mining sector diverge.

Let us first review the restructuring process in the coal mining sector. It is estimated that the mining industry employed almost half a million miners in the 1980s, which was reduced to a quarter of this by 2003. A widely shared opinion among domestic and international experts is that, regardless of any effort undertaken, the mines will never be able to become competitive and therefore should all be closed down (Towalski, 2005). Half a dozen successive restructuring plans have been drawn up but most of them were never fully implemented due to industrial conflict. The mines were turned into individual state-owned enterprises in 1990, then grouped again in 1992-1993 into a joint stock company and a holding, both remaining with the State Treasury. After some positive developments in 1993-1995, the financial situation of the mines started to worsen again and ever more rapidly from 1996. In 1998, a generous package for miners made redundant was adopted but failed to improve the loss-making situation of the mines. In 2002, an agreement was finally found on a plan designed by the government in 2000, and financed a loan from the World Bank. It included privatisation and a freezing of wages, but some disputes continued over the list of plants to be privatised.

Most redundancies in the mining sector are concentrated in two periods: 50,000 miners were made redundant in 1993-1994 and another 90,000 between 1998 and 2001. Conflicts over collective dismissals were avoided by granting relatively generous packages. There are reports of sums exceeding 10,000 euros against to secure a definitive exit of mining employment (Gadowska, quoted by Gardawski, 2003). The successive lowering of the unemployment benefit no doubt also explained why miners were so eager to push for negotiating high severance payment, rather than relying on the standard unemployment benefit, for which they lost their eligibility on that occasion (Gardawski, 2002).

This contrasts with the fate of the steel industry. While the coal mines were thought from the start to have no future, the expert opinion on the Polish iron and steel sector emerging from a sectoral study in 1992 was that, following appropriate measures, it had a chance to become competitive on international markets (Towalski, 2003). The first restructuring programme was adopted along those lines in 1992. As with the mines, the plant had already been individualised and made independent from each other in 1990. Between 1993 and 2001, employment in steel plants was reduced from 123,000 to approximately 36,000 (Towalski, 2003). Until 1998, around 45,000 jobs were lost, principally to retirement or disability benefits, transfer to other entities or else (Towalski, 2003). From 1999, a social package financed on the state budget and international aid allowed an acceleration of workforce reduction: 47,000 further jobs were lost, among which slightly less than half were transferred to other companies and the rest made redundant. Downsizing continued at a slower pace until 2006, but there are opinions that the resulting workforce size is still above the efficiency level. In 2003, a second social package for steelworks, focusing on activation was adopted by the government and endorsed by the sectoral tripartite team. One major innovation of this package was its goal to facilitate re-employment in other industries, by granting severance payments primarily in the framework of training contracts.

By Polish standards, restructuring in the steel sector is an unusually positive example of working social dialogue in a developmental perspective. In comparison to the mining sector, restructuring was remarkably peaceful and conflicts were scarce.[28] Cooperation between the actors allowed to set the conditions of restructuring. In the mining sector, on the contrary, attempts to bring the various actors together produced merely stalemates and it was difficult to obtain agreements on any restructuring plan. The differentiated path of restructuring between the two sectors can be traced back both to the different role played by the unions (obstructing restructuring of the mines while cooperating in a constructive way in the steel sector), and to the ultimate objective of restructuring (closing down the mines as opposed to reducing workforce to build smaller, competitive steel-melting plants). Incidentally, the measures agreed as part of the social packages in both sectors reflect an interesting divide between activation measures and passive compensation, which belong to two different worlds of adjustment.

Conclusion

The chapter has shown that, in lieu of a policy for socio-economic change, Poland relied mainly on *ad hoc* measures until at least the mid-1990s, before the basis for more comprehensive, new-style labour market policies was laid down around 1997. Building on the established typologies of socio-economic policies and welfare regime, it can be argued that in the period considered, Polish welfare policies and institutions approximate a trajectory going from a short-lived universalist system (initially extensive eligibility, unconditional and generous unemployment benefits coupled with a continuation of parts of the communist welfare system) with some corporatist and rent-seeking distortions (eligibility for special schemes restricted mainly to a few

[28] Most strikes in this sector date back to the first half of the 1990s.

well-organised and well-represented sectoral groups), before gradually reaching a minimalist or residual one (eligibility restricted to deserving categories, less generous benefits coupled with more obligations). Policies dealt with unemployment as a political problem more efficiently than with unemployment as a social problem: unemployment was institutionalised with little protest or opposition and the broad direction of socio-economic change was not challenged, but the unemployed remain extremely vulnerable given that they tend to stay in unemployment or inactivity with limited chances to move back to employment and hardly any access to a replacement income. While the political pressure was rightfully anticipated and dealt with, the social problem was not.

Two broad waves of policies were introduced partly successively: first, predominantly passive labour market policies to manage unemployment by alleviating its effects until the mid 1990s; followed by an increasing emphasis on active labour market policies (ALMP), aiming to redirect people to work, but with limited effectiveness. Active and passive measures do not benefit the same categories of people at all. Eligibility for income support (unemployment alleviation) is based on the need to compensate income loss while eligibility for ALMP (anti-unemployment measures) is based either on a presumed higher risk of remaining unemployed, or on a sense of unfairness or worthiness. Ultimately, the divide between active and passive policies reflects two radically distinct worlds of un/employment policy-making. Passive policies follow a logic of compensation and income replacement. Active policies instead follow logic of "activation", aiming at a return to employment and emphasizing measures consistent with the monetarist economic policy paradigm: "active" policies increasingly dominate the debate on labour market policies across Europe. However, even when there has been a clear will to target social assistance to the needy by means of income-testing, protective measures have continued to be pursued for the employees made redundant (Golinowska, 2005: 43). Irrespective of whether these measures are adopted as a national policy or in a small-scale plan, two distinct worlds of labour market adjustment that are nearly mutually exclusive can be distinguished: on one hand, a so far marginal, but expanding, forward-looking one, aiming at employment and relying on active labour market policies and on the other one, a backward-looking one, aiming to make unemployment bearable and relying on compensation and inactivity, which is in the process of fading away.

Aside policies with a universal scope, attempts to negotiate social pacts over restructuring were contained to a few specific sectors in which restructuring was seriously impaired by the hostility of workers who were well-represented by their unions and geographically concentrated. In the steel and mining sectors, only a negotiated solution could sectoral and regional restructuring to proceed. Conversely, it is by and large only in those cases of workers' mobilisation, that sectoral restructuring plans have been negotiated in Poland. The most powerful groups managed to obtain extraordinary compensation, sometimes generous but always short-lived. Outside these particular events, organised labour had little influence over the definition of policies for employment and unemployment, while the latter often remain the sole instrument to accompany workforce reductions.

These findings have at least one important implication. In comparison with other European countries, social and labour market policies do not currently provide much income security or support towards re-employment for a Polish person who loses his or her job for economic reasons. Some groups may enjoy more help than others and a number of well-intended reforms have taken place, but it is not obvious that this will led to a better and more universal protection against the risk of unemployment in the short term. This means that, if the kind of firm restructuring likely to occur today in Poland or in old EU Member States are much closer than in the past, the situation of workers affected by them remains radically different given that workers in old EU Member States can rely on more encompassing welfare states and better functioning labour market institutions.

References

AVDAGIC, S. and CROUCH, C. (2006), "Organised Economic Interests: Diversity and Change in an Enlarged Europe" in HEYWOOD, P., JONES, E., RHODES, M. and SEDELMEIER, U. (eds.), *Developments in European Politics*, Palgrave Macmillan, Basingstoke, pp. 196-215.

BAFOIL, F. (1996), "La question silésienne: autonomie et restructuration industrielle", *Courrier des Pays de l'Est*, No.413, pp. 63-75.

BAFOIL, F. (2006), *Europe centrale et orientale. Mondialisation, européanisation et changement social*, Presses de Sciences Po, Paris.

BALCEROWICZ, L. (1995), *Socialism, Capitalism, Transformation*, Central European University Press, Budapest.

BARBIER, J.-C. (1998), "Les politiques publiques de l'emploi en perspective: pour un cadre de comparaison des politiques nationales de l'emploi", in BARBIER, J.-C. and GAUTIÉ, J. (eds.), *Les politiques de l'emploi en Europe et aux Etats-Unis*, Presses Universitaires de France, Paris, pp. 383-410.

BARBIER, J.-C. and LUDWIG-MAYERHOFER, W. (2004), "The Many Worlds of Activation", *European Societies*, No.6, pp. 423-436.

BARR, N. (2004), *Economics of the Welfare State*, Fourth edition, Oxford University Press, Oxford.

BARR, N. (ed.) (1994), *Labor Markets and Social Policy in Central and Eastern Europe: The Transition and Beyond*, World Bank, Washington, DC.

BAXANDALL, P. (2002), "Explaining Differences in the Political Meaning of Unemployment Across Time and Space", *Journal of Socio-Economics*, Vol. 31, No.5, pp. 469-502.

BLAZYCA, G. (ed.) (2002), *Restructuring Regional and Local Economies: Towards a Comparative Study of Scotland and Upper Silesia*, Aldershot, Ashgate.

BOERI, T. (1997), "Labour-Market Reforms in Transition Economies", *Oxford Review of Economic Policy*, Vol. 13, No.2, pp. 126-140.

BONI, M. (2002), "Poland's Experiences in Constructing a National Employment Strategy", *Polityka Spoleczna*, December 2002, pp. 29-32.

BRUSZT, L. (2001), "Market Making as State Making: Constitutions and Economic Development in Post-communist Eastern Europe", *Constitutional Political Economy*, No.13, pp. 53-72.

CLEGG, D. (2005), "Activating the Multi-tiered Welfare State: Social Governance, Welfare Politics and Unemployment Policies in France and the United Kingdom", PhD Thesis, European University Institute, Florence.

CZARZASTY, J. (2004), "Youth Employment Measures Assessed", *EIRO Feature*, 4 November 2004.

CZEPULIS-RUTKOWSKA, Z. (1998), "Changes in Pension System", in GOLINOWSKA, S. (ed.), *Social Policy in the 1990s, Legal Regulations and Their Prospected Results*, IPiSS, Warsaw, pp. 194-209.

CZEPULIS-RUTKOWSKA, Z. (1999), "The Polish Pension System and its Problems", in MULLER, K., RYLL, A. and WAGENER, H.-J. (eds.), *Transformation of Social Security: Pensions in Central-Eastern Europe*, Physica, Heidelberg and New York, pp. 143-158.

EKIERT, G. (2001), "The State After State Socialism: Poland in Comparative Perspective", *IWM Working Paper*, No.6, Institut fur die Wissenschaften vom Menschen, Vienna.

ESPING-ANDERSEN, G. (1990), *The Three Worlds of Welfare Capitalism*, Polity Press, Cambridge.

EUROPEAN MONITORING CENTRE ON CHANGE (EMCC) (2006), Company restructuring. Info sheet, European Foundation for the Improvement of Living and Working Conditions, Dublin.

FREGE, Z. (1997), "The Changed Welfare Paradigm", *Social Policy and Administration*, Vol. 31, No.1, pp. 20-44.

FRITZ, V. (2004), "State Weakness in Eastern Europe: Concept and Causes", *EUI Working Paper*, European University Institute, Florence.

GARDAWSKI, J. (2002), "Unemployment Benefits Examined", *EIRO Feature*, 29 October 2002.

GARDAWSKI, J. (2003), "Difficult Restructuring of Coal Mining Continues", *EIRO Briefing*, 1 October 2003.

GOLINOWSKA, S. (1994), *Social Policy and Social Conditions in Poland: 1989-1993*, IpiSS, Warsaw.

GOLINOWSKA, S. (ed.) (2005), *The Social Report Poland*, Friedrich Ebert Stiftung, Warsaw.

GOLINOWSKA, S., PIETKA, K., SOWADA, C. and ZUKOWSKI, M. (2003), Study on the Social Protection Systems in the 13 Applicant Countries, Poland Country Study commissioned by the European Commission, DG Employment and Social Affairs.

GOLINOWSKA, S. and UNDP (1997), "National Report on Human Development: The changing Role of the State: Poland 1997", New York, Warsaw, United Nations Development Programme/Regional Bureau for Europe and the CIS, Centre for Social and Economic Research.

HALL, P. A. (1993), "Policy Paradigms, Social Learning, and the State. The Case of Economic Policymaking in Britain", *Comparative Politics*, Vol. 25, No.3, pp. 275-296.

HALL, P. A. and SOSKICE, D. (ed.) (2002), *Varieties of Capitalism. The Institutional Foundations of Comparative Advantage*, Oxford University Press, Oxford.

HEMERIJCK, A., MAARTEN, K. and RHODES, M. (2006), "European Welfare States: Diversity, Challenges and Reforms" in HEYWOOD, P., JONES, E., RHODES, M. and SEDELMEIER, U. (eds.), *Developments in European Politics*, Palgrave Macmillan, Basingstoke, pp. 259-279.

KABAJ, M. (1996), "Programmes and Strategies for Counteracting Unemployment and the Promotion of Productive Employment", *ILO-CEET Report*, No.15, ILO, Budapest.

KABAJ, M. (2000), *Programme Przeciwdzialania Ubostwu i Bezrobociu*, IpiSS, Warsaw.

KORNAI, J. (1992), *The Socialist System: The Political Economy of Communism*, Princeton University Press, Princeton, N.J.

KORPI, W. (1983), *The Democratic Class Struggle*, Routledge, London and Boston.

KRYNSKA, E., KWIATKOWSKI, E. and ZARYCHTA, H. (1998), "Polityka panstwa na rynku pracy w Polsce w latach dziewiecdziesiatych", *Report IPiSS*, No.12, Warsaw.

KSIEZOPOLSKI, M. (1993), "Social Policy in Poland in the Period of Political and Economic Transition: Challenges and Dilemmas", *Journal of European Social Policy*, Vol. 3, No.3, pp. 177-194.

MICKIEWICZ, T. (2005), *Economic Transition in Central and Eastern Europe and the Commonwealth of Independent States*, Palgrave, Houndmills.

MINISTRY OF ECONOMY AND LABOUR (MEL) (2005), *Employment in Poland 2005* (English translation of: Zatrudnienia w Polsce 2005), Ministry of Economy and Labour, Warsaw.

MLONEK, K. (1999), *Bezrobocie w Polsce w XX wieku w swietle badan*, Krajowy Urzad Pracy, Warsaw.

MPiPS (1995), *Promocja aktywnosci zawodowej mlodziezy. Programme przeciwdzialania bezrobociu wsrod mlodziezy*, Ministerstwo Pracy i Polityki Socjalnej, Krajowy Urzad Pracy, Warsaw.

MÜLLER, K. (1999), *The Political Economy of Pension Reform in Central-Eastern Europe*, Edward Elgar Publishing, Cheltenham and Northampton (MA).

OFFE, C. (1991), "Capitalism by Democratic Design: Democratic Theory Facing the Triple Transition in East Central Europe", *Social Research*, Vol. 58, No.4, pp. 865-893.

OFFE, C. (1993), "The Politics of Social Policy in East European Transitions: Antecedents, Agents and Agenda of Reform", *Social Research*, Vol. 60, No.4, pp. 649-663.

ORENSTEIN, M. A. (1995), "Transitional Social Policy in the Czech Republic and Poland", *Czech Sociological Review*, Vol. 3, No.2, pp. 179-196.

ORENSTEIN, M. A. (2001), *Out of the Red: Building Capitalism and Democracy in Postcommunist Europe*, University of Michigan Press, Ann Arbor.

PALIER, B. (2005), "Ambiguous Agreement, Cumulative Change: French Social Policy in the 1990s", in THELEN, K. and STREEK, W. (eds.), *Beyond Continuity, Institutional Change in Advanced Political Economies*, Oxford University Press, Oxford, pp. 127-144.

RASHID, M.; RUTKOWSKI, J. and FRETWELL, D. (2005), "Labor Markets", in BARR, N. A. (ed.) *Labor Markets and Social Policy in Central and Eastern Europe. The Accession and Beyond*, World Bank, Washington DC.

RUTKOWSKI, J. (1998), "Welfare and the Labor Market in Poland: Social Policy During Economic Transition", *World Bank Technical Paper*, No.417, World Bank, Washington DC.

SPIESER, C. (2007), "Labour Market Policies and Union Politics in Post-Communist Poland: Explaining the Peaceful Institutionalisation of Unemployment", *Politique Européenne*, No.21, April 2007, pp. 97-132.

STANDING, G. (1996), "Social Protection in Central and Eastern Europe: A Tale of Slipping Anchors and Torn Safety Nets" in ESPING-ANDERSEN, G. (ed.), *Welfare State in Transition. National Adaptation in Global Economies*, United Nations Research Institute for Social Development (UNRISD)/Sage Publications, Oxford.

SZYLKO-SKOCZNY, M. (2004), *Polityka spoleczna wobec bezrobocia w Trzeciej Rzeczyspospolitej*, IPS-UW, Warsaw.

TOWALSKI, R. (2003), "'Activation Package' Agreed to Accompany Iron and Steel Restructuring", *EIRO Briefing*, 30 October 2003.

TOWALSKI, R. (2005), "Labour Unions and Restructuring Processes in the Hard Coal Sector in Poland", *EIRO Briefing*, 18 April 2005.

VAUGHAN-WHITEHEAD, D. (2003), "Protection sociale. Une peau de chagrin dans l'Europe élargie?", *Courrier des Pays de l'Est*, pp. 4-15.

WRIGHT, S., KOPAC, A. and SLATER, G. (2004), "Continuities within Paradigmatic Change. Activation, Social Policies and Citizenship in the Context of

Welfare Reform in Slovenia and the UK", *European Societies*, Vol. 6, No.4, pp. 511-534.

ZIMMERMANN, B. (2001), *La constitution du chômage en Allemagne*, Éditions de la Maison des Sciences de l'Homme, Paris.

Conclusions

Jean-Jacques PARIS

Consultant at Alpha Group (France) and responsible for the Brussels site

The new Member States are now practically an integral part of the common market of goods, assets and persons.[1] Considered purely from the economic angle, the enlargement first consisted of a "liberalization of residual protections mainly in the form of dumping measures".[2] The global effects[3] of this liberalisation were limited or relatively reduced in the former Member States compared to the new ones which felt the effect of integration more strongly "to the extent that they joined an area (the fifteen Member States) already strongly integrated". An area which had become, even before the first of May 2004 the main trade partner of the CEECs, and in which companies had already, before this date, implemented readjustments through strategies of direct foreign investments and relocation of production units that largely contributed to the debate on deindustrialisation in the former Member States (EU-15).

For Guglielmo Meardi and Michael Fichter, the fears of the EU-15 countries linked to impact on employment relocating production units ("direct relocations")[4] should be put in perspective. According to the European Restructuring Monitor), only about 5% of job losses during the 2003-2005 periods could be attributed to relocations. The results of a European Commission study done in 2006 in three countries (Germany, Austria and the Netherlands) also tend to show that one must not overestimate the impact of relocations on labor in these countries.

1 With the exception of some temporary restrictions on migration flows.

2 For example, the protection in agriculture opposed by the EU to Polish exports represents a tariff equivalent to 77%; see Edi Bchir, M. and Maurel, M. (2002), "Impacts économiques et sociaux de l'élargissement pour l'Union européenne et la France", *Dossier du CEPII*, No.2002-03, Centre d'études prospectives et d'informations internationales, Paris.

3 And not just in some states or areas that most strongly felt the impact of integration.

4 It is heard in a strict sense as the transfer of production unit of a former Member State to a new Member State.

However, the authors invite us not to underestimate "indirect relocations", even if their scope remains hard to evaluate: for example in branches such as the automobile industry and chemistry, the center of gravity of investments moves towards the new Member States with possible substitution effects on the long run and effects on employment in the countries where the investments come from.[5]

It remains however that the social consequences for the new Member States are without comparison with those in the EU-5 countries. The fundamental restructurings of companies in the East (transition from a socialist economy to a market economy and opening to international competition in the context of the enlargement process) have led, and sometimes continue to do so, to considerable job losses in these countries, more particularly in Poland.[6] At the end of 2003, the average unemployment rate was 14.7% in the so-called candidate countries (at the time). The main victims of unemployment are the least qualified jobs, as well as certain specific categories of workers, such as women, younger and elder people (Catherine Spieser, Daniel Vaughan-Whitehead).

Since 1989, the inflow of direct foreign investment from Germany and Austria, in the enlargement countries (more particularly the Czech Republic, Hungary and Poland) contributed to these economic and social transformations. Guglielmo Meardi and Michael Fichter point out that for Germany, these countries are the first destination for investments, before Asia.

Although relocations are mostly the result of cost reduction strategies,[7] the foreign direct investments are often explained by other considerations, such as the horizontal extension of capacities (in the automobile industry where conducts are also dictated by the behaviour of consumers, manufacturers often following their clients) or the extension of networks (for example in banking, trade or the food industry) that have weaker or less immediate effects on employment.

Taking the example of Hungary and the food industry (the biggest employer in the country), Yordanka Chobanova aptly shows the complexity of the strategies of MNCs (Nestlé, Kraft foods, Interbrew (now

5 For example, in case of overcapacity in the market (in particular automotive) companies tend to preserve investments in countries with low social costs at the expense of sites in the EU-15, especially when products and services re-exportable are concerned.

6 In Poland, where economic restructuring carried out since 1989, have resulted in a rise in unemployment rate reaching around 20% in 2004 (Catherine Spieser).

7 A recent survey (in Germany) shows that the primary criterion for relocating for German companies (85% of respondents) is the cost of production (Guglielmo Meardi and Michael Fichter).

InBev), etc.) that cannot be boiled down to cost reduction aims. The Hungarian government has multiplied initiatives to improve the conditions of attractiveness of foreign investments while strengthening the capacity of territories (by involving universities and research centres, for example) to absorb the investments and acquire the knowledge and the know-how of MNCs. As Yordanka Chobanova, or Guglielmo Meardi and Michael Fichter show, this does not necessarily mean that these corporations actually invest in local development (by promoting training, for example). Strategies of relocation and outsourcing remain attractive to them. New ideas are starting to emerge, like setting up clusters around an integrator (Suzuki, General Electric, Audi, for example) to allow a better transfer of knowledge (Guglielmo Meardi and Michael Fichter).

The restructurings done in the context of enlargement had consequences on industrial relations and on the working conditions of workers in the EU.

For Daniel Vaughan-Whitehead, the mere threat of outsourcing or relocation of activities puts immediate pressure on salaries and labor norms. More generally, restructurings have an impact on employment and working conditions in the UE-15 countries as well as the new Member States: the reappearance of compulsory part-times and other forms of atypical types of work contracts in Europe is an illustration of that, as is the increasing use of migrant workers to minimise social costs[8] (Daniel Vaughan-Whitehead). The permissive nature of the law, especially on working hours (Katharina Bluhm) increases theses risks.

The intensification of competition on international markets contributes to the creation of new categories of vulnerable workers, such as managers or white-collar workers which are increasingly the victims of health and security risks. By affecting territories in different ways, these globalisation phenomena are capable of increasing the gap in socio-economic development between the new Member States or within the same country (Daniel Vaughan-Whitehead).[9] These changes have an effect on the evolution of industrial relations within the new Member States as well as in the EU-15 countries. In the latter, companies have a tendency to use social dialogue as an engineering tool within their flexibility strategies, like the decentralised agreements on flexibility in Sweden, negotiated in 2005 in exchange for a salary increase (Daniel Vaughan-Whitehead). Moreover, in countries such as Germany, restruc-

---

8 In the United Kingdom, the use of migrant workers from the new Member States (Poland, in particular) has contributed to the policy of wage moderation in the UK.

9 In Poland, for example, the unemployment rate stood at 40% in the municipality of Lobeski, it is 6.3% in Warsaw.

turing and relocation processes tend to lead to a workforce decrease in the production sector (the cradle of industrial relations), thus leading to an erosion of onsite industrial relations, but also capable of leading to the creation of new forms of representation (Guglielmo Meardi Michael Fichter).

Foreign investors who have the experience of structured social dialogue in their own country (France, or Germany) could play a positive role in the promotion of a social dialogue still in search of itself within the new Member States. From the perspective of worker representatives, there is little done in terms of creating stronger links with colleagues in the other Member States, because, among other things, of linguistic barriers. The European Works Councils could be a way to reinforce solidarity between worker representatives. Of course, this applies to EU-size companies, and not to small and medium-sized ones.

Some MNCs criticise state intervention in social regulation within the new Member States (Heribert Kohl and Hans-Wolfgang Platzer) and the weakness of social dialogue. However, Guglielmo Meardi and Michael Fichter show that, as far as Germany is concerned, companies can accommodate themselves very well with a non-regulated system such as the Hungarian one. For Katharina Bluhm, the social relations system in these countries offers considerable flexibility allowing management to take unilateral decisions. According to the author, the existing gap between formal rules and socio-economic reality makes this system very permissive.

As happens within the EU-15 countries, companies sometimes make the signature of an agreement with worker representatives a condition for remaining in a new Member State. In 2005-2006, the management of Fiat-GM (Poland) required a negotiation on the reorganisation of labor within the company as a prerequisite for maintaining their 81 million euro investment project to increase the capacity of the factory, thus creating 300 new jobs.[10]

The management let it be known that in the absence of a deal, investments could be moved to India, Turkey or Brazil.[11] Even companies that were present, even embedded within CEECs well before the enlargement have started to adopt relocation and cost-reduction strategies, like Kraft Foods which relocated to Bratislava[12] from Hungary, despite being market leader in that country, or Univeler which closed its

10 In a very tense social climate with the threat of relocation, the negotiations between union and management have failed in February 2006, the independent trade union "Solidarnosc", with majority in the company, having refused to sign the agreement.

11 E-europenews, 2005.

12 300 workers affected by the move.

Budapest[13] site to produce in lower cost countries (Yordanka Chobanova, Nikolett Hös).

The weakness of unions and of worker representation in companies is certainly a major obstacle in the creation of an influential social dialogue within the new Member States. The decrease in the number of union members is a common characteristic to these states; it can be explained in many ways (diminution of standard of living in the transition period, increased unemployment especially in the manufacturing industry which was traditionally highly unionised, privatisation process and fragmentation of big public companies, absence of unions in small and medium-sized companies, criticism sometimes leveled by workers themselves against organisations). In Poland, the decline has been important: it has fallen to 18%, like in Spain (Katharina Bluhm). Moreover, the conventional protection within the new Member States remains law (Guglielmo Meardi and Michael Fichter), compared to that of the EU-15 countries.

As for employer organisations, they still lack the unity and the representativeness to be considered as valuable social dialogue partners. In 2003, the employer organisation s of the then candidate countries only represented an average of 30 to 40% of industrial companies.

Faced with heavy restructurings in the steel sector, social partners were sometimes able to negotiate the consequences on employment of restructurings on their territory: in Poland talks on redundancy plans in the steel sector led to the signature of territorial agreements and the implementation of a sectorial[14] and bilateral social dialogue that is still missing in other new Member States (Nikolett Hös). This bilateral social dialogue could reinforce the representativeness of social stakeholders and in the end be of help to tripartite social dialogue, which is still in search of democratic legitimacy (Daniel Vaughan Whitehead, Katharina Blum).

Such contractual practices are also encouraged by EU social policies that put forward the concept of social partnership (Katharina Bluhm). At the same time, European organisations (OECD, EU) promote the implementation of active employment policies (Nikolett Hös).

In the particular context of restructurings, several authors (such as Nikolett Höss, Daniel Vaughan-Whitehead, Guglielmo Meardi Michael Fichter, Katharina Bluhm) have pondered the impact of the *acquis*, and more particularly the "restructuring" directives, in the transformation of

---

[13] 200 workers affected.

[14] Such a dialogue could not be established by control in the mining sector as a result of confrontational social relations in this sector.

industrial relations within the new Member States. What is the impact of these directives in countries where the industrial relations models are still influenced by practices stemming from state centralism?

The implementation of the *acquis* in the field of labor law has increased the pace of often important reforms in these countries. It gave rise to substantial debates on the tools used by social dialogue when faced with restructurings. In Poland and Estonia, the implementation of the framework directive on information and consultation (2002) sparked considerable debate (Nikolett Hös) on the necessity to anticipate restructurings through social dialogue. The scope of redundancy plans and the increase of social conflicts (Catherine Spieser), the multiplication of externalisation practices within companies, the increased risk of bankruptcy, all these tendencies have made it all the more useful to apply the so-called structural directives on the protection of workers' interests in case of mass redundancy plans, transfer or insolvency of companies.

Nikolett Hös considers that the enlargement is also a test for the application of the directive on European Works Councils (EWC): on the existing 737 EWCs, more than 500 involve companies having activities in one or more of the new Member States. Moreover, several companies from the new Member States (35) have already created an EWC.[15] Their role however remains limited. According to Guglielmo Meardi and Michael Fichter, the role of EWCs is mostly a defensive one, local actions being preferred over coordinated transnational actions. Therefore, also economies are linked, social relations remain compartmentalised, which leaves room for competition between sites and the weakening of the social bond in a transnational context.

However, the effective implementation of the *acquis* presupposes specific structures common to the Member States. Thus, the application of the "insolvency" directive requires the creation of a salary guarantee fund in all the Member States to protect the salaries of workers affected by the insolvency of their company. In the same way, directives on "mass redundancies" or "transfer of companies" cannot be implemented without the establishment of information and consultation procedures, and the existence of an effective worker representation within the company. As several of the contributions show (particularly that of Katharina Bluhm), one cannot fail to observe that the conditions for the implementation of the *acquis communautaire* are not always met.

In Poland for example, the establishment of worker representation bodies in the companies of more than 50 employees is recent (April 2006) and was done through the Polish law of implementation of the

---

15 According to data from the European Trade Union Institute.

2002 directive on information and consultation of worker representatives. In companies where there is union representation, the members of the works councils are nominated by the unions. In the absence of union representation, the members of the works councils are elected. Thus, this dual system of representation is completely new but contains the risk of creating competition between the representation bodies in terms of information and consultation. Even more so since the *acquis communautaire* has often been understood in these countries as a partial diminution of existing standards and union prerogatives: unions often see the works councils as a threat to their existence (Katharina Bluhm).

The Czech Republic adopted a different solution: a works council is set up in companies having more than 50 employees only if there is no unions representation; the works council can claim a right of information and consultation, but cannot negotiate. The works council is dissolved if appears union representation (Katharina Bluhm).

In the field of governance, the systems in the new Member States favor worker representation within the managing bodies of the company (surveillance board or executive board). Tensions between works councils and unions also exist in the EU-15 countries but are not so strong.

More generally, the various authors adequately show that the new Member States are facing similar social and economic problems to those in the old Member States. What changes is the intensity level of the problems and the fluctuating capacity of stakeholders to deal with them. On this point, there are numerous structural and cultural obstacles to the implementation of the *acquis communautaire*: the directive, in its application, moves away from the existing industrial relations culture within the new Member States (Katharina Bluhm) and the weakness, or even absence, of structures and institutions that are a necessary part of the implementation of the *acquis*, such as worker and employer representation, tribunals, or industrial inspectorates, can actually have the opposite effect of the original aim.

Notes on Contributors

María Esther Blas López is Dr. and Senior Lecturer of European and Constitutional Law at the University of Saragosse (Spain) and Postdoctoral researcher at the Catholic University of Louvain (UCL-Belgium) in the framework of the research project RECWOWE. She holds a PhD in Law, has been Visiting Researcher at the European Law Research Center at Harvard Law School (2002-2003) and Jean Monnet Fellow at the European University Institute in Florence (2003-2004). She has been recently working on the scientific coordination of the Research Project AGIRE (2006-2008) in collaboration with Marie-Ange Moreau. Her main research interests include European Law, EU social Law, Social Europe, Private International Law and the social dimension of restructurings in Europe.

Katharina Bluhm (PD Dr.) holds a full professorship for Economic sociology at the University of Osnabrück and studied philosophy at the Humboldt-University (Berlin), where she also obtained her doctoral degree in 1987. After the German unification she worked in a research project at the "Soziologisches Forschungsinstitut" (SOFI) in Göttingen, followed by a postdoctoral position in a research group on East German transition of the Max-Planck-Society in Berlin. Since 1997 she has been working in Jena where she also finished her "Habilitation" in sociology. From 1999 to 2000 she spent an academic year at the Minda de Gunzburg Center for European Studies of the Harvard University. Main research interests are the economic and organisational sociology, Central Eastern Europe, management and multinational corporations.

Yordanka Chobanova (B.Sc.) holds a bachelor degree from Varna University of Economics (Bulgaria); a Master degree from Central European University, Budapest and a PhD in Political and Social Sciences from the European University Institute (Florence) on the strategies of MNEs in Central and Eastern Europe. She is currently Senior Fellow, Economic programme, at the Center for the Study of Democracy, Sofia (Bulgaria). She has been working as a research collaborator in different research projects among which "Capital Controls" from Harvard University and "Labour Markets in CEE" from the EUI. Her research interests are Foreign Direct Investment, MNEs, Investment policies, International Financial Institutions.

Michael Fichter is Dr. and Senior Lecturer and researcher in the Center for Labor Studies at the Department of Political Science, Freie

Universität Berlin. He has published widely on German trade unions and co-authored studies on the revitalisation of unions and on right extremist attitudes among trade union members in Germany. A second focus of both his teaching and research has been on labor relations and employment practices in the transformation processes of the countries of Central and Eastern Europe, especially in regard to the practices of foreign investors in manufacturing. Currently, he is assessing the impact of business restructuring on employment relations within the European Union and the options available for cross-border trade union policy development.

Nikolett Hős is currently researcher at the European University Institute at the Law Department. After researching the European Directive on the transfer of undertakings and its implementation in Hungarian law, she started a PhD program at the Pázmány Péter Catholic University, Faculty of Law (Budapest). Her thesis focuses on the question how to find a healthy balance between the interests of the employers and employees in the case of business restructurings. Last year she was giving lectures at the Pázmány Péter Catholic University, Department of Social and Labour law. From September 2005 onwards she studied Comparative and European Law at the Andrássy Gyula German Language University (Budapest).

Annette Jobert is Annette Jobert is Sociologist and Research Director at the CNRS, Institutions et dynamiques historiques de l'économie (IDHE), University Paris X Nanterre. Her research focuses on collective bargaining in France and Europe in particular in the area of restructurations and territorial social dialogue. She is the author of *Sociologie du travail: les relations professionnelles* (with Antoine Bevort, Armand Colin, Paris, 2008).

Maarten Keune has a PhD in Political and Social Sciences from the European University Institute in Florence and Senior Researcher at the European Trade Union Institute (ETUI-REHS). From 1995 he has been Senior Expert, at the International Labour Office (Geneva) working on Central and Eastern European Countries. Among his publications are, *Relocation. Challenges for European Trade Unions* (2005), *Collective Bargaining Systems in Europe: A Schematic Overview* (2006), *Collective Bargaining and Working Time in Europ*e (2007) and has worked in several international and European research projects.

Guglielmo Meardi is Associate Professor of Industrial Relations at the University of Warwick (UK). He obtained a PhD from the European University Institute (Florence) and has been a Visiting Scholar at the Academies of Sciences of Poland, Hungary and Slovenia. He is currently researching industrial relations in multinationals in Central and Eastern Europe, as well as Polish migration to the UK.

Marie-Ange Moreau is Professor at the Law Department (Social Law Chair) of the European University Institute (Florence). She has been Full professor at the University of Rouen (1987-1990), University Paris-Dauphine (1990-1993) and the Institut de Droit des Affaires at University of Aix-Marseille III since 1993. She is also working with the *Centre de recherche interuniversitaire sur la mondialisation et le travail (CRIMT)* of which she is one of the charter members, on globalisation and labour law. On this theme recently she has organised links on research in India. She also has focused her research in the fields of European labour law and comparative labour law by participating in a European report on the *Evolution of Labour Laws in Europe (1992-2003)* for the French and Luxembourg reports. She is a member of several editorial boards of journals on labour law, industrial relations and international law reviews. She has been the scientific coordinator of the European research project AGIRE (2006-2008). She is the author of *Normes sociales, droit du travail et mondialisation. Confrontations et mutations* (Dalloz, Paris, 2006).

Jean Jacques Paris has been researcher at the European University Institute in Florence and Administrator at the Directorate General V, for Employment, Social Affairs and Equal Opportunities of the European Commission. Actually, he is consultant at Alpha Group (France) working with representatives of the employees of the enterprises and participating in the whole restructuring process, assisting representatives of works councils with respect to any changes that can have impact on the living and working conditions of the employees. Within the Alpha Group, he is responsible of the Brussels site.

Catherine Spieser (MSc LSE) is a researcher in the Department of Social and Political Science of the European University Institute and Lecturer in Political Science at the University of Strasbourg, France. Her primary research interests are in comparative social policy, labour market policies and the politics of social policy, with specific reference to central Europe and Poland in particular. She is currently working towards a PhD on the construction of social and employment policies in Poland in the period 1989-2004 under the supervision of Professor Colin Crouch. Prior to that, she has worked as a policy analyst specialised in the economic aspects of EU enlargement in Brussels and Warsaw. She is also interested in the territorial aspects of socio-economic governance in an institutionalist perspective, which feeds into a study on EU regional policies for the AGIRE project.

Daniel Vaughan-Whitehead obtained his PhD in Labor Economics at the European University Institute (Florence). In the mid-1980s he worked as adviser to the European Commission's President Jacques Delors, mainly on Social Europe, before joining the ILO in 1991. From the ILO regional team based in Budapest between 1993 and 1999, he worked on more than 16 Central and Eastern Europe countries since the beginning of the transition. In this capacity, he advised governments, trade unions and employers' organisations in their reform processes, mainly in the areas of wages and incomes policy and industrial relations in general. He then put this experience (1999-2003) at the service of the European Commission (DG Employment and Social Affairs), where he was in charge of social dialogue in the EU enlargement process and thus acted as a negotiator on social issues with the EU applicant countries. He returned to the ILO in 2004, where he is today responsible for employment and working conditions around the world.

"Work & Society"

The series "Work & Society" analyses the development of employment and social policies, as well as the strategies of the different social actors, both at national and European levels. It puts forward a multi-disciplinary approach – political, sociological, economic, legal and historical – in a bid for dialogue and complementarity.

The series is not confined to the social field *stricto sensu*, but also aims to illustrate the indirect social impacts of economic and monetary policies. It endeavours to clarify social developments, from a comparative and a historical perspective, thus portraying the process of convergence and divergence in the diverse national societal contexts. The manner in which European integration impacts on employment and social policies constitutes the backbone of the analyses.

Series Editor: Philippe POCHET, ETUI-REHS (Brussels), Director General and Digest Editor of the Journal of European Social Policy

Recent Titles

No.64 – *Pensions in Europe, European Pensions. The Evolution of Pension Policy at National and Supranational Level*, David NATALI, 2008, ISBN 978-90-5201-460-9

No.63 – *Building Anticipation of Restructuring in Europe*, Marie-Ange MOREAU (ed.), 2008, ISBN 978-90-5201-456-2

No.62 – *Jobs on the Move. An Analytical Approach to 'Relocation' and its Impact on Employment*, Béla GALGÓCZI, Maarten KEUNE & Andrew WATT (eds.), 2008, ISBN 978-90-5201-448-7

No.61 – *Les nouveaux cadres du dialogue social, Europe et territoires*, Annette JOBERT (dir.), 2008, ISBN 978-90-5201-444-9

No.60 – *Transnational Labour Regulation. A Case Study of Temporary Agency Work*, Kerstin AHLBERG, Brian BERCUSSON, Niklas BRUUN, Haris KOUNTOUROS, Christophe VIGNEAU & Loredana ZAPPALÀ, 2008, 376 p., ISBN 978-90-5201-417-3

No.59 – *Changing Liaisons. The Dynamics of Social Partnership in Twentieth Century West-European Democracies*, Karel DAVIDS, Greta DEVOS & Patrick PASTURE (eds.), 2007, 268 p., ISBN 978-90-5201-365-7.

No.58 – *Work and Social Inequalities in Health in Europe*, Ingvar LUNDBERG, Tomas HEMMINGSSON & Christer HOGSTEDT (eds.), SALTSA, 2007, 538 p., ISBN 978-90-5201-372-5.

No. 57 – *European Solidarities*, Lars MAGNUSSON & Bo STRÅTH (eds.), 2007, 355 p., ISBN 978-90-5201-363-3.

No. 56 – *Industrial Relations in the Small Scale Entreprises*, Christian DUFOUR, Adelheid HEGE, Sofia MURHEM, Wolfgang RUDOLPH, Wolfram WASSERMANN (eds.), SALTSA, 2007, ISBN 978-90-5201-360-2.

No. 55 – *The European Sectoral Social Dialogue. Actors, Developments and Challenges*, Anne DUFRESNE, Christophe DEGRYSE and Philippe POCHET (eds.), SALTSA/Observatoire social européen, 2006, 342 p., ISBN 978-90-5201-052-6.

No. 54 – *Reshaping Welfare States and Activation Regimes in Europe*, Amparo SERRANO PASCUAL & Lars MAGNUSSON (eds.), SALTSA, 2007, 319 p., ISBN 978-90-5201-048-9.

No. 53 – *Shaping Pay in Europe. A Stakeholder Approach*, Conny Herbert ANTONI, Xavier BAETEN, Ben J.M. EMANS, Mari KIRA (eds.), SALTSA, 2006, 287 p., ISBN 978-90-5201-037-3.

No. 52 – *Les relations sociales dans les petites entreprises. Une comparaison France, Suède, Allemagne*, Christian DUFOUR, Adelheid HEGE, Sofia MURHEM, Wolfgang RUDOLPH & Wolfram WASSERMANN, 2006, 243 p., ISBN 978-90-5201-323-7.

No. 51 – *Politiques sociales. Enjeux méthodologiques et épistémologiques des comparaisons internationales / Social Policies. Epistemological and Methodological Issues in Cross-National Comparison*, Jean-Claude BARBIER & Marie-Thérèse LETABLIER (eds.), 2005, 2nd printing 2006, 295 p., ISBN 978-90-5201-294-0.

No. 50 – *The Ethics of Workplace Privacy*, Sven Ove HANSSON & Elin PALM (eds.), SALTSA, 2005, 186 p., ISBN 978-90-5201-293-3.

No. 49 – *The Open Method of Co-ordination in Action. The European Employment and Social Inclusion Strategies*, Jonathan ZEITLIN & Philippe POCHET (eds.), with Lars MAGNUSSON, SALTSA/Observatoire social européen, 2005, 2nd printing 2005, 511 p., ISBN 978-90-5201-280-3.

No. 48 – *Le Moment Delors. Les syndicats au cœur de l'Europe sociale*, Claude DIDRY & Arnaud MIAS, 2005, 2nd printing 2005, 349 p., ISBN 978-90-5201-274-2.

No. 47 – *A European Social Citizenship? Preconditions for Future Policies from a Historical Perspective*, Lars MAGNUSSON & Bo STRÅTH (eds.), SALTSA, 2004, 361 p., ISBN 978-90-5201-269-8.